**Symbolizing
America**

SYMBOLIZING AMERICA

Edited by
Hervé Varenne

Foreword by
George and Louise Spindler

University of Nebraska Press
Lincoln and London

Copyright 1986 by the University of
Nebraska Press
All rights reserved
Manufactured in the United States of
America

The paper in this book meets the guidelines
for permanence and durability of the Committee on Production Guidelines for Book
Longevity of the Council on Library Resources.

*Library of Congress Cataloging-in-
Publication Data*
Main entry under title:
Symbolizing America.
   Bibliography: p.
   Includes index.
   Contents: Creating America / by Hervé
Varenne—Doing the anthropology of
America / by Hervé Varenne—Freedom to
choose / by William O. Beeman—
[etc.]   1. United States—Social life and
customs—1971-   —Addresses, essays,
lectures. 2. United States—Popular cul-
ture—History—20th century—Addresses,
essays, lectures. 3. National characteristics,
American—Addresses, essays, lectures. 4.
Ethnology—United States—Addresses,
essays, lectures.
I. Varenne, Hervé.
E169.02.S974 1986   973.92
85-24694
ISBN 0-8032-4656-0 (alk. paper)

To Margaret Mead, pioneer

Contents

Foreword

American anthropologists have of late been "coming home" to study their own country's culture. Some never really left, for beginning with Franz Boas and Edgar Hewett there have always been anthropologists observing and writing about the American scene. But such activity has never been the distinguishing mark of the profession. There is no doubt that the exotic, remote, isolated, non-Western, nonurban, tribal, and preferably—though no longer really possibly—"unpacified" peoples and places would provide the major symbols on an anthropological coat of arms. This orientation influences our behavior when, for example, we teach introductory courses in our discipline. The anthropology of America, the United States, usually gets only a nod, if that. As editors of the Case Studies in Cultural Anthropology, we generated seventeen titles on segments of American culture written by anthropologists in good standing who had done significant work in the United States as well as elsewhere. Most of these titles have gone out of print because not enough anthropology professors would use such material in their courses. It is clearly the case studies about exotic cultures that have been used widely enough to stay in print.

When we anthropologists do come home we find that we must make the familiar strange—a repeated theme in *Symbolizing America*. We must be "thrice-born," to use Sriniva's words (V. Turner 1978). We have our physical birth, we are born again when we do our first fieldwork in some culture other than our own, and we are thrice-born when we again face toward our culture, now seeing it as something strange. We might say that when anthropologists objectify and translate someone else's culture they must make the strange familiar, and when they study their own they must make the familiar strange (Spindler and Spindler 1982). They must exoticize their object of study. How could they exercise their art if they did not? And who would read their writings? In varying degrees and in various ways the chapters in this volume do make the familiar strange enough to give the reader perspective and make the material interesting.

What is it that the authors of these chapters have studied? Each author is clear about this, and the reader will enjoy discovering the answers. But is what they have studied *American* culture? Hervé Varenne grapples with the problem in his Introduction. Is there an American culture? There need not be one to justify studying in America, but there must be one if we claim, as some of us do, that we are not merely studying *in* America but studying American culture.

As students of American culture, we think there is one. Or perhaps we should say there is an American dialogue. Though the dialogue is not the whole culture, it is both a representation and a determinant of it. The dialogue is more than talk, for it influences behavior in countless situations and settings. It is expressed most directly in settings where the coordinating symbols of Americanness are at center stage, as in the campaign speeches of presidential candidates (Steele 1957). Careful listening to what they say every four years will demonstrate that the reference points for good and bad are not as polarized as the candidates would have us think. The political content of their speeches may be at odds, though within a constricted range of real options, but the actual values they promote and defend are essentially similar, such as hard work, independence, optimism, and progress.

Since 1951 we have collected responses from Stanford students to twenty-four open-ended sentences arranged around pivotal areas of American mainstream culture (Spindler 1974). Others have used our "values projective test" in other places and with other populations within our country. The results indicate that there is indeed an American dialogue about success, work, individualism, honesty, sociability, the future, time, competition, sexuality, and equality. It is not the only dialogue, but it is one. Though it changes through time, the changes tend to be cyclic rather than linear. (Right now we are in a conservative cycle that is already beginning to shift direction.) And it is not merely a mainstream dialogue. Responses from ethnic minorities are indistinguishable from those produced by the mainstream—except that minority respondents tend to be more traditional, more "American" in their value orientations.

It is not necessarily true that people wholly believe in the dialogue they participate in and often defend. In fact, they may be antagonistic to many of the sentiments expressed as it unfolds. We think this is also a major theme of American culture—conflict within the boundaries of a national dialogue. It is, we hypothesize, one of the reasons why in America violence on a mass scale is rarely political, and why the advocates of sociopolitical violence and revolution in the 1960s and early 1970s were largely unsuccessful. They had stepped outside the boundaries of the national dialogue. The dialogue is open-ended enough to be flexible and absorptive, but centered enough to be recognizable and constraining.

The chapters in this book are in themselves part of the American dialogue. As American culture is told, crafted, improvised, resolved, and done, to follow the titles of the five parts, at least two kinds of dialogue are simultaneously displayed: the dialogue(s) of America and the dialogue(s) of the anthropologists writing about America. A thoughtful reading of this book will inform one about both.

In the 161 publications by anthropologists writing about American culture that we reviewed in 1983, there is nothing quite like *Symbolizing America*. In making American culture strange enough to be interesting, some writings have gone too far. The contributors to this book do not go to excess, but they express very well the variety that is integral to our dynamic, multifaceted, yet surprisingly unified American culture.

George and Louise Spindler

Preface

Editing this volume of essays on America involved me in making explicit a third stage in my response to life "in these United States." Fifteen years ago, when I began working on what would become *Americans Together* (1977), I was an unattached graduate student from France, lost in wonder (or was it culture shock?). Three years later, when I began working on *American School Language* (1983), I was married, soon to be a father, a junior assistant professor. I now had responsibilities beyond myself, but not much had really been trusted to my "foreign" hands. More years passed, and as I worked on this book and my contributions to it (chaps. 1, 2, and 10), I received tenure, was promoted, and became chairman of my department.

From being an onlooker at the periphery, I have thus moved to the position of one with responsibility for maintaining the center. Some might see this as a movement of assimilation, if not enculturation. I see it, rather, as a transformation of my relation to the American institutions I first encountered when I applied for a student visa at the consulate in Marseilles.

Yes indeed, I have changed, and this change is reflected in the way I approach America in these pages. But I have changed only to the extent that institutions, through the people who enforce them and, often, struggle with them, have opened possibilities and I have responded. Since the day in 1968 when my passport was noisily stamped at Kennedy Airport, I have been assimilated by America first as student and then as researcher, faculty member, husband, father, and administrator. All in all, it is the quality of the assimilation rather than its level that has changed.

There is also a voice in me saying that, through all these years, I have not changed. I am still the "I" who rode his bicycle to class in Chicago.

What I wrote in *Americans Together* is still what I would write. Most of the voices around me, and some within me, disagree and emphasize the discontinuity. I am now known by my family in France for my American accent. Those who meet me for the first time in the United States no longer treat me as a foreigner. When students quote certain pages of *Americans Together* I wince, and I was partially pushed to do this book by the voices in me that want me to correct certain impressions that book might leave. Most important perhaps, major institutions are relying on me to maintain them in front of those to whom they are responsible. My assimilation has proceeded hand in hand with the transformation of the ways my responses have been co-opted.

I have of course generally been a willing participant in this co-optation. I have worked hard to earn my doctorate, gain tenure, and serve the students who come to me as chairman. I have been given new voices, and I have used them. This, certainly, is change.

These changes have inevitably been echoed in my writing on America. From the wonder I experienced when I began to hear the dominant voices in a small town sing in unwitting harmony, I moved to an ability to hear the complaints, and then to notice the attempts to find new voices. In the process my vision of the United States has clearly become more complex. I can discriminate better among the many shades produced by the various ways of encountering America. I can hear more clearly the subtexts that link, and often contradict, the performances that are so striking to newcomers. To that extent at least, my earlier works stand corrected by what this one emphasizes.

It remains that those transformations in my knowledge of America that I can easily chronicle are not simply a movement from error to a greater truth. Undoubtedly I am now much closer to the "native's point of view"—and thus closer to what some think is the goal of cultural analysis. I am also much further from another point of view that I can no longer incorporate in my writing. And yet I am quite sure there is more to be learned by contrasting the various texts that I, and all the others who have written about America, have produced than there is in looking for the ultimate one. Depth in cultural understanding depends less upon full participation than upon the ability to compare what various types of participation lead one to produce.

I hope that my contribution to this volume, and the contributions of the other authors, reveals the complexity of a cultural vision. We are not simply in the business of more accurately describing an object ("American culture"). Rather, we are striving to present a richer picture of life in the

United States; that is, of the cultural process that reproduces, and changes, America—a picture that must include the pattern that stabilizes American history.

It is the theme of this book that no act stands by itself, that we are always one with those who spoke before us and those who will speak after us. In this context, acknowledgments take on a new meaning, for indeed this work would not have existed without the many who have talked with me—informants, friends, colleagues, critics. In fact, how could I separate who is who among those who have been with me these past years?

It is particularly hard for an anthropologist to separate friends from informants. Informants must be friends to be informants. So it is only tradition that makes me single out "Ted," who let me use the taped fragment of conversation analyzed in chapter 10. I think of him as informant, but also as friend.

I also thank the many friends and acquaintances who have made America for me these past seventeen years. I hope that the voice with which I recast their speaking in these pages does not betray them too egregiously. The small town that, together, we have recreated in the middle of New York City is a testimony to their collective strength.

Even though it is not conventional, I would like to thank those who have established the tradition of anthropological studies in American culture. They have blazed a trail that has made our own work so much easier. It is in recognition of our collective debt that I dedicate this book to Margaret Mead.

Closer by are those with whom I have discussed my essays, particularly Roy D'Andrade, Walter Dickie, Clifford Hill, John Kirkpatrick, Raymond McDermott, Susan Montague, George Spindler, and of course those who have contributed to the volume.

It is not tradition only that makes me close this list by recognizing the participation of Susan, David, Michael, and Catherine—"my" family— or rather the family to which I belong. Together we have discovered new possibilities in America. We have made good music, and I look forward to the music we will make.

Hervé Varenne
New York,
September 1982—May 1985

Anthropology, the science of man, is often held to be a subject that may satisfy our curiosity regarding the early history of mankind, but of no immediate bearing upon problems that confront us. This view has always seemed to me erroneous. Growing up in our own civilization we know little how we ourselves are conditioned by it, how our bodies, our language, our modes of thinking and acting are determined by limits imposed on us by our environment. Knowledge of the life processes and behavior of man under conditions of life fundamentally different from our own can help us to obtain a freer view of our own lives and of our life problems.

Boas 1940, v

Introduction

Hervé Varenne

This book might have been subtitled "Cultural Constraints on Everyday Life in the United States." It is a book about how people conduct their lives in this country and in relation to its institutions. It is also a book about America—about some of the things that can happen when people who live in the United States confront what makes it a particular kind of place. To live in the United States is to participate in a unique historical process that has solidified into a set of laws, customs, habits, and rules for behavior and the interpretation of behavior—that is, into what we call a "culture," *American* culture.

This book also shows what a particular intellectual tradition can contribute to the study of survival in the United States. This tradition is the one that, for close to a century now, has insisted that to know Man, one must know human beings in their multifaceted, historical circumstances while resisting any easy move to universal and eternal "natural" verities. This tradition is closely associated with the discipline of anthropology, though it is of course much broader. Philosophers, historians, and sociologists have taken this perspective on what human beings produce. But anthropology, more than any other discipline, has been founded on the principle of the variability of human adaptations, a broad matter usually glossed by the term "culture." Anthropology, however, is not well known for what it can contribute to the understanding of modern life, and one may wonder what the anthropologists who have written for this volume can in fact say about America and the people who live there.

There has never been much anthropology of the United States. When anthropologists come back home it is often as quasi outsiders, what Freilich called "marginal natives" (1970). As such they may appear naive or superficial, particularly when their work is compared with that of the native ritual specialists. What can those who observe life tell those who live it?

Many, such as John Dewey, Josiah Royce, George Herbert Mead, or more recently David Riesman, Philip Slater, and John McDermott, or again John Kennedy and Martin Luther King, Jr., to name a very few, have written and spoken about America as Americans trying to understand, and improve, what they are passionately involved with. What kind of educational system suits and nurtures democracy? What is the relation between Christianity and the building of community? What is the modern world doing to the rugged individualism that has made America? What are the risks of an overemphasis on satisfying individual needs? What is the "American dream"? What should America do to remain the "city upon a hill"? In their various ways and from many points of view, these prophets, like all those who speak from conviction within the dominant dialogue, directly address the American imagination with the particular efficacy that a myth well told always has for its audience. Indeed, what they do is express in words appropriate for public settings the yearning and puzzlement that most people in the United States, at one moment or another, could also express, albeit perhaps not in the same vocabulary. The work of people like Studs Terkel should convince us again that wisdom is not dependent upon rhetorical competence.

Confronted with such competition, the anthropologist is at a disadvantage if he is expected to contribute to the same kind of conversation with the same vocabulary. In the prophetic mode, there is probably little that anthropology can contribute when it is being itself. The anthropological task presents itself as a scientific one—as descriptive and analytic. It is also a task that is oriented to the universe, to all men rather than to some of them. When the scientist prophesies—that is, when he draws implications for our philosophical discourse from generalizations—it is because of political responsibilities that frame science but are not quite part of it. To produce the theoretical work that makes a bomb possible is a different activity from warning the polity of the dangers of building the bomb. The anthropologist, thank God, is not in a position to wreck our planet. But there still is a distinction between the prophetic and the analytic tasks that, at different times, anthropology may be called on to perform.

When all this is said, one might still wonder why anthropologists should claim the right to be heard along with the sociologists, psychologists, historians, literary critics, and the like, who have traditionally been given the task of holding up a scientific mirror to America. In fact, few anthropologists would disagree with what Boas wrote in the epigraph to this Introduction. Most refuse to be imprisoned in dark and dusty museums purveying exotica for curiosity seekers. Anthropology's destiny is to *US,* if not to the *U.S.*—natives and intellectuals who wish to participate in the contemporary conversations about what it means to be human. Anthropology will "help us to obtain a freer view of our own lives and our life problems." How? the skeptic may ask.

The task of the social sciences is to contribute to the general understanding of human behavior. Traditionally, anthropology has taken on the task of doing this by seeking what, to Western eyes, appears exotic, human, but somehow more different from what we take to be humanity than can be encountered among us. The value of this journey into the most Other lies in what it contributes to the broader, interdisciplinary conversations that together constitute the social sciences and, beyond them, our humanistic knowledge of ourselves. In these conversations anthropology has generally appointed itself the gadfly that challenges any statement about human nature built solely from observations of people in our societies. From Margaret Mead to Clifford Geertz, this has been a main theme of the discipline's contribution when addressing the other disciplines that also speak about humanity.

There has also always existed within anthropology a movement to take a determined look at our societies and to underscore what others would see as exotic. This movement has a long history. Americanists will accept the work of the Lynds in the late 1920s as "anthropology" (1937, 1956 [1929]). Lloyd Warner, on his return from research into the social structure of an Australian aboriginal society, conducted in the thirties and forties what remains the most massive community study of an American town ever done (1941–48). There is less work from the fifties and early sixties, but in recent years interest in an anthropology of America has blossomed, as the Spindlers' recent review demonstrates (1983).

Anthropology has always been "on the way back home," as people like to say. All the contributors to this volume, in one way or another, are coming home. Most of them have worked intensively in other cultures: Beeman in Iran (1976, 1977, 1986), Drummond in Guyana (1977a, b, 1980), Myerhoff among the Huichol Indians (1974, 1976), Singer and Moffatt in India (Singer 1980, [1972], 1984; Moffatt 1979 a, b), Greenhouse in Mexico (1979). Some have published extensively on their work in America (Drummond 1978; Greenhouse 1982; Myerhoff 1977, 1978; Singer 1977, 1984; Varenne 1977, 1978, 1982, 1983). All are keenly aware of the paramount importance of an awareness of the Other. All would insist that the journey back home cannot be completed. The movement that takes the anthropologist away is central to a useful return. While traveling, the anthropologist develops approaches to understanding the exotic qualities of the Other, approaches that are well suited for analysis of our own behavior in its exoticism.

The different, the surprising, the exotic has always been the prime candidate for what we usually call "the cultural." But anthropologists also insist that the nonexotic, the unsurprising, everything that does not strike us as "different" is also a product of cultural processes. Planning a parade in Los Angeles must be understood in the same terms as a Balinese cockfight. Both are the result of historical processes and also of a continuous human activity. Both are constructed; both are "artificial" in the classical sense. Neither is "simply" the product of natural drives that would mechanically determine behavior. The natural drives that do act upon us are little more, and little less, than the material we build our lives with. Because of this building, the end product is thus always elaborated in unexpected ways that go beyond necessity.

Measuring the distance between nature and some state of culture is a task for which anthropologists have trained themselves in encounters with the Other where the artificiality of such apparently "natural" structures as those that govern male/female relationships, for example, could be more easily revealed. This training, the contributors to this book believe, is particularly useful in revealing the constructed aspects of the life people live in America. It is useful in suggesting new ways of understanding the processes through which people end up producing statements, behaviors, institutions, and life careers that will somehow look more "American" than, say, "French." In fact, it might be said that the contribution of anthropology to the social sciences has been the demonstration that human beings are indeed creative of their world, thereby strengthening the humanistic insights that the nineteenth-century mechanistic biases had threatened. What anthropologists can now offer are exemplary analyses of the conditions of this creativity.

This overview of the contribution of anthropology applies, in one way or another, to all anthropological work. What I offer here is the product of a general tradition and also an argument for the usefulness of a specific approach within this tradition. While there are many nuances of outlook among them, all those who contribute to this book start with the assumption that one can learn about human beings only in terms of their creative capacity for symbolizing. Symbolizing, as understood here, is the activity of transforming an object, an experience, a social encounter into "something else"—a word, a story, a myth. Symbolizing is an imaginative activity. It is creative. It is also a very practical art. It is something that human beings concretely do when they are together. It is an aspect of their behavior.

Such an approach has many consequences that differentiate it from approaches, in anthropology and in other disciplines, that collapse the symbolizing capacity into personal fantasy, what people believe (which would rarely be "true" or "adequate") versus what they do (which would reveal their "actual' reality). If symbols—say, the American flag and the ritualism that surrounds it—are visible, then they have the same reality as, say, eating a hamburger. This, at least, will be assumed by the contributors to this book, whatever their own theoretical positions on a host of other problems.

One corollary of an interest in symbolizing as an act is the search for a multiplicity of symbols that respond to each other. No symbol means "by itself." Symbols are powerful only as they relate to each other. When looking at symbolizing in the United States, one cannot look at any one setting in its separate terms. One must see, in the specific organization of any setting, echoes of other settings it must answer to. Thus families echo schools, whites echo blacks, individualism echoes egoism, and community values echo conformism. This system of echoes is what we will call "America."

Some will consider our decision to talk about America as a constraining pattern—that is, as a culture—to be the most controversial aspect of our work. Whatever happened in the 1960s, it clearly transformed the paradigms that had dominated the study of America from an assumption of holism to an assumption of more or less radical heterogeneity. Since Glazer and Moynihan (1963) at least, it has been very difficult to argue that there may be something limiting in the statement that a multiplicity of cultures are maintaining themselves in the United States. By the later seventies, thoughtful observers were left trying to reconstruct a field for American Studies that would be based mainly on local analyses of regional processes (Wise 1979). In fact, this movement away from assumptions of homogeneity was a profoundly popular one, and scholars may not have done much more than express what became the common sense. "After all," people will say, "we are all different. Just look around you!"

Let me say at this point that the authors of the essays in this volume do not accept the radical implications of these developments. People who live in the United States do speak in many voices that are easily identifiable. Methodists do not speak like Catholics, males like females, second-generation Italians from New York like tenth-generation Boston Brahmins. Each voice, however, has a place in the chorus. Indeed, the signs that help identify the voice, and the system of connotations each carries, are controlled by the other voices and ultimately by the chorus itself: ethnicity, religion, and any of the other qualities in terms of which people can be distinguished in the United States, are not simply produced by internal processes. Rather, they are developed in interaction: Italian ethnicity is controlled by the political forces that have granted Columbus Day, the Mafia, pizza, and pasta to "Italians." People who have migrated from Italy do not have the power to refuse to place themselves in relation to such signs—even if they deny their relevance. All Italians are related to the Mafia because non-Italians will make it so.

As will be explained further, such an approach to America requires us to strongly differentiate people from the cultural patterns they live by. We take seriously the phrase with which I opened this Introduction: this book is about *people who live in the United States*; it is not, strictly speaking, about "Americans." We are not simply returning to the old search for statements about the American "mind" (as in American studies) or the American "character" (as in culture and personality work). "America," here, is the pattern in terms of which human beings must construct their lives when they interact in the United States. American culture is whatever one cannot escape in the United States. Some, like me, feel more strongly than others about the usefulness of searching for systematic distinguishing features of Americanness. We are convinced, however, that there is something "different" about some of the things that happen in the United States, something that is so stable historically and so widespread geographically that it cannot be ignored.

The authors of the essays are a varied group. They look at different things. They emphasize different aspects of what they look at, and they do not make the same things of their observations. But they are all out to put concern with "America" back where it belongs, at the center of what anthropology is in fact all about. Another premise they all accept is that making the quotidian exotic is not easy. It is not enough to mention that Americans don't eat horsemeat and the French do. It is not enough to mention that there is something "not natural" in the crises our adolescents go through. Such observations are our problem, not our solution. Finally, it is a fundamental argument that culture is action. It is found in the practice of everyday life.

This volume is committed to an anthropology of America that emphasizes difference, constraint, and opportunities in the construction of everyday life. To emphasize this point, the book is organized into several sections framed by a series of action verbs intended to alert us to the variety of creative situations within which we act. America is told (part 1), it is crafted (part 2), it is improvised (part 3), it is resolved (part 4), it is done (part 5). Telling a story, crafting a statement, improvising a scene, resolving a dilemma, doing anything are all aspects of action. The organization of the chapters as illustrating one aspect rather than another is thus somewhat arbitrary, and any of the case studies could be understood as illustrating other aspects of the acts that produced the events examined, be they advertisements, movies, ethnic parades, church minutes, dormitory parties, sexual activities, or invitations to "drop in."

Action in culture must always involve a careful replication of traditional categories, displaying dominant themes that appear uniquely powerful as they act on our imaginations and also on the imaginations of others we may wish to manipulate. Action in culture is also always improvised. We never speak our minds except in words that others have used. But we never replicate, either. To make our audience pay attention to what we are saying, we must ring a change on the expectations. Any action in culture is at the time of its performance an "achievement," something actively constructed. In some ways, however, such action is also the end of a sequence—an attempt at closing an episode that may have been developing in threatening ways. Groups are not paralyzed by existential dilemmas produced by the clash of cultural prescriptions; they usually resolve them. These resolutions, of course, are temporary. The statement that attempts to bring a discussion to closure is soon followed by another statement that reframes it and keeps the group alive. There is no stopping action in culture.

Finally, action in culture is told. Nothing is more human, perhaps, than telling each other what happened yesterday, what happened in our absence, and then placing these descriptions in broader mythical, religious, or ideological frameworks. As I mentioned earlier, there are many settings in the United States where such tellings occur. The one I reflect upon in the first two chapters of the book concerns the telling of action in America that has evolved within anthropology and some closely related disciplines. These essays are theoretical and methodological inquiries intended to make explicit the relevance of the detailed studies that follow. We decided it might be better to separate the discussion of this relevance from the case studies themselves so that the argument could be made in more depth and less repetitively. The case studies thus must stand in the context of this Introduction, and vice versa.

The studies are presented in four groups. First (part 2), we have two studies of highly crafted cultural artifacts: commercials (Beeman, chap. 3) and James Bond movies (Drummond, chap. 4). Here the attention is on products in which nothing is left to chance. We know that every object appearing on the screen has been specifically chosen, that every word of an ad has been carefully edited. In the process, some of the dominant themes that have always been associated with America—individualism, choice, progress through machines, the state and the corporation—are particularly clearly articulated. And yet even here uncertainty and the transformative quality of cultural performances affirm themselves. The advertiser is never sure of the power of a campaign. The ensemble of myths to which people in the United States respond presents a complex, shifting image that does not allow for much standing still.

In the second set of essays (part 3), attention is on improvising in difficult situations. These chapters look at people as they try to deal with the identifications the culture offers: as "American" and as "ethnic." "How can one affirm one's Americanness when one is identified as an 'ethnic'?" Singer asks (chap. 5). "What can one do to reaffirm one's ethnic separateness when one is in danger of disappearing from the general consciousness? What will work?" ask Myerhoff and Mongulla (chap. 6).

The chapters in part 4 deal with temporary resolution of paradoxical aspects of American culture. What does one do with politicoreligious disagreements if one's reading of the Bible says recourse to the law is sinful (Greenhouse, chap. 7)? What can one do not to affirm one's whiteness in an integrated college dorm (Moffatt, chap. 8)? Greenhouse details the process that silenced certain Southern Baptists as they struggled with the dual prescription of "freedom of expression" and "consensus." Moffatt observes what happens when the prescription for "freedom of assembly" and "universal openness" (nonsegregation) have to be followed at the same time in a racially mixed dormitory.

Part 5 consists of two chapters detailing the effect of culture on two types of moments in everyday life when no time is given for crafting or improvising, when tensions cannot be resolved, when blows must be taken. The chapter by Canaan (chap. 9) shows how the American symbolizing of sexuality is lived by teenage girls in a suburban school as they continue the old struggle with slippery definitions of legitimate and illegitimate sexual acts. The chapter by Varenne (chap. 10) analyzes a few seconds of conversation when an invitation to "drop in anytime" that is not made is rejected. This analysis suggests a method of demonstrating the basic assumption of all anthropology, the assumption that culture does organize behavior in its details.

Each essay can be read by itself. Our intention, however, is to present a collective effort to which each contributes something. We do hope that they will be read together for what they say about the enterprise as a whole. This Introduction, the brief introductions to each part, and the Epilogue (Caughey), are intended to encourage a holistic reading. The effort presented, obviously, is still an early one. Much remains to be done. Much, however, has been accomplished already.

P
A
R   Telling
T   America

I

Editor's Introduction

It is the collective stance of the authors of this volume that symbolizing as a creative, and constrained, activity is at the heart of the cultural process. The next two chapters consider different problems associated with the scholarly telling of this process as it unfolds through the people who live in the United States and relate to its institutions. This process is what we call "American culture." To remain consistent with our assumption that this process is a very general one from which it is difficult to escape, we must also insist that what is usually referred to as "description" or "analysis" is itself a symbolic activity made possible and constrained by the environment in which it is done. An analyst cannot retreat behind the pretense that he or she is simply using the language of pure description that Western culture would somehow have developed. As I explain in the first chapter, the anthropologists' participation in a culture does not mean a total inability to go beyond what is offered. Such oversocialized views of humanity have been left behind. What our condition requires, however, is that we continually reflect on the operations we are conducting when we tell our observations and analyses to an audience. It is for such reasons that I say, anthropologists do not "describe" America, they "tell" it.

To the extent that they "tell" America (if not tell on it), anthropologists also create it for specific purposes. America is not an event to be mapped, as Lévi-Strauss taught us long ago (1963a [1958]), it is a model crafted to help (some of) us understand what happens around us. America does not tell itself. It must be told *by* human beings, *through* specific rhetorical means that will appear convincing *to* a special audience. This recognition of the conditions of work on America is not a justification for ethnographic license. Rather, it is a call for greater rigor in the overall task of the social sciences, the deepening of our understanding of human beings. The development of these sciences could in fact be seen as the evolution of these calls for various types of rigor. At the end of the nineteenth century sociologists and philosophers established that human beings could be understood only in terms of their sociability. The Boasians moved on to insist that rigor in this new endeavor consisted in recognizing that human sociability can proceed in many different ways. Human creativity in society was thus reaffirmed against determinist biases. In the course of this insistence on the role of culture, new questions were raised about the nature of observation and the link between observation and theory. The 1950s and 1960s directed our attention to this issue. This led to the more complex view that insists it is necessary to take into account the participation of the observer and his cultural baggage. Given this evolution toward a more exacting view of the total research activity, it is not surprising that we now insist on the need to pay attention to how the observer relates to his audience through the symbolic means (writing, lecturing, etc.) at his disposal.

The two essays that follow attempt to make explicit the theoretical, analytic, and ethnographic grounds that allow anthropologists to make certain types of statements about what happens in the United States. In the process, I point out those statements I consider inappropriate. Given the abstract character of this search, I begin with a common, concrete "observation" that is often reported by those who tell America—the observation that, as it is normally put, "Americans are friendly." I show under what conditions this statement might be accurate, what it is a reflection of, and how it might be put so as to throw more light on everyday action in the United States. This leads me to raise fundamental questions about the relation of action to structuring constraints, the place of differentiation, homogeneity, and diversity—matters that must be addressed in any model of, or tale about, America.

The second chapter focuses on the actual ethnographic tasks and on the constraints, resources, and possibilities that frame the work anthropologists can perform when they encounter the United States.

An Apache Portrait of the Whiteman

[J answers a knock at the door, and finds L standing outside.]

J: Hello, my friend! How you doing? How you feeling, L? You feeling good?

[J now turns (to) K and addresses her.]

J: Look who here, everybody! Look who just come in. Sure, it's my Indian friend, L. Pretty good alright!

[J slaps L on the shoulder and, looking him directly in the eyes, seizes his hand and pumps it wildly up and down.]

J: Come right in, my friend! Don't stay outside in the rain. Better you come in right now.

[J now drapes his arm around L's shoulders and moves him in the direction of a chair.]

J: Sit down! sit right down! Take your loads off you ass. You hungry? You want some beer? Maybe you want some wine? You want crackers? Bread? . . . How 'bout it? . . . Maybe you don't eat again long time. . . .

[At this point, J breaks into laughter. K joins in. L shakes his head and smiles. The joke is over.]

K: *indaa? dogoyááda!* ("Whitemen are stupid!")

Basso 1979, 46–47

1 Creating America

Hervé Varenne

"American"?

"Whitemen" may not be stupid, but the Apaches are on to something when they caricature their American neighbors by overemphasizing the displays of openness, friendliness, and concern that Indians would not perform in similar settings. When the white men were still only a rumor among the Apaches, Tocqueville was writing that, in America, the "manner" of men who meet by chance "is . . . natural, frank, and open" (1969, 567). Since then, many others have pointed out that in America people who barely know each other use first names, that they smile at each other and otherwise display signs of goodwill. Some, like Vidich and Bensman (1968), have also wondered at the way people who know each other very well as adversaries, if not enemies, will still, in public, smile, joke, and in all other ways *not* display their enmity.

If any pattern of behavior can be said to be "characteristically American," this is the one. Using first name with strangers, joking good-naturedly with political adversaries, is not typical of the "manner" of all men and women across the world. On the other hand, few if any general commentators on America have failed to mention the "importance of friendship." This unanimity is enough to make one suspect an artifact. But if, besides Apaches and Frenchmen, Britishers (Gorer 1948, chap. 4) and others have noted with more or less insistence the importance of friendship and a friendly demeanor, it must be because of some experience they have had in the United States.

It is the nature of this experience that is at issue among those who are at work on America as a culture. If so many have felt a "difference" when they encounter the United States and its institutions, we can feel confident we are not pursuing a figment of our imagination. What we cannot do, however, is rely on this common sense to tell us *what* was experienced. What else must we do with such observations? This is the methodological question we must start with. To do this, I think it will be useful to examine at some length what is implied when one talks about American friendliness, whether one is a native or an outside observer, whether one is using it to praise or to criticize. Friendliness is a relatively simple behavior, and a brief discussion of the American mode will help me introduce the kind of issues that must challenge all cultural anthropologies of America. What are Apaches, Tocqueville, Vidich and Bensman, and other observers of American greeting patterns saying when they argue that "openness" is "American"? Who are the Americans? What exactly are such observers saying? Are they saying that:

—Americans are friendly? Is friendliness in greeting the expression of the state of mind of (most? many? more than elsewhere?) people who live in the United States?

—it is common for Americans to greet people in a friendly manner? If we were to count instances of greeting behavior cross-culturally, would we find that people who live in the United States use first names most of the time? More than people in other countries?

—one should expect all people who live in the United States to either be friendly or act friendly? Or should we expect only people who have been born and raised there to exhibit the trait? Should we expect third-generation Americans to be more friendly than first-generation immigrants? What about blacks, southerners, women addressing men, and so on?

—friendliness is above all a problem that all those who live in the United States have to deal with?

These are the kinds of questions that any general characterization of the typically American will raise, whether it concerns "individualism," "democracy," "conformism," "materialism," or any of the other "isms" that are applied to the culture.

I will eventually argue that only by asking the last question can we move in a fruitful direction. At present, let us continue our discussion of the methodological issues raised in characterizing Americans as "friendly" by further examining such greetings. This will provide us with a concrete basis for the more theoretical discussion that follows. Notice that the analysis of friendliness in greeting starts with the observation of an event that is somehow surprising. Tocqueville's remarks are made in a chapter where he contrasts his experiences in England with his experiences in America. Vidich and Bensman are surprised because they expected adversaries not to be friendly, even in public. Initially at least, what "American friendliness" refers to is *an event that contrasts with other likely events in similar settings*. Without a contrast the event would not be noticeable. Perhaps it could be interpreted, as ethologists like to do, as something that all primates do to display nonaggressivity. One could then go no further, and we would have to dismiss a common intuition. Something more is going on.

To stress contrast is also to stress context. The event of using first names soon after meeting for the first time, an item of behavior sometimes used to justify a statement about American friendliness, does not stand alone. Whether or not the analyst is conscious of it, the analysis of the event depends on what happened before and after the greeting. It also depends on what might have happened but did not. It is important that the first names are used soon after the two persons have met for the first time or that it is happening even though they are locked in a political fight for domination in their town. We must know that these two persons have last names, that each knows the other has a last name and what it is. This tells us that both are explicitly *not* using these last names. We also want to know what the participants can say about the use of first and last names (to each other, in interviews, etc.). Finally, we want to know what other people might do with the same event, particularly people who do not live in the United States.[1]

Notice, at this stage, that we have ceased looking at the behavior itself, or at the setting itself, and are now looking at its historical and political context. We are looking at what the greeting is a response to and at the way it can be answered. We started with the two events that traditional ethnography gave us (individuals using/not using first names); we now have two sequences involving several participants. The first step of each sequence starts with the same behavior:

STEP ONE

Two men meet for the first time;

we know that two different utterances make sense as responses:

STEP TWO

2a	2b
They use first names in direct address (though they know each other's last names);	They use last names in direct address (though they know each other's first names);

We now also know that this sequence can have two sets of contrastive endings depending on an overarching code for proper conduct:

STEP THREE

First names	(2a) Use	(2b) Do not use
	3a.1	*3a.2*
Character-istically "friendly" culture (America?)	This is interpreted by others (or by themselves) as "friendliness" and "openness."	This is interpreted by others (or by themselves) as "cold formality."
	3b.1	*3b.2*
Character-istically "unfriendly" culture (Apache?)	This is interpreted by others (or by themselves) as "rudeness" and "improper familiarity."	This is interpreted by others (or by themselves) as a sign of "respect" or "consideration."

It would not take much more investigation to find out that the third step in the sequence could take many other forms. In any event, this step is rarely the final one if the situation is of any political import. In an American setting, one possible step four would include a discussion of the "authenticity" of an appropriately friendly greeting: Did the people "mean" it? Were they only pretending? This could be followed by commentaries on how terrible it is that people would pretend, perhaps followed by hypotheses about the cause of such pretense.

The ideal typical case I just drew is not completely artificial. It could be seen as a schematic summary of the process Vidich and Bensman (1968) followed as they moved from watching people greet each other in the streets of Springdale and maintain unanimity in political meetings, to a mention of the people's view of themselves as "friendly," to a stress on the shallow character of this friendliness, to a hypothesis that friendliness is an escape from the realization of powerlessness. Ted, my informant in the case I examine in chapter 10, followed a similar narrative structure as he told of his ambiguous encounter with a friend.

Two things are important here. First is that the issues we must raise are fundamentally interactional, social. A greeting pattern obviously requires at least two actors. In fact, to expand on Arensberg's analysis of the minimal unit of culture study, we must consider that, looking over the shoulders of the couple greeting, there stand an "enforcer"—the political institutions that make one, or both, pay a price for a misgreeting—and an "interpreter"—the ideological institutions that are given the task of identifying a particular greeting as a token of a general type.[2]

The second matter of importance that must be emphasized at the outset concerns the early entry of matters of "philosophical" importance into the development of any discussion of a particular instance of greeting. Obviously, in most instances questions of "authenticity" are not raised by a "hello!" However, if any issue is to be raised, then authenticity or other symbols of the same type will soon become the topic. It is not so much that all greetings are "important," but rather that a close linkage can always be established *by the participants* between items of behavior that analysts commonly consider unimportant and some of the "major themes" of the culture. The reality of this linkage is central to the work being presented in this volume, and I will return to the issue presently. But let us first go back to our questions about "American" friendliness.

Observationally, we have the case of observers (some native, some professional) who watch people greet each other, using first names and maintaining an open manner, and who then question their authenticity. We finally have the case of some observers who give such a sequence as an example of the American. These observers suggest this sequence is not "conservative European" or, for that matter, "Apache" if the joke I used as an epigraph is a good suggestion for another way of handling greetings.[3] Even if the sketch above were presented as the final stage of an exhaustive cultural analysis—and the material in chapters 8 and 10 suggests this would not be outrageous—the evidence would still be based on the single-case analysis that is at the core of ethnographic, anthropological approaches. Tocqueville and Vidich and Bensman imply that they have seen many instances of the use of first names. I could vouch that it is "prevalent" in all American institutions I know, from small-town churches to big-city universities and business corporations. I could even vouch for the "importance of questions of authenticity." I could call upon the reader's own experience. But I could not be explicit about the boundaries of the population that could be characterized as friendly.

Many argue that the only analyses worth making are those that produce a probabilistic statement about the relative frequency of a trait within a specified population. If this is one's position, then it is clear that any generalization of a pattern to a population must be based on a rigorous comparative statistical analysis. Some who should know better sometimes write as if ethnographic approaches could provide the grounds for such generalizations, as they claim to validate their statements by claiming that "many" or "most" of their informants exhibit the trait. In fact, any probabilistic analysis must be organized by two principles that are of interest here because ethnographic approaches can never fulfill them: (1) the population to be characterized must be sharply bounded on a priori criteria (e.g., all the people who are citizens of the United States, or any specifiable subgroup within this population); (2) the behavior that is to be considered characteristic of the population must be so operationalized that it is clearly distinguishable from other events.

Clearly, one could design a research project that would establish how often, within the boundaries of the United States, people use first names. This could be stratified by setting, race, sex, social class, national origin, citizenship, length of stay in the country, and hundreds of other "variables." Such a survey might suggest directions for research. But it would not answer the basic anthropological questions about the place of this "trait" in relation to other traits in the production of everyday life—that is, about "cultural patterns."

It is well known that anthropology has developed itself in contradistinction to probabilistic kinds of research questions. Sometimes it has been because the field situation made it materially impossible to ask them (the natives would not sit for the questionnaires, the limits of the population were not clear, the "trait" could not be unambiguously operationalized, etc.). The rejection of quantification goes deeper in fact. In the United States people certainly do fill out questionnaires, even if they sometimes grumble about it. The only justification for ethnographic approaches in this country must thus lie in the radical assertion that the patterns of importance are not statistical events. Since all the authors in this volume use ethnographic, or quasi-ethnographic, methods and, by default at least, find themselves on the side of the more extreme form of the argument, I will now make the case for this argument.

America!

In brief, for me what makes it necessary to understand a specific behavior in terms of the concept of culture in its particularistic sense is any evidence that the behavior is the starting point for a particular type of "political" problem in the oldest sense: it must be a concern for the polity, that is, for the institutionalized social order. Whether or not the behavior is "prevalent" is irrelevant to this analysis. Some of the most interesting behaviors in any culture are rare events—think of voting, for example. What is characteristic of the culture a person has to deal with is the institutionalized pressure exerted on his behavior. It is the resources the person can find around him as he works out his response. Such constraints and resources are relevant anywhere they are active and useful, and only there. The tautology is intended: the constraint is a structure, in Dumont's sense, and as such it is either there or not there (1980b [1966], 219). It is not more or less there.

Think, for example, of what it may mean to watch an American movie in France. The movie could not have been produced there. But it can start an interaction between itself and a French audience and, less abstractly, among members of the audience. The movie, given its particular form, has a certain power over the interaction it starts. This is the power that puts the French "at risk" of being American. But the rest of the interaction, for example, the conversation one may have about the movie with friends, is now going to be controlled by the French polity. At this point the movie can easily be transformed into a "French" cultural event as it becomes a token of "America," though it now is an America that Americans often will not recognize. Contrast this to the situation of someone who first walks the narrow hallways of Kennedy Airport. This person, perhaps a tourist or an immigrant, is in a position radically different than at home, since any misstep will now trigger an American institution—for example, the immigration officer who insists one stand in an "orderly" line. The person may personally "not understand," but even the revolt, if it leads to an interaction, will be responded to as an American event. It will be a token of "American racism" or of "foreigners with strange customs, who must learn."

The demonstration that there is an "American" way of doing anything must involve an analysis of the processes linking a complex set of behaviors that permit certain struggles, and games, to be conducted. It must be demonstrated, for example, that "friendliness" is powerful—so powerful, in fact, that it can be used to *lie* about the implicit relationship that is being established. We are on our way to our analytic goal when we can show that, while first-name greetings do imply "friendliness" and "familiarity," they can also be used when there is no friendliness or familiarity, when the underlying relationship is antagonistic and when the actors are aware that they are struggling. It then becomes clear that friendliness is so powerful that people must fear it.

Paradoxically, friendliness is never so culturally relevant as when one notices it is not there. Someone who can be said not to be acting friendly, someone we suspect of not being friendly, is acting in an American fashion, whatever his intentions, his national origin, or the extent of his personal "enculturation," to the extent that his friendliness is questioned. Any statement to the effect that someone is "not friendly" implies the existence of institutional pressures that make an absence of friendliness have consequences for the future of the interaction.[4]

"Absence of friendliness" cannot be operationalized. One cannot simply count people who do not smile when greeting strangers, since the absence of a smile is significant only if we are operating within the pattern that makes it a consequential event. A stern face is an item only when a smile is possible. This is to say that friendliness is a significant symbol, a pattern of behavior. It is itself related to complex patterns of other behaviors (e.g., those glossed as "individualism," "democracy," or "conformism"), all of which are politically consequential, from passing exchanges in the street to presidential campaigns and intellectual argument. I label this overall pattern "American" (rather than X, or "Nacireman"— American spelled backward, as Miner [1975 (1956)] suggested we do) to follow commonsense usage. *I do not do this to gloss a statistical frequency of traits in the United States.*

Such a stance does not resolve the questions we may want to ask about the extension of "America." Even if we agree that America is a pattern, we can still wonder where we encounter it, how we can test for its presence, when it began to be consequential, and how it can transform itself. Cultural anthropologists have not given these questions the attention they deserve. It can first be said that these questions are of a different nature from the ones we started with. They assume that we *first* construct a plausible pattern and then compare actual events to the pattern to determine whether they make sense in terms of it. Such an investigation could produce relative boundaries, but it would not establish the properties of the structure itself. Establishing a pattern is a hierarchically superior task, since it is a precondition to testing its extension in space and time.

Cultural anthropologists also have not been very interested in answering questions about geographical and temporal extensions of patterns, because good rules of thumb for guessing at such an extension are available. If we accept that, as I have been suggesting, a cultural pattern consists in the relationship between routine everyday behaviors ("smiling") and the consequences these may have in many different domains, including the philosophical questioning of the behavior ("Does he mean it?"), one may assume—until proved wrong—that, for example, if personal authenticity is at issue then "friendliness" is also at issue. If we continue climbing levels of generality, we can plausibly argue that anywhere the dominant political institutions of the United States are operative, we are "in America" (*whether or not* we are physically in the United States). America is where the Constitution of the United States, its legal and customary interpretations, and the problems it raises are consequential.[5]

In brief, a behavioral sequence is "American" in a structural sense if it can be shown to be a transformation upon a form that is politically relevant in the United States. These forms include not only those that are related to "politics" in the narrow sense (the Constitution, the two-party system, voting patterns), but also those that have consequences in social action (greeting patterns, food consumption, dress, presentation of self in public). What allows us to say that a greeting structure is American is the demonstration that (1) it can be related to "democracy" (or "individualism," "authenticity," etc.) as a "cause" for it, a "sign" or "symbol" of it, or a "consequence" from it; *and* (something that may be most starkly evident to those who come in contact with the United States for the first time) that (2) it is a political act that defines the terms of an interaction, even before it is an expression of a personal feeling.

America and Americans

I began my discussion of friendliness with a list of questions. The first was "Are Americans friendly?" This, as far as I can tell, is the normal way of asking questions about culture in an American conversation. It is a question about people and about their mental states. It is a question about an individual, a person with feelings that may or may not be friendly. It is not a question about a social fact. The last of my questions was "Is friendliness a problem?" The preceding pages began showing what can be done if we decide to answer yes to this question and look at culture as the product of institutional processes that organize politically significant relationships.

If American culture is a political event, if it is the pattern or structure of the temporal unfolding of complex interaction between many people, then America constrains *all* human beings that relate to the United States, whether they live there or not, whether they "understand" what is happening to them or not, whether they are "American" in the usual sense or not. In this perspective, the personal constitution of the individual as a separate entity ceases to be a central tool for understanding the culture itself. What remains is the intuition of difference, contrast, and reproducibility we started with. To separate culture from personality (or cognition), America from Americans, is not to reduce culture. On the contrary, it is to recapture our interest in "prior customs" that "form the habits [of individuals]," as Dewey might have put it (1930, 55). But the customs that are "prior" to any historical individual are themselves *human* creations. To be interested in patterns of customs—culture—is to be interested in what is particularly "human" about human beings.

"Humanity," in this context, concerns the ability to vary modes of ecological adaptation, to institutionalize these variations, and to reproduce them. Above all, producing varied adaptations to environments is a group event. No human being adapts "by himself." The modalities of the adaptation, that is, its pattern or "structure," become imperative to the members of the group only as a secondary step: we adapt to our group *after* our group has adapted to its environment. The fundamental questions concern the way a group pattern gets established, institutionalized, and then reproduced through individual members who are not, strictly speaking, "the group" and are not directly "wired in" with each other. Whether this adaptation comes to generate the personal psychological constitution of each member should be considered still another question.

As has been recognized from Dewey to Geertz, the institutionalization and reproduction of variable adaptations constitute a problem of "communication" or, in modern jargon, "semiotics" or "dialogue." What has not been so readily recognized is that communication or semiosis depends on patterns of signification (the recognition that a message is "meaningful," that its behavioral base "makes a difference" and has consequences) that are institutionalized by sociological processes. It is tautological to say that members of a group "share" a communication structure. They do so by the simple fact that they are in political relation to the group *whatever their psychological (or cognitive) makeup.*[6] What makes a message a message is a response, any response. It is not the "meaning" "given" to the message by the speaker (or hearer).

Our problem is that questions about the structure of communication systems ("culture") and questions about the cultural constitution of persons ("personality") have been confused by most of those interested in human variability. When we look at the most immediate philosophical roots of American cultural anthropology, the movement toward psychological concerns is easy to understand, for such concerns have always been dominant in the pragmatist writings that, directly or not, shaped the anthropological tradition. Paradoxically, perhaps, it was all the more difficult for these concerns not to dominate, since in the statements of philosophers like Dewey, Mead, or Royce the emphasis was precisely on the sociocultural constitution of the personality. That such questions are very "American" does not make them less important.[7] The problem for anthropology is that these questions made it lose sight of the previous question, that of the constitution of culture itself.[8]

The question this book addresses, then, is not "Americans" in their psychological plurality. It is America itself, the environment that may transform some human beings *into* Americans. Unless we adopt a radically mechanistic and deterministic stance, we must expect to find that most people who live "in terms of America" (rather than "in" it, since it is not a physical entity) are *not* "American." But we blind ourselves to the very humanity of our condition if we refuse to consider that individual lives are constrained. "America" is a gloss for a particular patterning or structure. It ⁓ is not an object, nor is it a population.

The Integration of America

When Ruth Benedict talked about cultural patterns, she also talked about "integration." When her students and critics thought about integration, it was to make the concept a hypothesis about psychological sameness. This is not the place to argue whether Benedict "meant" to do this. But since the demise of the "culture and personality" school in the late forties, any claim to have described a pattern, or structure, in a holistic, integrated fashion has been greeted with the routine criticism that such an approach "cannot handle diversity" and that it assumes a "homogeneous" population. In fact, there are no grounds for expecting any population to be homogeneous in the traditional sense.

I would now like to move from criticizing the dominant ways of studying culture to presenting the position I consider useful. I will approach the issue of structural integration first formally and then from a point of view that preserves temporality and process.

The Structure of Culture

In formal terms, the concept of structure as used here has nothing to do with the simple repetition of a single trait. A structure is, as Piaget and Bateson said repeatedly, a system of *transformations* (Piaget 1968) that operates because of internal *differentiations* (Bateson 1972, 317–18). Adapted to a theory of culture, such statements imply that we must expect internal differentiation, differences that make a difference, to be the very condition for the integration of a culture. A description of America must point out the significant differences that are the product of cultural structuring. To give a cultural account of America is to highlight the ways bureaucracy is not family, for example, machines are not men, Italians are not Jews, being ethnic is problematic with regard to being American.

In the past an interest in such differentiations often led to a focus solely on the "categories" themselves. If the category father is different from the category mother, what is the feature that distinguishes each category? In traditional semantic analysis this feature is treated as a substantive, univocal quality of the object the symbol simply refers to: father is differentiated from mother based on the reality of "sex." Sex itself is a substantive reality differentiated from "age," and so on. In sociology and psychology, this distinguishing feature is treated as a variable, a property an individual possesses that, hypothetically, makes him or her behave differently from other individuals.

The structuralists I mentioned approach the problem differently. First of all, the categorical difference, to be effective, must have a behavioral base. The maintenance of the category bureaucracy depends on the performance of certain acts that can be differentiated from the performance of other acts that have the property of signaling "family." However, the differentiation is not produced through a replication of some objective, finite property of the category. Rather, the differentiation is the result of (symbolic) operations performed on the indefinite properties of the behavior or object. Neither bureaucracy nor family has absolute properties. It has been said of the family that "the more one looks at [it], the more it isn't there" (Leichter 1978, 567). It could also be said that in America the more one does not look at the family, the more it *is* there, as what one is looking at is *not.* The American cultural structure is *in* the operations that distinguish between the two: fatherliness is not motherliness, whoever performs whichever for whatever reason.

These principles would apply to the study of any culture. The issue of integration through differentiation is in fact more complex in America because the culture is articulated around such categories as freedom, choice, individualism, difference, which to manifest themselves must be per-formed so as to contrast with the performances of despotism, obligation, socialism, and sameness. If my analysis holds, these must not simply be "ideas" or "values" to Americans. Above all, freedom or despotism must be something that they *do,* symbolically. For freedom to be relevant, Americans must construct an environment in which they will see the signs of freedom (and thus the signs of despotism). If we are to be able to choose, Beeman reminds us in his essay on advertising (chap. 3), a variety of ob-jects must be offered for sale. Choice must have a concrete, material basis: it must direct industrial production. To demonstrate the existence of "free-dom of assembly," there must be occasions for people to meet separately from others and do different things. As Moffatt suggests (chap. 8), the con-crete problems people may have in a racially integrated dormitory reside not in the personality trait of "racism" but in the behavioral paradox that makes it impossible to distinguish the symbols of "freedom of assembly" (selection of a group of friends from among one's acquaintances) from the symbols of "racism" (segregation of some people among one's acquain-tances with whom one is *not* friendly).

The manifestation of difference is thus itself a symbolic event within the cultural structure. It is characteristically American to be different in the sense that it is characteristic of an institutionalized environment. It is both a positive prescription and a danger. "Difference," like friendliness, is sacred and thus dangerous. It is an issue in interaction. As I have shown elsewhere (Varenne 1977), it is characteristically American for a small town to offer twelve different ways of worshiping God with your friends and acquaintances and twelve different ways of not worshiping God. Such a display makes for an integrated structure, even though the end product of the cultural process is people who can be seen by any outsider as "very different" from each other. The participants themselves are aware of these differences—not surprisingly given that the culture is tuned to highlight them.

Integration, from this perspective, refers first to the patterns that institu-tionalize domains of human life, link a set of symbols to each domain as "what it is all about," and then differentiate people by using these prop-erties. America, for example, has institutionalized something it calls "ethnicity" (by insisting that the Census Bureau preserve appropriately symbolized statistics,[9] that appropriately designed rituals such as parades be performed, that local or national political struggles be fought through appropriately based groups, etc.). It has linked to the domain a set of other symbols and stories: ethnicity is a matter of descent (where your grandparents were born), it is a matter of life-style ("culture" in the popular sense—see Moffatt, chap. 8 for more on this), it has to do with the supposed human propensity for wanting to live with people who are "like" oneself. "Ethnicity," with all its connotations, is institutionalized as a human universal. This analysis is then justified by demonstrating how "different" Jews are from blacks—something they have no choice but to be at moments when ethnicity is made interactionally, that is, politically, relevant. Gentiles are not welcome in Jewish parades (Myerhoff and Mongulla, chap. 6).[10]

Integration also refers to the patterns of patterns that establish linkages and correspondences between apparently disparate domains. "Ethnicity" is institutionally different from "religion" or "education." Yet as Schneider has suggested (1969), the matters highlighted in each domain correspond closely to those highlighted in others. Most of the American interpretations of the process that multiplies religious denominations are essentially similar to the interpretations that explain the multiplication of ethnic groups. The institutional constraints that maintain symbolic differentiation between the denominations are essentially the same as those that maintain the groups: demonstrations of differences in life-styles (spaghetti versus lox and bagels), rituals where the totems of each group are prominently displayed (infant/adult baptism, parades), rituals of cross-group solidarity (the hyphenation of ethnic identification as [ethnic adjective]-*American*, community church services), use of the differences in national politics, and so forth. Finally, the symbolic performances that establish the existence of a multiplicity of nonmelting ethnic groups and of a multiplicity of churches, along with any evidence that suggests that organizational difference in the United States is a fact and increasing, are also a justification of America as "the land of the free."

Structure in Process
Such structuralist arguments, however, do not highlight the historical processes that are continually at work transforming the relationships between the different domains and their properties. It is easy to present structures as if they were absolute facts that mechanically determine behavior. As Drummond emphasizes at the end of his analysis of the tension between man and machine in various forms of popular culture (chap. 4), even such apparent polar opposites as "man" and "machine" are not fixed referentially or semantically. The distinction between the two is problematic. For a man not to be a machine must mean that in some way he can be compared with a machine. Any new machine (the computer, for example), any

new statement about the nature of man (out of biology, for example), challenges our performative understanding of both man and machine.

We must go further. The development of structuralism has been accompanied by a running commentary that challenges its analyses of human behavior in the name of the acts of speaking and behaving. I am thinking here of people like Bakhtin (1981), phenomenologists like Merleau-Ponty (1973 [1969]) or Ricoeur (1976), pragmatic philosophers and their modern descendants (Geertz 1973b; Singer 1984). In many different ways, they insist that at the moment of speaking, in what might be called the radical present, all social structures suddenly hang on the future activity of an individual that cannot be understood mechanistically. This radical present is a theoretical point, since all action takes place within a context that immediately responds to the act of the individual and thereby resocializes it. The experience of uncertainty, however, is one that we all have and that is well documented. As Bakhtin emphasized, the most serious of statements is only as strong as the laughter that may follow it. We have only to watch old movies to see that what used to be taken as the most sincere display of deep emotion will now be taken as parody. We may also come to the uncomfortable realization that our own displays of serious concern will soon be laughed at. In general terms this is simply a restatement of the relative arbitrariness of the signs we use to communicate. In time this arbitrariness will reveal itself, since things do change.

Outside the social sciences, the possibility that cultural arbitrariness will suddenly be exposed is evoked by the tale of the emperor's new clothes. For a while, people refuse to trust their eyes; instead, they trust the crowd. Culture has won over Man, but Man eventually wins in the person of the little child who asks why the emperor is naked. At that moment, it is implied, the consciousness of the kingdom is radically transformed, and enlightened rationality triumphs. In real life, I suspect, the child's mother would have said something like, "Of course the emperor is naked, but don't mention it or you'll get us in trouble!" If Bakhtin (1968 [1936]) is right, only the clowns in the marketplace could mention the emperor's nakedness, and only so long as they were not imprisoned. We reach the limits of the ability to perform the truly different when we encounter the highly institutionalized. At this moment the consequences of a performance other than the one expected will be so uncomfortable that few are likely to risk it. But this is true only if the performance is itself symbolically marked as a direct threat. If it falls in the gray area of the simply unusual, possible but never done before, somewhat challenging but not aggressively so, the institutional responses may try to incorporate it. The act that was unique now becomes legitimate. Other people may come to perform it, and everything else may change to accommodate this "new" event.

This analysis is only an extension of Saussure's view of linguistic change. If he is right, all utterances deviate somewhat from the structural norm. They are effective in interaction to the extent that they are recognized as institutionally appropriate. Practically, this means that the difference is ignored. At any time, however, the difference may be institutionalized, and a variant is then born. As this happens, all other aspects of the system that were dependent on the original form of the utterance must themselves change so as to maintain the necessary structural differentiations. This model for change is not a critique of structuralism. On the contrary, structuralism was produced by the need to deal with the kind of change in which nothing can happen without consequences for everything else. The history of languages and, I would argue, the history of cultures is the history of such changes. We need a structuralist theory to understand them.

A Hierarchy of Differences

One aspect of such a theory of change that is most important for understanding people in culture, Americans among them, is that it is hierarchical. French and Italian are "different" languages. They are also "the same" languages ("Romance") *at the same time.* The Romance languages are different from the Germanic languages, but at the same time the two sets are the same. And so on until we have defined a family of languages labeled "Indo-European." Dumézil and his students (Littleton 1966) have demonstrated that this linguistic analysis could be transformed into an "ideological" analysis, what anthropologists call a "cultural" analysis. I believe that such a hierarchical analysis could also be conducted from the level of a "national" culture (e.g., America) down to the level of regional, family, and even personal cultures.

If culture consists in institutionalized responses, it follows that cultural structures are constraining, strictly speaking, only to the extent that a particular item of behavior is responded to by a particular institution. To take an example from my recent work on family literacy (Varenne et al. 1982; Varenne and McDermott, 1986), there are different institutional responses to the various kinds of reading Americans do in everyday life. In particular, there is a radical split between the reading we do in the course of such activities as shopping, deciding which television program to watch, or leaving a note on the refrigerator door and the reading we do as part of school activities—for example, "homework." The difference lies, we argue, in the fact that homework, whoever is doing it, whatever his social class or ethnic group, however "successful" he is, is an event controlled by the school, which responds to it in specific terms, making an issue of "competence" in particular. Competence is not an issue "at home" unless one is doing homework.[11]

The implication of this analysis is that there is much less variation across families in doing homework than in other areas of family life. While doing homework, whether you are the child of recent immigrants from Laos or a daughter of the Daughters of the American Revolution, the spotlight will be on your competence. It is "your" homework that is being done; you are in constant danger of making errors; these errors will themselves be spotlighted. At home while not doing homework, it may make a lot of difference whether you are a recent or an old American, whether you are working class or middle class. Indeed, the constraints that constitute a "class" themselves respond to, and thereby control, only some of the family's activity. Two families of the same ethnic group, living within a block of each other in the same neighborhood, can differ radically on those items that are not directly controlled by the school, the church, or the political and economic systems. For example, these families may differ in the way they handle "intrusions" of other tasks into homework (the blaring of the television, the baby brother's requests for attention, the telephone). Such intrusions are not directly structured by any institutional representatives other than family members. It is thus not surprising that families develop special ways of dealing with them.[12]

Within the family itself, members' ability to be "different" beyond what is prescribed by the systemic differentiation of roles is controlled by the response of the other members, who preserve the institutionalized patterns that constitute the family in its own arbitrariness relative to other families. In other words, the same kind of structural analysis that can be used to sketch a "culture," to ground the possibility of such a pattern and place the limits of its power, can be used to sketch a family "style" and understand its power and limitations.

More important for our discussion of "variability" in the United States, this analysis argues for the need to sort out the "differences" we may find as we travel across the country, encountering its classes and ethnic groups. Greetings have a different quality in the South and in the Middle West, we are told. People in California are "laid back" whereas in New York City they are tense and aggressive. Black middle-class religiousness does not have the same expression as white middle-class religiousness. The dress styles that sell on the West Side of Manhattan will not sell in a Kalamazoo shopping center. What sells in Peoria may sell everywhere, but don't be too sure!

The list of such "differences" could go on forever. Regional differences, class and ethnic differences, family styles, all are relevant at a certain level of analysis. But none that we can document are cases of absolute variability until they have been analyzed further. In summary, an instance of "difference" may be a case of (1) the production of the structure as it differentiates to stabilize (bureaucracy/family); (2) the production of the particular aspects of American culture that requires displays of difference at appropriate times (Jew/Irish, Methodist/Presbyterian); (3) the production of a new institutionalized form allowed by the relative independence from institutionalized pressures of the particular instance (a family method to deal with intrusions into "doing homework"). An instance of "difference" could also be a true first occurrence, a "new" form that will challenge the old forms into a realignment that transforms the culture at some level. But we are entitled to be skeptical of anyone who claims to have found such a form.

In any event, it is probably the third type of differentiation that is of most interest to those who want to challenge any generalization to "America" of what happens in the United States. They present data from Indian reservations, obscure Appalachian valleys, recent immigrants, or marginal urban groups. Quite properly, they argue that the existence of such cases disallows any statement that a behavior trait is "typical" of the population. Claiming this would deny the relevance of the everyday life realities of these groups and thus prevent us from understanding them. It is a mistake, however, to stop our analysis with demonstrating what, at this level of context, may indeed look like absolute differences. We must also investigate instances where such differences are in fact active to get a feeling for their relative independence from the broader institutional forces: we should not mistake the differences between Jews and Irish as these are controlled by American interpretations of such differences for the differences that can develop because the internal organization of a particular situation is irrelevant to the general polity. It may be possible for people in the Appalachians to develop family or religious forms quite different from those institutionalized in the national media or the suburbs because they do not need to interact in those situations where national models on these matters are used. It is improbable that they would develop alternative economic relationships to the extent that they depend upon national and indeed multinational corporations for their livelihood. As has been shown by such di-

verse writers as Meillassoux writing about the systemic relationship between European industrialization and African family systems (1981) or
Drummond writing about the relationship between the "nanny-takers"
and "nanny-givers" of nineteenth-century England (1978), radical difference in everyday life-styles or ideologies can go hand in hand with social
complementarity. In such cases, however, there is no doubt that one part
of the group in interaction defines the relationship involved. The British
aristocracy that hired working-class women to take care of their children
defined them as nannies, whereas nowadays the Manhattan executive
who hires a Dominican woman defines her as a baby-sitter to make her
employment appropriate to the institutionalized images offered by the late
twentieth-century imagination (Lubin 1984).

At this point I could invoke Bourdieu and Passeron's ideas of "symbolic
violence" (1977 [1970]). In cases of economic exploitation of certain people by others legitimated through the use of appropriate symbols, Bourdieu's ideas are certainly applicable. My own goal is broader, however,
since I consider that all human relations, even nonexploitative ones, are
governed by similar principles. Culture, in my view, is relevant to the relationship of people to each other, individuals to individuals, groups to
groups, nations to nations. Power considerations cannot be ignored.
"America" is "typical" of the United States because it is powerful there in
the sense that a change in the organization of America will probably ne-
cessitate a change in the organization of Appalachian family life. That the
contrary would be true is doubtful. A French audience at an American film
is still independent enough from America to do things with the movie that
would not often be done in the United States. But most of these transformations will not return to haunt people in the United States, because they will
probably never have to deal with them unless they decide to open their
doors as certain intellectuals may do in film studies. France, on the other
hand, may have little choice but to open its doors. America, whether we
like it or not, is hierarchically dominant.

[Whitehead] congratulated Russell on his brilliant exposition "and especially on
leaving . . . *unobscured* . . . the vast darkness of the subject."
   All science is an attempt to cover with explanatory devices—and thereby to
obscure—the vast darkness of the subject. It is a game in which the scientist uses his explanatory principles according to certain rules to see if these principles can be stretched
to cover the vast darkness. But the rules of the stretching are rigorous, and the purpose
of the whole operation is really to discover what parts of the darkness still remain, uncovered by explanation.
   But the game has also . . . [the purpose of making] clear some part of that most
obscure matter—the process of knowing.

                                                         Bateson 1958 [1936], 280

2   Doing the
           Anthropology of
           America

           Hervé Varenne

Toward an Anthropology of America:
Dangers, Challenges, and Opportunities

The following is not a review of the work anthropologists have produced
over the past half-century.[1] But a brief discussion of the kind of work that
has been published will help me place more accurately what is presented
in this volume. In particular, I want to explore the processes that have led
anthropologists to focus where they have so far generally focused. Bateson, optimistically, warns us about the cover-up games scientists play. He
challenges us to look at the uncovered darkness and wonder at the analytic
operations that have prevented its covering. By doing so, he suggests, we
may be able to clarify (cover up?) the process of knowing. Anthropologists
of American culture have proudly announced that "by investigations of
. . . simple societies [they are] able to equip [themselves] better for the
analysis of more complex forms of human society" (Warner and Lunt

1941, 3). It is only fair that we also look for what can be missed when a society—any society—is studied "from an anthropological point of view." To do so, as Warner himself suggested, there is no better method than to look at what has been *done*, for "an account [of 'facts' and 'results'] is also an implicit statement of the changes taking place in the thinking and other activities of the researcher" (Warner and Lunt 1941, 6).

What anthropologists have done, above all, is to look at small towns, small neighborhoods, and subgroups that are clearly differentiated from the mainstream because of regional isolation, ethnic separateness, odd occupations, and the like. This was a great advance, for it made audible the voices of people who were easily forgotten by those for whom "culture" was a privilege of the elite, to be studied solely in the great literary, political, or religious texts of the time. However, there was also a danger in this democratization of cultural research when anthropologists failed to establish the connections that cannot fail to exist between the different voices as they struggle and as some win. This has made the anthropology of America slightly eccentric compared with the activities of the other disciplines that deal with the culture (sociology, history, philosophy, literature, "American studies," "popular culture," etc.). This makes the relevance of many anthropological analyses debatable: Is it really true, we may ask, that we learn something about the general issues that concern us—issues of political power, economic doctrine, racial strife, educational failure, life and death—when we read about drunks (Spradley 1970), rock stars (Montague and Morais 1976; Drummond, chap. 4), and Memorial Day rituals (Warner 1953)? My answer to this question is yes, but I am aware of the dangers involved. It is with these dangers that I want to start.

Dangers

As I see it, two major temptations confront anthropologists on their way to a proper anthropology of America. There is first the temptation of exoticism. There is also the temptation of parochialism. By the temptation of exoticism, I mean the movement toward those forms of life in the United States that to intellectual, middle-class eyes seem almost as exotic as the people anthropologists normally study. By the temptation of parochialism I mean the tendency not to place anthropological analyses in the context of the work on America that has been done by other disciplines. "America" is by no means virgin territory, particularly for those interested in imagination and symbolism. There is much to be learned from the abundant work produced by the disciplines that have occupied the territory until now.

Fifty years and more of work in what has called itself "American studies" is not to be dismissed, particularly when we come to realize how closely the evolution of this work parallels the evolution of culture theory in anthropology.[2] There cannot be much use in rediscovering "individualism" unless we can also specify how our statement of the pattern is more useful than the traditional ones.

Anthropologists, however, generally do not start from, or return to, the performances that are the symbolic focus of American uniqueness. They rarely look at literature, art, or religious thought, the staples of work in American Studies and in much anthropology of the non-American. It may even be that this lack of interest in performances that other scholars find so interesting is a deliberate political act—as finding them interesting is for the others. Doing anthropology is often said to be an act of rebellion. Anthropologists are sometimes described, and like to describe themselves, as people who stand slightly outside their own culture, who are more comfortable with the foreign than with the familiar. They are "marginal natives" (Freilich 1970).

In this context, the familiar within which one is not comfortable is the kind of everyday life that is strongly marked rhetorically as *the* "American way": the suburb, the shopping center, genteel liberal Protestantism, polyester administration. More often than not, a student will choose to work in anthropology because the discipline offers an escape from America. If fate (in the form of funding agencies, faculty advisors, etc.) pushes this student into working within the United States, the temptation is strong to search for the most exotic within the nonexotic: the regional poor, the ethnic, the drug addict. It is then easy to recapture the dominant anthropological attitude: the researcher places himself between "his people" and an audience. He assumes that the audience will be shocked and that it must be educated to a proper understanding of the rationality of exotic lifestyles. Alternatively, the temptation will be to look at items of the "popular culture,"—movies, the mass media, mass entertainment, and sports—precisely because they challenge elitist tendencies within the disciplines that hold mirrors to the United States and construct America.

It would be too easy to caricature the heroic stance that anthropologists can take when defending "their" people against ethnocentric, elitist attacks. There is a strong dose of hyperelitism in certain critiques of elitism. In fact, the work on what is exotic to middle-class consciousness within the United States has the value of ethnographic research in general. As Geertz would say, it "makes available to us answers that others, guarding other sheep in other valleys, have given, and thus [allows us] to include them in the consultable record of what man has said" (1973b, 30). It is work that makes our imaginary museum more complete. Given the prejudice against lower-class and fringe ways of life, the demonstration that such lives have a complex structure at least partially controlled by the people themselves has a clear political role. Labov's research on Black English (1972) is paradigmatic of the work that will have to be done again and again. Similarly, there is a definite value in demonstrating that products the masses appreciate have in fact a definite expressive power (Drummond, chap. 4).

Pure ethnographic work, polemic demonstrations of rationality in difficult circumstances, and the demonstration of popular wisdom are not, however, enough to establish the anthropology of America. To understand US we must go back home all the way to those areas that *are* US. "We" (anthropologists and other such intellectuals who like to place themselves at the margin) are not at the fringe, we are the center. An anthropology of America must be an anthropology of the center. It must be an anthropology of the center because the center is an ethnological location and we want to enter it into our "consultable record" of what men said there.

Above all, an anthropology of America must be an anthropology of the center because, whether we like it or not, America is, if not "the" center of cultural life on the globe in this second half of the twentieth century, at least one of the two or three most powerful centers. To study the center of America is, by implication, to study the whole world, since in a very direct sense the whole world is constrained by what happens there. Indeed, one cannot understand the fringe, as fringe, unless one also understands what makes it a fringe. The problem for Black English, for example, is not that it is not a full language. It is that it is a language in relation to an institutionalized language. Without understanding the place of Standard English in the economic and political institutions of the United States, we will not see what hides behind the popular argument that Black English is not a "good" language. Above all, we may not understand why a linguistic demonstration that Black English is just as useful for personal expression as Standard English is does not have the political consequence, in schools and out of them, that we might expect such a demonstration to have.

To do the anthropology of the center of America is to do something that has immediate political implications. Such implications will always be critical, whatever the writer's political orientation. We need only look at Warner's heroic efforts at arguing that his class analysis is not an attack on the American political system (Warner et al. 1949, 297–98) to see how difficult it is not to be critical even against our will. There is, however, a methodological paradox in doing a proper anthropology of America.

Whether or not Malinowski was able to achieve it, he will remain in the history of anthropology as one of those who taught that to learn about a people is to live their life in their own terms. To learn we must empathize. We are after the "native's point of view," initially at least, and that means we must mute our criticism, fight against our prejudice. Even if we do not like our natives, we must act as if we did.[3]

Above all, we must analyze the behavior of our American "natives" in terms of an institutionalized, cultural rationality. For American anthropologists this, interestingly enough, is what is most difficult to accomplish. Most anthropologists of America have probably been tempted to write something in the style Miner adopted for his analysis of American "body rituals" (1975 [1956], 1956). This parody of anthropological analysis is itself a caricature of what too often happens on the way "back home." Miner tells us that "The Nacirema [American spelled backward] are people who are . . . punctilious about care of the mouth." And yet they have "a rite involving a practice which strikes the uninitiated stranger as revolting. It was reported to me that the ritual consists of inserting a small bundle of hog hairs into the mouth, along with certain magical powders, and then moving the bundle in a highly formalized series of gestures" (1975 [1956], 11).

The natives, of course, call this ritual "brushing the teeth." It is certainly cultural, and Miner is right to point this out. But must he also imply that the only value of the "ritual" is the value that magic has among all primitive men (1975 [1956], 13)? Given the struggle anthropology has conducted to show that men are never "primitive," that all men are somehow rational within their constraints, must we now be told that Americans are primitive, irrational, and given to magical incantations?

Miner, I believe, does not want to suggest that Americans do not make sense. But he does not tell us how they do make sense. Above all he does not tell us how his observations about body rituals might possibly relate to the issues that must eventually interest anthropologists if they are to participate in the scholarly and political discussions that justify the work in its own context. How is brushing teeth related to democracy, capitalism, social class, children's failing in school? These are the questions addressed by the other disciplines that deal with America. Anthropologists cannot ignore them even if they do not answer them in the traditional vocabularies.

Challenges

There are two steps to a full return to US, at the center of America. First, we must actually go to what I would like to call the "symbolic suburbs" of the United States, those places where the dominant political institutions of America play themselves out most smoothly—at least superficially. There we must learn to listen as sympathetically as anthropologists try to listen anywhere else. We must do this not simply because the center is the center, but also because the analytic problems that confront us are fierce. As we listen sympathetically while nice suburban ladies tell us about their difficulties with their teenage children, as we try to transform what we have heard into an account that is relevant to what we are seeking, we soon discover that the traditional phrasings of anthropological theory are inadequate. We then discover that our analyses lead us to concerns that are shared by many in other disciplines, and that we have something to say. It is at this point that the real difficulties arise, for we still do not quite know how to contribute to the scholarly and political discussions at whose periphery we are now standing. Learning to participate in those discussions is the second step toward a full return to US.

Look, for example, at what happened with the publication of David Schneider's *American Kinship* (1980 [1968]). Schneider tells us that he talked almost solely to "white, urban, middle class informants." And yet he dares to use the word American. He tells us that, though the fieldwork that was the first stage in the work produced six thousand pages of notes, and though he has a compilation of all the quotations that support his generalizations, he refuses to incorporate them into the published analysis because he is afraid they might be taken as proof—which would be cheating, since there is no way he could specify how the examples were chosen (1980, 123–24). His analysis, like the analyses by all other cultural anthropologists, must thus stand on its internal coherence and on its fit with the theory of culture and action that underlies it.

One does not have to be a cold-blooded empiricist to realize that in making such statements Schneider is tackling many sacred cows. He is pressing the attack on many fronts at once, and the attack is all the more controversial because the field is middle-class America. Schneider's even daring to write about "American" kinship challenges any theory of culture we wish to espouse. The arguments we can use against him are not simply the arguments of theory ("This doesn't make sense") or of ethnographic particularism ("My natives don't do it that way!), they are the arguments of the participants: "My mother doesn't do it that way!" No analysis of American material can hide itself behind the eyewitness defense, "I was there and you weren't." When we read Leach's critique of Malinowski's analysis of tabu among the Trobriands (1958), only four or five of us can match it to a direct experience with the Trobrianders. When we have to consider the relationship between father as a "kinship" term and father as a "religious" term, the traditional disputes about primary meanings and metaphorical extensions take on a very different character. For an anthropologist to deal with American phenomena is thus always doubly dangerous: the professional critics are also the natives.

What is more, some of these critics have themselves produced an extensive body of writing that is not very different in genre from anthropological writing. Anthropologists are newcomers to the direct study of America, a field with a long history. As newcomers with a mission often do, they easily adopt a superior know-nothing attitude toward most of the work done on the United States in history, sociology, political science, and so on, as if this work were irrelevant to the kind of study now to be conducted. In fact, a vast amount of altogether good "anthropology" already exists not only in sociology, but also in history, American Studies, popular culture, and education. Anthropologists cannot reinvent the wheel and rediscover "individualism," for example. It will initially be difficult to improve upon complex statements on the relationship between individualism and the search for community such as those made by Riesman (1955; Riesman, Glazer, and Denney 1961 [1950]), Bellah (1970, 1975, 1985), Marty (1970), or McDermott (1976, 1983) in sociology, theology, and the history of philosophy. Anthropologists of America cannot ignore forever the traditional disputes in history about the early Puritan settlements and the extent to which they foreshadowed modern institutional organization (Higham 1974; Murrin 1972). They should know about the ongoing disputes about the role of nineteenth-century schooling in keeping American society open (Ravitch 1977) or closed (Katz 1971; Bowles and Gintis 1976).

Opportunities

If anthropologists cannot participate in these conversations, they will remain on the periphery. To converse with historians, sociolinguists, or literary critics, however, should not mean uncritically surrendering to the terms of the conversation as traditionally constituted. When addressing sociologists, for example, particularly with the dominant "empirical" forms, care must be taken not to succumb to the suggestion that all generalizations must be based on trait analysis. Unhappily, much ethnographic writing carelessly suggests that the "proof" of the analysis lies in a statistical observation. This may work when addressing other anthropologists, but it is catastrophic in the context of American studies. Ethnographic work can only produce "bad" trait analysis ("four out of my sample of five say that x is y, for which I deduce that saying so is characteristically American"). Either we abandon ethnography or we deal with the need to make a general argument that is not statistical. Similarly, while historians have found it useful to organize their observations in the shape of community studies (Lockridge 1970; Zuckerman 1970), it is also the case that anthropologists can contribute to their theory of social action (Varenne 1978).

In such confrontations lie great opportunities. When traditional phrasings are applied to American phenomena, their inadequacy soon becomes overwhelming, and the search for new phrasings can only be good for all the disciplines involved. I have repeatedly discussed the difficulties involved in talking about America as a structure constraining all who live in the United States. Clearly, we cannot do it by a commonsense reference to "shared values." Few natives, few scholars in the other disciplines that deal with the United States, will accept it. As Moffatt shows (chap. 8), one of the features of Americanness may be the refusal to accept group identification apart from a projected act of individual agency (or "choice" as it is phrased in the language of advertising investigated by Beeman, chap. 3. How can "we" be described as "sharing values" if some of us are Democrats and others Republicans, some liberals and other conservatives, some white and others black, some Catholics and some Fundamentalists? That these questions can be phrased in the language of "scholarly" debate (e.g., Feinberg 1979) cannot make us forget that they are also asked outside such debates, and often in terms of this concept of "culture" that we believe is our own when it is clear that it is also one of the dominant symbols of the American conversation. We can try to escape the implications of the debate by talking about pluralism, regionalism, multiculturalism, ethnicity, and subcultures, but this only postpones the problem. No talk of black, Irish-American, Catholic, or southern (sub)cultures in the traditional modes can stand very long before being challenged by some person who can claim participant status and refuses the postulated generalization. At this point, either we proclaim the "death of culture" or we go back and try to reformulate our traditional intuitions about cultural determination and difference.

I addressed these questions earlier (chap. 1). Let me finish by restating what I think will be the contribution of anthropology to the general conversations about America. Anthropology is about what has come to be known as "culture," a concept through which we attempt to capture the arbitrariness of human adaptations to the environment and the constraints placed on further action within this environment. Practically, this has meant a constant concern with variability and comparison and also with the details of everyday life. The fundamental insight is that variability of adaptation is not an abstraction. Rather, it is a constraint on the humblest acts. Given culture, we must analyze "how to ask for a drink in Subanun" (Frake 1980), for there is no way for us to know what is involved in getting the drink.

Given such a stance, Miner's interest in toothbrushing is not so far-fetched. It is not that his conclusions are strikingly new. Other observers of America have come to the conclusion that "the fundamental belief underlying the whole system [of body rituals] appears to be that the human body is ugly" (Miner 1975 [1956], 10). The simple fact of the custom does not allow the probabilistic statements he derives from it: "[The Nacirema] believe that, without the rituals of the mouth, their teeth would fall out, their gums bleed, their jaws shrink, their friends desert them, and their lovers reject them" (1975, 11). How would he know what the Nacirema really believe? The usefulness of the analysis lies rather in the demonstration that a detail of everyday life is powerfully constrained by arbitrary forces. There are Nacirema who do not brush their teeth or use deodorants; there are powerful voices that criticize the use of these devices. But they are still used because using them is a rational response: black teeth and bad breath do put you at risk of having your friends desert you. In "another culture" this may not be so. But people in the United States, whatever their background and personal belief system regarding the body, do not live in "another culture." They live in America. It is American culture that is consequential for them. And, in late twentieth-century America there are probably no dirtier four-letter words than "body odor."

We can go further. Besides translating Miner's reference to "magical beliefs" into a reference to an intelligent response to a constraint, let me suggest how we might in fact relate everyday rituals of the body to more general issues regarding American culture. First, brushing teeth is not simply an exercise intended to disguise natural bodily processes such as odor, decay, and fall; the process has a distinct mechanical aspect: to prevent odor, decay, and fall, it is necessary to treat the body directly, on its own terms, that is, "scientifically." The body must be treated as a machine so its processes can be disguised. Furthermore, the disguise of body processes is accomplished by attempting to maintain the body at what is considered the peak of its "natural" state: the ultimate goal is to keep teeth looking like those of a healthy sixteen-year-old. One does not disguise teeth by decorating them. One does not disguise the rest of the body by scarification, body paint, and so on. Thus it is not only that "Americans do not like body odor," it is that "body odor" itself is constructed through the activities that eliminate it.

We can go still further. It is well known that American culture is "dualist." It separates the body from the soul, the material from the spiritual, the evil from the good, the mechanical from the human, sex from love, and so forth. Such accounts are generally made in the philosophical mode. They rarely specify how such generalizations about American ideology are lived out in everyday life, except perhaps by suggesting, as did Miner, that it is a matter of "values." What anthropology can contribute, if it remains true to its ethnographic roots, is the demonstration that general themes are indeed lived in the routine of everyday life. I do not want to say that toothbrushing is a significant expression of the "great tradition" in America, but I do want to say that even the routine, apparently unimportant incidents of everyday life are constrained in very specific ways that raise the same issues that are raised when cultural consciousness is pushed to its breaking point at the most sacred, least routine moments.

In fact, the best in the anthropology of America has always done this. Warner's inquiries into the daily experience of class as his informants came home from cocktail parties, his unpacking of symbolic processes in parades (1959; Warner and Lunt 1941), Mead's linking details to "the American way to war" (1965 [1942])—debatable as it is in the form she uses—all point us in the right direction. The best of recent American anthropology continues to operate in this tradition. The power of ethnography has probably rarely been so well displayed as McDermott's linking the single gesture of a child volunteering to read in such a way to avoid getting caught not knowing how with the arbitrary cultural constraints that make it consequential to fail in school—a rational consequence in a meritocracy completely organized on individual competence (McDermott and Gospodinoff 1979; McDermott and Tylbor 1983). And while we might wish Schneider had given more thought to what would constitute the "proof" of his analysis, it may be that we do have this proof in Garfinkel's analysis (1967) of what is at issue when an ambiguously sexed person attempts to pass for a culturally appropriate "woman."

Part of anthropology's role is to demonstrate that America is indeed integrated and that the intuitive generalizations we can make from limited cases or texts do correspond to active constraints on the conduct of everyday life. Democracy is not simply an ideal, relevant only to philosophical musings and ritual speech. It is also a constraint on everything that happens in the United States, down to the level of casual greetings. The role of anthropological research is to demonstrate the performative relevance of America—that is, the usefulness of thinking in cultural terms about behavior in the United States.

Anthropology, in fact, will do more for studies of America. Funny things can happen on the way back from everyday life. It may seem naive to say that democracy is relevant to everyday life in America. It certainly would be naive to say that American life "is" democratic. It may be much more disquieting to say that in confrontation with everyday life what emerges most clearly is the ambiguous nature of something like "democracy." Life everywhere is uncertain and problematic. The conditions of life can be described. Democracy is a condition of life in the sense that individual merit is always at issue in school, that personal involvement—"friendliness" (Varenne, chap. 10), "love" (Canaan, chap. 9)—is always at issue when people greet or court. Describing these conditions is the first task of anthropologists.

Such descriptions do not exhaust what anthropologists can contribute. Unless they blind themselves, they will also see their informants' struggles against the conditions and the first signs of the transformations that are to take place. Toothbrushing may be something most of us do without thinking about it, but it is also something that can be brought to consciousness—when we go to the dentist, for example, or while watching commercials for toothpaste or denture adhesives or reading newspaper articles about fluoridation. At such times the questions about nature, machines, and the dominance of the spiritual over the material become concrete and easily contradictory. After all, if the body is to be invisible through being culturally manipulated into its natural state, we must treat it like a machine. To treat it like a machine we must know how it works, and this requires that we make the body visible. But making the body visible is precisely what we do not want. What are the makers of denture cleaners or adhesives to do? They must be offensive (mention odors and toothless gums) so we will not be (not smell and display youthful teeth that are not recognizable as dentures). But the more they make dentures a mentionable subject, the more they transform the institutional consequences of tooth loss.

That we are so intimately concerned with the tension between man and machine may explain why, in our explicitly mythological life, the dynamic tension between the two is a dominant theme. Drummond's essay on James Bond and his gun, John Henry and his sledgehammer (chap. 4), is an example of the next step in the analysis that will allow us, eventually, to move from the small details of everyday life to the great concerns of history and philosophy and to do so in a manner that will transform these concerns. Using an approach related to Moffatt's (chap. 8), Drummond does not simply say that James Bond movies "are" American. He says that the possible responses to the expression of certain themes put those themes in danger of change.

The task outlined here is a huge one that the work of the contributors to this volume does not pretend to fulfill. Anthropological work on America is still preliminary. But what has been done holds the promise of breakthroughs that could transform our understanding of America.

**P
A
R
T**

**I
I**

Crafting
America

Editor's Introduction

In a controversial critique of Marx's use of "labor" as an absolute reference point for social organization, Boon (1982, 85–97) emphasizes that the eventual question, if we are interested in the distribution of coats across a society, lies only secondarily in the *social* labor necessary to produce a coat; it is primarily the *cultural* imagination that makes it necessary for people to wear coats tailored of woven material. The shape of the labor is partially organized by the need to wear symbolically appropriate coats. If coats are to be worn, then the labor of keeping warm in winter must be divided between weavers and tailors. If, further, it is symbolically appropriate that these coats *not all look alike,* then the machinery that produces them will have to be so organized that it yields different kinds of coats.

This is one of the fundamental points made in the next two chapters. They examine massive economic events—advertising and mass-market movies—in their symbolic organization, as places where American culture best reveals itself, perhaps precisely *because* it is being used for ulterior reasons (greed, power, domination). Advertising, as Beeman emphasizes, is communication. "Addressors" send "messages" to "addressees" through a medium that establishes the "contact," using a special "code" in a certain "context" (to paraphrase Jakobson's classical model of the factors involved in communication [1960, 353]). As a message, a commercial is a total social fact that intimately involves all the participants as they make something out of it. As Drummond says of James Bond movies, they would not attract crowds if they did not represent to their audience common experiences transported into the world of myth where they can be made starkly explicit. Whatever our reaction to any commercial, this reaction participates in establishing the legitimacy of the message as something that can be both said and done.

There is no doubt that such products as commercials and popular movies are tools of the dominant commercial interests of our society and, through them, of those who want to master us. In fact, as Beeman reminds us, advertisers are absolutely frank about this. Advertisement is not art, it is a marketing tool. Its function is fully rhetorical. It is above all meant to convince. It is propaganda. The advertisers know this. Those who watch commercials know this. The advertisers know that we know that they are lying. We know that they know we know, and so on. Ultimately, there is no lie in advertising. But there is much of what McDermott and Tylbor (1983, 278) have called "collusion," an activity that "refers to how members of any social order must constantly help each other to posit a particular state of affairs, even when such a state would be in no way at hand without everyone so proceeding."

The economic function of the commercial thus is only a partial key to the interpretation of advertising as an activity. It is the problem of the advertisers and, through them, those who struggle for social power, as they attempt to control us: What can be so designed that it will make us participants, however unwilling, in our own control? We know that a message will not convince us, or hold sway over our imaginations, if it does not have a form appropriate to a specific historical and cultural condition. The commercial of yesteryear would not work. Mass-market movies produced in India or Japan do not begin to have an audience in the United States.

In fact, as soon as we move beyond generalities about "shared values," we do not know how cultural appropriateness is concretely achieved. Beeman and Drummond advance this search by emphasizing the fundamental ambiguity of the most carefully crafted messages. The advertisers do not know whether they are "successful." The moviemakers, even while they provide us with sleek tellings of our myths, are caught in the historical drift that redefines these myths as they are being told and appropriated. The producers of mass speech are in the peculiar position of having all the technical elements that allow them to shape their message completely. Nothing in a commercial is left to chance. Nothing is improvised; everything has been weighed. If the organization of symbols for sense and persuasion were a mechanical affair, then the advertisers would always be successful. In fact they rarely are, and not for long. The very mechanisms that the commercial uses (choice, novelty, segregation of different groups of like-minded individuals) must kill the commercial when the approach ceases to be new and the product is so widely distributed that it can no longer be pretended that owning it makes us part of an exclusive group.

Drummond goes on to suggest that themes of "man versus machines" and "man versus the state or corporation" that seem to pervade such myths as the James Bond saga, football and rock stardom, are themselves products of a puzzlement produced by our historical condition. This point is not new. Leo Marx concludes his classic study *The Machine in the Garden* with these words: "In the end the American hero is either dead or totally alienated from society, alone and powerless, like the evicted shepherd of Virgil's eclogue. . . . The resolutions of our pastoral fables are unsatisfactory because the old symbol of reconciliation is obsolete" (1964, 364). For Drummond there cannot be reconciliation—and not simply because "the old symbol" is obsolete. The old symbol was never new. Any statement of the myth, any appropriation of it by an audience, threatens the balance, if only because any use of the myth articulates possibilities that can now be examined for their fruits. Man, machine, state, corporation are not neat and mutually exclusive categories. The gunfighter, like the race-car driver or the test pilot, is the mythical representation of the historical event that suddenly offered industrial man sophisticated machines that made individual mastery possible. It also made man dependent on the machine, so that more machines had to be produced. The machine is the tool of individualism, equality, democracy. It is also the paradoxical Trojan horse that might make us finally dependent on the inhuman. Machines are human products that human beings bring to life, but they are not human. Here is a problem that no movie, even if its aim is simply to entertain, can resolve.

There is only one freedom
Freedom of Choice
Advertisement, Sun Oil Company,
New York Sun, 5 January 1948

3

Freedom to Choose: Symbols and Values in American Advertising

William O. Beeman

Introduction

Few areas of American life provide such easy access to a steady flow of varied symbolic communication as advertising. People in America are overwhelmed with its messages every day. Advertising is the one area of symbolic communication that has a clear sense of its own effectiveness, partly because its communication goals are limited. "Successful" advertising is thought to produce increased sales; unsuccessful advertising has no effect or a negative effect on sales.

Despite its ready accessibility and potential value as an object of study for those interested in symbolic communication in America, advertising presents several methodological difficulties for analysts. First, it is extremely difficult to separate effective from noneffective advertising simply by inspecting the final product. Paradoxically, advertisers do not really know whether their messages produce a positive response in consumers—the purchase of the product advertised. Advertisers of course know what effect their messages are supposed to produce—more sales—and, they gauge the success or failure of their communication by measuring those sales. But unfortunately for researchers outside the industry, it is difficult to obtain information on which advertising messages have succeeded and which have failed. Often advertisers themselves do not know—almost no one can tell the difference until long after the fact, when sales go up, go down, or stay level.[1]

As a consequence, the average consumer sees about as much good advertising as good television programming or good reading in magazines and newspapers—very little. Moreover, there is a difference between good advertising and good art. What the consumer thinks is good advertising, because it is visually attractive or entertaining, may actually be bad advertising because it does not get him to buy the product.

The standard literature on advertising training and interviews with professional advertising people reveal that advertisers know what kind of response they want. They often believe they can tell when they have achieved this response. But they are not able to predict with any certainty which messages will be successful and which will fail. This inability to predict the fate of one's messages is not necessarily characteristic of other types of communication in American life. Although they may depend more on hope than on certitude, most people enter ordinary verbal interaction with the expectation that their mundane greetings will have the intended effect, that people will laugh at their jokes, that stern warnings will produce sober responses, and that routine requests will bring action.

Advertisers seem to have no such certainty. Their messages are complex, to be sure, and the variables are extraordinarily difficult to control. Using a single message to sell soap to millions of people with diverse tastes and behavior routines is hardly the same as getting one's spouse, whose habits, quirks, and weaknesses one knows all too well, to fetch a cup of coffee. Nevertheless, most advertisers generally agree that advertising carries out a set of communication functions that center on two principal activities: informing and persuading.[2]

Both these activities are geared to one end: affecting consumer choice. As Cowling et al. (1975, 197) conclude in a sober econometric study: "Advertising has direct welfare effects when it leads consumers to modify their choice behavior and also in the sense that, assuming there is scarcity of resources, more advertising means less of something else. As has been reported, we did find evidence that advertising affects consumer choices at all levels." As a working description of what advertising is, then, I offer the following:

Advertising is a system of communication that aims through information and persuasion to modify the choice behavior of individuals operating in the economic marketplace.

Inspecting instructional materials, manuals, and "how to" books in American advertising, I was struck by the degree to which advertisers see consumer choice as the object of information and persuasion.[3] Here I will examine consumer "choice" as a central theme in advertising communication. I contend that "choice" is a successful focus for American advertisers precisely because it coincides with "choice" as a central symbolic theme in American culture. As I will argue below, "choice" constitutes a symbolic action that allows Americans to assert their commitment to individualism. In emphasizing choice, advertising not only suggests that this value is being upheld by the exercise of consumer preference in the marketplace, but also allows consumers to uphold a culturally valued but diametrically *opposed* value: conformity.

In exhorting consumers to exercise choice in the marketplace, advertisers have the potential to deliver an extremely powerful double message: they can invite American consumers to fulfill two powerful but contradictory cultural tendencies — to be independent and to conform.

Advertising: Communication Dynamics

In treating advertising as a form of communication, it is useful to adopt a sociolinguistic perspective. Advertising can be considered a "communication event" in Hymes's sense of the term (1974). Taking this perspective, one can see that the accomplishment of successful advertising can be measured by its effectiveness in modifying behavior. Thus, Hymes's inventory, derived from an elaboration of Jakobson's now classic enumeration of the functions of speech (1960), is useful for cataloging the specific elements of advertising communication that contribute to its effectiveness.

Hymes's unpacking of the components of communication uses a mnemonic device constructed on the word SPEAKING: Situation, Participants, Ends, Act Sequence, Key, Instrumentalities, Norms, and Genres. Of these components, Act Sequence, Key, and Instrumentalities are most problematic for advertisers. Act sequence includes message form, or how the message is presented, and message content — what the message *is*. "Key" is the tone, manner, or spirit in which a communication is carried out: mock, serious, perfunctory, painstaking, flip, advisory, and so on. "Instrumentalities" involve both *channels,* including oral, written, television, radio, mail, and the like and *forms*—dialect, stylistic registers, and special codes, as well as different nonverbal visual forms almost infinite in variety.

One can also speak of different "Genres" in advertising, but these are less well defined. Television commercials have developed several distinct forms (Geis 1982), and print advertising also seems to fall into categories. Stand-up pitch, testimonial, dramatization, demonstration, humorous piece, problem solution, and mood piece are all terms that advertisers themselves use to describe television commercials (Betancourt 1982, 124–25). Humor is seen as the most difficult and risky genre. As Betancourt states, "People will generally laugh at the commercial and forget who is the advertiser" (1982, 125). From a sociolinguistic standpoint, it is not difficult to understand why. Humor is another form of communication, and it interferes with understanding that the communication event is a "commercial" that aims to inform and persuade.

For both print and electronic media the choice of channel is becoming more and more complex, since different placements of a commercial reach different audiences and attract different rates of attention from consumers.[4] Television programs at different times and on different subjects attract different viewing audiences. Barbie dolls are never advertised after the late evening news, and feminine hygiene products are never advertised on Saturday mornings. Similarly you do not find handguns advertised in *Bride* magazine or quiche pans in *Field and Stream.* Most publications now offer regional editions and can even target a pattern of zip codes throughout the nation so that issues carrying a specific set of advertisements aimed at affluent readers, single women, middle-class black families, students, or Hispanic males can most effectively penetrate the target audience. Even point-of-purchase advertising (in stores where the goods are purchased) divides up the merchandising area of a store into target areas so as to place displays in the most effective locations.

All this is part of the craft of advertising. One must assume that advertisers have some technical competence in manipulating channels, codes, and genres to reach and get the attention of their target audiences. Message form and content are the trickiest areas of all, since this is where cultural factors come into play most strongly. It is this area I will treat next.

Symbolic Aims and Effective Advertising

Advertisers have long understood that in constructing images that will attract interest in a particular product, abstract consumer interests centering on personal cultural, physical, and emotional needs are more effective than straight product information. As Martineau stated (1957, 147–48): "Sometimes the rational sales story represents extremely important constituent parts of the product image. But mostly . . . it is the overtone of affective meanings and subjective imagery which constitutes by far the most forceful elements of the symbol. . . . Even in the cases where the advertiser insists that success is due to common sense sales arguments, there are psychological overtones and affective meanings injected into the product image which are playing a key role."[5]

Recent research by Ann Keely of Ann Keely/Ideational Research, a marketing research firm in New York, shows that a series of abstract principles govern 50 to 60 percent of the consumer decision-making process.[6] Moreover, these principles show a high level of involvement at a social/cultural level of concern. They are summarized as follows:

1. Abstract and general options preempt specific and concrete ones.
2. Impersonal and socially oriented options preempt ones that are personal and idiosyncratic.
3. Ideas preempt considerations of style and fashion.
4. Physical needs have greater priority than attitudinal preferences.

According to Keely, the values underlying choice are arranged hierarchically. The more influential the value factor, the less change will occur among options. The more compelling the factor, the higher it is on the value scale. Advertisers can modify consumer behavior at the top of the scale by slow reeducation, but they must engage in constant persuasion to change customer action at the bottom (Keely 1982, 10).

By this criterion, the highest motivating factors in advertising are those that are abstract, socially oriented, and ideational but that also deal with physical needs. Thus an ideal advertising campaign would center on some product that meets a real physical need but can be portrayed in symbolism that depicts choosing it over others as fulfilling important social values in society.[7]

Leo Burnett, the highly successful head of the Chicago agency bearing his name, echoed Keely's findings in this advice on the general aims of advertising:

1. *Emotionalize—Offer the reader something in terms of one of the two basic laws of human nature:*
    A. Self-Preservation
    B. Self-Enhancement
    "Don't tell people how good you make goods; tell them how good your goods make them."

2. *Rationalize—Give the reader an "excuse" to buy.*

Under these two general laws, psychologists have defined forty-four different motives for buying (appetite, health, sex attraction, approval of others, home comfort, etc.). The appeal must be based on one of these emotional motives. Frequently, however, the consumer will not admit the real reason for his action, and the advertisement must enable him to "rationalize" his purchase. (Burnett 1961, 243)

Martineau, Keely, and Burnett underscore the importance of communication at the symbolic level in making advertising effective. Creating symbolic communication that allows the consumer to justify a purchase in terms of higher, abstract social goals becomes the principal communication task advertisers must address. To do this well, then, they must understand what Americans feel is important in their cultural universe and address that level of response.

What Americans Want: Be Integrated—Be Unique

In the broad symbolism of complex societies, values that can be seen as polar opposites often form a dynamic axis against which actions and ideas can be measured. Iranian society seems to swing ideologically between devotion to the pure, intimate inside and the corrupt public outside (cf. Bateson et al. 1977; Beeman 1976, 1977, 1982, 1986). Japanese society seems caught in the difficulty of balancing individual feelings and desires (*ninjo*) against social duty (*giri*) (Nakane 1968). These opposed symbolic dimensions are more than the musings of superannuated culture and personality specialists. They are demonstrable cognitive standards against which individuals weigh their own and others' behavior, reflected in literature, language, and moral philosophy.

For the United States, one key opposition that has gained widespread recognition is the opposition between *individualism* and *conformity*. As George and Louise Spindler explain: "it appears that individualism, and the opposition (and complementarity) of the individualism/conformity duality, is a central feature of American culture. The recognition of it has been surprisingly constant for about two centuries" (Spindler and Spindler 1983, 64). Numerous field studies, such as the study of Appleton by Varenne (1977) and of U.S. soldiers by Spindler (1963 [1959]) illustrate this polarity. Hicks, in his study of an Appalachian community, demonstrates how these two polarities can function at the same time in what he terms an *ethic of neutrality,* where members of the community must act independently but must not be assertive or aggressive or call attention to themselves and must seek agreement in disputes (Hicks 1976, 90).

The contrast between the two polarities is aptly reflected in the appellation commonly used for the United States form of government: a democracy in a republic. As Tocqueville pointed out, the American notion of republic was "the tranquil reign of the majority" (1969 [1948], 395). He goes on to note that Americans have a strong tendency to conform to the practice and opinions of the majority: "The Americans' conception of a republic is singularly easy to apply and has lasting qualities. With them, though in practice a republican government often behaves badly, the theory is always good, and in the end the people's actions always conform to it" (1969, 396). Democratic principles are, by contrast, principles of individualism, a point also recognized by Tocqueville: "Individualism is of democratic origin and threatens to grow as conditions get more equal" (1969, 507).[8]

Tocqueville traced these contradictory tendencies to the same source: the American ideal of equality. This same ideal caused the isolation of individualism, since every person was free to pursue his own destiny unfettered by rank or family origin. It also fostered rule of the majority, since "the nearer men are to a common level of uniformity, the less they are inclined to believe blindly in any man or any class. But they are readier to trust the mass, and public opinion becomes more and more mistress of the world" (1969, 435).

I quote Tocqueville extensively here because, as students of American culture have often discovered, his remarks are still amazingly apt in description of contemporary culture, even in so mundane an area as consumer choice in the marketplace.

The polarity between individualism and conformity gives Americans a double message:

1. Be independent: achieve, be unique!
2. Be well integrated: conform!

Because these two dicta are fused in American ideology, they are able to coexist with equal moral weight. One can easily support both, citing situations when one or the other should take precedence. As I will show below, however, advertising demonstrates that it is possible for consumers to fulfill *both* dicta at the same time. The means for doing this lie in humble, routine purchases of consumer goods.

Choice: Prime Expression of American Symbolic Culture

There are few things all Americans can agree on. Near the top of the list, along with mother and apple pie, lies "freedom of choice." The power of this concept is shown by its ability to be adopted without public comment by groups as diverse as the Advertising Council, pro-abortion forces, and the anti-busing movement. This concept comes close to being sacred for Americans.

"Freedom of choice" at first blush seems to be a concept that defends individualism against conformity. As Spindler and Spindler maintain: "Individuals are . . . rarely committed to community, and when individual satisfaction, free choice, or particularly "happiness" is threatened by commitment or membership, the individual withdraws to find new alignments. The emic concept of individualism is the ability to make free choices. There is, therefore, a constant opposition between individual and community, even though the existence of one depends on the other" (1983, 63). Nevertheless, in the United States choice is also the basis for the formation of groups. One could almost claim that people are what they choose in life—profession, household goods, and all.

There are few nations on earth that have so many organizations where membership is based solely on personal decisions concerning careers, hobbies, and even purchases. There have always been organizations of people who all happen to have purchased the same make of car or boat. Now there are dozens of organizations of people who happen to own the same type of computer equipment. These groups meet largely to exchange information concerning use of the objects they have chosen to own.

In the United States, having chosen to purchase the same item creates an immediate affinity among Americans if they meet.[9] People with the same model and color of car honk at each other; people with the same brand of food processor enter into rapt discussions on how to use it; people contemplating choices seek out advice from others—indeed, personal recommendation and word of mouth are the best sales techniques of all.[10]

All this shows that in the United States, through exercise of original choice, people not only demonstrate their uniqueness, they also recognize and actualize their integration with others. They do this by making, acknowledging, and perpetuating social ties based solely on the affinity that arises through making the same choices.

Choice in Advertising

Advertising in the United States, as I mentioned above, is enormously varied. Much is ineffective. Moreover, with little predictability about effectiveness of the channel, message form, or message content, it is difficult to generalize with any certainty about what advertisers do or about what American advertising purports to be. Nevertheless, certain techniques are well established. They are widespread and seem to pervade advertising campaigns of long currency, indicating at least that the companies paying for the advertising perceive some positive effects.

In successful advertising, consumer choice and its implications may be the most pervasive overall theme represented. It is heavily disguised at times and is rarely treated directly. The general message for consumers is: *If X is chosen, then Y benefit will be realized.* This basic message may be formulated in many ways, some of which follow below:

1. "Choosing X is the same as action A (which is beneficial)."
   An example might be a recent commercial for Prince spaghetti that declared: "Choosing is caring, and I choose Prince."
2. "People who have B quality choose X (so if you choose X you will also have B quality, which is beneficial or desirable)."
   The Jif peanut butter commercial "Choosy mothers choose Jif" is a good example. Another is the associative testimonial, as in a recent campaign where glamorous, energetic Lauren Bacall endorsed High Point decaffeinated coffee.
3. "By choosing X you are in fact doing something else, action C, which is desirable."
   This is different from 1 above because it is not a direct equation of the two actions. A good example is "Join the Pepsi generation" or "Be a Pepper—drink Dr. Pepper" or "Join the first team, reach for Winston." In these examples, note that what is implied is that by choosing a particular product one is joining a special group. This will be dealt with below.
4. "When you choose X you obtain an added indirect benefit, D."
   This is the "rationalizing" factor, saying in effect, "Besides obtaining the product, you also get D." An example is a recent Metropolitan Insurance campaign: "If you buy Universal Life from Metropolitan, you won't have to worry whether you've done the right thing." OR a Brim coffee commercial: "Our new rich roasted taste makes your coffee moments so special. . . ." In effect what is being sold is not the product, but rather the added

benefit. The consumer is being asked in effect to obtain the added benefit in making the product choice.[11]

5. "When you choose X you become E."

A great deal of this kind of formulation involves images and pictures of glamorous or successful people who have chosen the product. The implication is that by choosing one will become that person, or become like that person. A well-known example is the Virginia Slims campaign, one of the longest running in advertising history, where a simulated Victorian or Edwardian lady in miserable circumstances (often because she dared to smoke in public) is contrasted with a stylish modern woman with the caption: "You've come a long way, baby." Only the name of the cigarette is mentioned; the identification of women who smoke Virginia Slims with the stylish model is implied.

There are many additional variations on this basic theme. Clearly, choice of the product, disguised as some other action, is easily and handily packaged. It is the "other action" that provides the generalized social, emotional, rationalizing appeal that Martineau, Keely, Burnett, and other advertisers' councils say must be the object of selling.[12]

Choice as a focus for advertising is most effective, however, when it is used to appeal to the two prime American cultural directives cited above: individualism and conformity.

Choice and Individualism

In all the reformulations of choice cited above, a powerful benefit offered to the consumer is the opportunity to demonstrate individuality or uniqueness through choice of a product. This may come through obtaining a unique benefit, or demonstrating a unique quality or capacity by exercising choice, or obtaining unique recognition through choice.

The small victories of life, like being "the best mom" or "showing the guys in the car pool," are common appeals to being individual and unique. Television commercials construct thirty-second dramatizations that demonstrate the small (but admittedly satisfying) ways people can stand out by using a coffee that someone will comment on or a cologne that someone will notice.

Further afield, one can become individuated merely by being the kind of person who would choose the product. The kind of choice that is "not for just anybody" has enormous appeal. One liqueur called Trenais, made of the unlikely combination of cognac and yogurt, declares itself to be "unexpected, unconventional, undoubtedly like you."

Still another variety of advertising message appeals to uniqueness by implying that only people with certain special qualities (like being rich and glamorous) are qualified to make the particular choice of product in the first place. Slavicks, a famous Los Angeles jeweler, declares flatly: "Diamonds so extraordinary, only one out of a thousand Americans will ever know the joy of owning one." If one out of a thousand actually did want these diamonds, Slavicks would sell a great many of them—but no matter. Everyone can aspire to being at least one in a thousand. One in a million might be a little too intimidating.

Judith Williamson, in her interesting semiotic study of advertising, notes that "in an advertisement, we are told that we do choose, we are free individuals, we have taste, style, uniqueness and we will act accordingly. In other words, having been attributed with the qualities connected with a product, we are projected as buyers of it precisely because 'given' that we 'have' the beliefs implied in the ad, we will act in accordance with them and buy the product that embodies those beliefs. It is a sort of 'double bind' " (1978, 53).

Advertising and Conformity

Conformity and social integration are the other great benefits advertisers offer for choosing a product. Again, this benefit can be seen in many different lights. One can benefit by submitting to duty in family, social, or work roles—the choice of a particular product being the means to bring this about. Christmas advertising plays on this kind of need to be integrated. Advertising copy that uses phrases like "Imagine the joy on their faces when they see . . ." or the classic 1948 ad for Macy's showing a woman embracing her husband with the headline: "Oh, Darling—you shouldn't have." The copy for this "masterpiece," as one commentator called it (Watkins 1959 [1949], 191) goes on to say: "we started to think about the light in her eyes when she scolds you for being so dear, so sweet, so foolishly generous. Honestly, we were so nervous 'way last Summer when we picked out the gift for you to give her." Another classic magazine advertisement for International Correspondence Schools shows a man handing his wife some money with the headline: "Here's an extra $50, Grace—I'm making real money now!" The copy goes on to say: "I've been promoted . . . and the first extra money is yours. Just a little reward for urging me to study at home." This advertisement first appeared in 1919 and ran for decades (Watkins 1959, 112–13).

Still another appeal to conformity and integration is the advertisement that implies that choosing a particular product automatically makes one a member of a group—the kind of people who use this kind of goods. Marshall McLuhan, in his classic book *The Mechanical Bride,* shows a famous advertisement for Lord Calvert scotch that features pictures of a number of famous men—Adolphe Menjou, Paul Lucas, Robert F. Six, Arthur Little, and others—with the caption: "For men of distinction." McLuhan declares:

> The present ad is only one of thousands which loudly insist on depriving men of their birth-rights by rating them in accordance with their supposed preference for some purchased product. And to do so is perhaps a weakness inherent in any market economy. If success can only be measured by purchasing power, then the intellectually creative men with whom the future of mankind always rests will be regarded only as floperoos. Living as they do on $3,000 or so a year without respectful attention to current merchandise, they are easily felt to be unpatriotic: "Oh, our ways aren't good enough for you?" say the satisfied consumers of well-known brands. (McLuhan 1951, 58)

The appeal need not be to snobbery. These days, people conscious of their health, "achievers," sensitive people, or any other group one can imagine can be invoked in an advertising message, where to make a particular choice is touted as a way to create an immediate self-identification with others who embody valued social qualities. This extends to families as well. As Schudson notes: "Families select target standard packages. They want to consume more and better things, but not endlessly, not insatiably. They seek not social superiority, as a rule, but social *membership* (1984, 145). Williamson notes that the nature of the group may be utter fantasy, existing only within the framework of the advertisement itself: "By buying a Pepsi you take place in an exchange, not only of money, but of yourself for a Pepsi Person. You have become special, yet one of a clan: however, you do not meet those others, except *in* the advertisement" (Williamson 1978, 53).

Uniquely Integrated Consumers

As Williamson implies, most advertising in fact presents double messages. As I have argued here, one of the most important double messages is the one implying that with a single consumer choice a customer is able *both* to become unique, special, and individual *and* to achieve integration and conformity.

Advertisements implying that consumers join groups when choosing products, like "those who have taken the Pepsi challenge" or "the Volvo owners," are most obvious in this. The choice of a particular product is a "tribute to the good taste" of the customer and thus is distinguishing. Still, the advertisement usually offers the assurance that thousands, if not millions, of others have the same good sense and in fact constitute a group of distinguished persons of discriminating sensibilities. One can even achieve integration by becoming associated with a place of business. One television campaign puts a team of grocers from Almacs (an East Coast food chain) in people's kitchens. By being a discriminating shopper, the housewife can "join the A team, for low low prices." Zayre's declares flatly, "you're going to make Zayre your store."

More interesting are some of the strong image advertisements. Marlboro is the largest selling U.S. cigarette, and yet it uses specific imagery of the famous Marlboro man, a rugged cowboy usually alone on the prairie. Cuervo tequila ran a series of highly successful ads where conventional people were shown letting down their hair on weekends and doing unconventional things, always well integrated with groups of friends and, of course, Cuervo tequila.

Combinations of integration and independence in the same advertisement can take other forms. Texas Instruments has capitalized on parenting roles in a recent campaign where parents are essentially told that they must help their *children* excel and achieve by buying home computers. Merrill Lynch's long-running advertising campaign featuring a lone bull going through his paces in isolated surroundings as "a breed apart" essentially is telling consumers that by establishing a relationship with this huge brokerage house they are tapping into some special pipeline of independence and uniqueness in managing stock portfolios. Even charity appeals emphasize joining a community of givers, such as the Foster Parents' Plan, in order to enable less fortunate individuals to achieve.

These double messages are remarkable in that they tell consumers they can achieve contradictory but laudable goals merely by exercising choice on a microcosmic level. Every time we choose one brand of liquid detergent or motor oil over another, we are subtly being told both: "you are unique and special" and "you are in the company of the millions of others who choose this." This is the opposite of a no-win situation. It is an always-win situation in cognitive terms, and it is as powerful as it is subtle.

The Symbolic Power of Advertising

It is small wonder, then, that despite uncertainty and inefficiency the advertising industry so dominates the United States economy. Some consumer goods would be as much as 50 percent cheaper without advertising. Some goods would never exist at all, since their appeal comes totally from their advertising campaigns.

The principles discussed above do not, of course, apply to all goods advertised. Many successful advertising campaigns depend on simply providing information on a unique product or service. In the hot world of personal computers, people frequently say their reason for buying magazines such as *Byte* is access to the advertisements for equipment and software they want to purchase. Price is another prime factor. An advertisement that features prices at 50 percent of market value will draw customers no matter how unsophisticated its symbolism.[13] Appeals to symbolic values and imagery such as those discussed above primarily pertain to sustained sales campaigns for goods that are difficult for customers to distinguish on their merits alone. Martineau summed up the dilemma nicely in a speech in 1956: "Basically, what you are trying to do . . . is create an illogical situation. You want the customer to fall in love with your product and have a profound brand loyalty when actually content may be very similar to hundreds of competing brands" (quoted in Packard 1981, 45).

For consumers everywhere, the easiest way to achieve that illogical goal is to provide a strong symbolic association between the act of choosing that product and the most highly valued ideals of their culture. If, as in some successful advertising in the United States, you can convince customers that they are actually achieving contradictory goals by exercising their choice, you have them in a cognitive hammerlock that is difficult to break. Customers are being offered a cultural, cognitive bargain that they cannot refuse. Finally, when you add to that the notion that choice itself is an action of high cultural value, there is no stopping the tremendous rhetorical forces thus unleashed.

4 The Story of Bond

Lee Drummond

Introduction

Why, in a book on American symbols, write about James Bond, a fictional British agent in Her Majesty's Secret Service and the product of a British novelist self-exiled to Jamaica? And if this initial doubt regarding the Britishness of Bond can be put to rest, one might still ask the general—and daunting—question: Why, considering the shallowness of Bond movies and their cheap exploitation of women and of foreign places and people, bother with a serious examination of such mindless fare? Surely such low-brow stuff contains little of interest to the symbolic anthropologist searching in his own culture for clues to the fundamental organization of culture.

The Britishness of Bond would have been a valid reason for excluding him from consideration had this book appeared twenty-five years ago, before John Kennedy called Bond to the attention of the American public in 1961 by revealing that *From Russia with Love* was one of his ten favorite books (keeping company with works by Stendhal and Churchill), and before Bond went Hollywood. The series of Albert Broccoli and Harry Saltzman-produced movies with their high-tech gadgetry and jet set locations has nullified Bond's parochial status and made it all but impossible to interpret his popularity as a function, say, of Americans' interest in things English.[1] The story of Bond has become fully incorporated in the saga not of the United States, but of America—that rich, gimmicky, and bizarre land that is less a place than a state of mind.

The second demurral to this study—that Bond movies are sensationalist, chauvinist trash and thus unworthy of serious consideration—bears inspection no better than the first. If a movie's success depends on its exploitation of sex and violence, then we must ask why Bond movies have been so tremendously popular while serving up relatively meager portions of both in comparison with the pornographic gore that can be found in movie theaters everywhere. Bond generates only a fraction of the gore that Dirty Harry routinely provides, and his sexual escapades are closer to the old Doris Day and Rock Hudson bedroom farces of the fifties than to current hard-core offerings. The Bond movies are not great art, but neither are they vile. To denounce this lightweight fare out of hand carelessly lumps it with movies that are very different and, by tarring everything with the same brush, dulls the edge of film criticism. Rather than dwell on generalities, this cultural analysis of Bond seeks to understand what makes him distinctive—a cinematic legend unlike any other.

James Bond is clearly a major folk hero of our time. Since he appeared on the world scene in 1953 in *Casino Royale*, Agent 007 has fought and seduced his way through fifteen books, which have sold over one hundred million copies, and as many movies, which collectively have earned far more than the most successful of the supergrossers—*Star Wars, Jaws,* and *E. T.* As the most successful movie series of all time, Bond movies provide the cultural anthropologist a means for exploring the incredible popularity and commercial success of several recent films. We live in an era of supergrossers. Nothing in our brief history as moviegoers has prepared us to deal with that fact, and there is little to indicate the future place of movies in American culture. But just as we were beginning to believe reports that television was cannibalizing that grand old institution, the weekend movie, along came a rash of movies of unprecedented popularity: *Star Wars, Jaws, Superman, Close Encounters of the Third Kind,* and *E.T.*

What accounts for the tremendous mass appeal of these movies? Are *Star Wars, Jaws,* and the others tied to anything of significance in American culture, or are they merely a final, whimsical spasm of a once-vital civilization? Although there are many who would argue for the latter alternative, I want to propose that the nonserious fare of our popular movies has serious implications for the study of American culture. As the largest oeuvre in American film (a *Star Wars XV* still seems unlikely), the Bond movies are a logical choice for developing this approach. The movies as a group make up an epic—la geste de Bond—of the first rank in the brief history of American film.

An American Dreamtime

The Bond movies have been neither produced nor consumed in a cultural vacuum. They have been commercial successes not because they are 100 percent cotton candy fluff, but because they manage to convey something basic about life as it is lived in late twentieth-century America. To borrow a term from Australian aboriginal religion,[2] the story of Bond forms part of an American Dreamtime: a mythical epoch in which everyday life yields to the secret appeal of a parallel and ever-present dream life of final causes and questions. To penetrate that Dreamtime realm it is necessary to suspend our usual critical disdain for such lowbrow productions as James Bond movies and instead put them through an intensive cultural analysis.

An anthropologist recognizes the dominant ritual of a people through the activities going on around him. And an anthropologist intent on studying modern America cannot fail to be impressed by the queues snaking away from downtown marquee advertising the latest supergrosser. If he came from someplace else—say, Mars—the very concept "movie" would soon acquire rich connotations of the spiritual life of his ethnographic subjects. Following up his observations, our Martian anthropologist would probably seek to determine which of those mass rituals called "movies" were most important and would then proceed to an analysis of the situations and characters they developed. By studying what the people around him find interesting the anthropologist hopes to understand their lives and society. And where in the cinematic realm could he find a character as interesting, ubiquitous, and enduring as James Bond, who has already exercised the talents of three novelists (Ian Fleming, Kingsley Amis, and John Gardner), three actors (Sean Connery, Roger Moore, and David Niven), and hundreds of studio personnel in a career spanning more than thirty years in Her Majesty's Secret Service?

It is true that Bond's career has been less meteoric than those of supergrosser characters like Luke Skywalker, R2D2, and E. T., but it is proving far more enduring. Because James Bond is no longer the sensation that hits the covers of *Time* and *People* or gets turned out in doll form by the hundreds of thousands in Hong Kong toy factories, it is easy to miss the fact that he is the figure of a genuine saga—a saga of our time—the cold warrior, the secret agent. And like E. T. and the others, Bond's appeal is not limited to societies with a particular sociopolitical configuration: from Indonesia to the Amazon he is known as some variant of Pauline Kael's "kiss kiss bang bang," the mythic emissary of a global, American-dominated technological culture (Kael 1968).

Besides, I have always liked the Bond thrillers. I read the books, I went to most of the movies, and I watch the reruns on television. Though unsympathetic friends have accused me of going to almost any length to rationalize my hopelessly lowbrow tastes, I find that the fun of Bond movies is inseparable from my interest in them as objects of cultural analysis. They are—or with a little academic obsessiveness can be made to be—instances of what Clifford Geertz (1973a [1971]) has described as "deep play": amusements that issue from a people's deepest sensibilities. Bond would not be fun for me or for his tens of millions of other fans if he did not strike a responsive chord in us all, something we hold in common despite the diversity of our experiences. This premise is enough to launch a cultural analysis of the story of Bond, for it holds out the promise that a close inspection of the saga will provide insights into the workings of our culture.

Doing Cultural Analysis: Preliminary Considerations

I think this process typifies the way, unscientific though it may be, that we undertake any cultural analysis: we are initially struck by the appeal or popularity of a movie, a television show, video games, purple mohawk hairdos, roller disco, or whatever, and the effect is to generate an acute puzzlement. Why in the world should *that* particular production acquire such a following? What is it about this peculiar culture we possess that installs some slipshod creation at the mythic core of things? This sense of puzzlement is like an itch, and when we scratch we discover aspects of our culture previously obscured beneath a cloud of facile, everyday assumption. I think this is where the fun of Bond leads.

The cultural analysis undertaken here is anything but a rigorous formal study of individual texts. Eco (1979) has already identified the narrative structures in Fleming's novels, and I will not attempt to add to that work. The movie Bond and the novel Bond are so different and yet so intertwined in the public consciousness that close scrutiny of the text of, say, *Goldfinger* that neglects the movie *Goldfinger* does some violence to the character of Bond. Rather than attempt to chart the intriguing transformations Fleming's character has undergone at the hands of scriptwriters and directors, I adopt the happy position that nearly everyone knows something about Bond and that this collective knowledge constitutes *the story of Bond*—a living saga, independent of any particular text. Much of what follows is consequently large-scale comparison of Bond with other mythic figures of our culture rather than minute dissection of literary and cinematic structures in the Bond corpus of books and movies.

It will be apparent, however, that the analysis is clearly biased in favor of the movie Bond. I believe this is entirely appropriate, since most people, myself included, now know Bond through movies rather than books. Whatever cultural significance attaches to Bond is communicated through film, and so a glimpse at the movies will direct attention to the mythic structure of the saga.

Every Bond movie is really two movies: a prologue and a main event. The prologue is a fast-paced action scene lasting about ten minutes and bearing little or no relation to the main event. However jaundiced one's view of Bond movies may be, it is hard to deny that their prologues have virtually perfected the dramatic device of the chase; packed into the opening minutes is enough high-speed, high-tech mayhem to fill out any conventional ninety-minute thriller.

Consider the opening scene of *The Spy Who Loved Me*. It takes place in a remote ski cabin high in the Austrian Alps. Bond is making love to a beautiful woman on a pallet of furs before an open fire. Suddenly there is a clicking sound and his wristwatch begins to feed out a teletyped message: Bond must report for duty. He dons a sleek ski outfit, pulls on a matching backpack, and is off down the slope. But his amorous companion is a KGB spy who has summoned an assassination squad, also on skis, that is just making its way to the cabin. The would-be killers could conceal themselves and, when Bond neared, cut him in two with their automatic weapons. But of course they do not. Instead, they give chase. The text serves notice, if any were needed, that it is a piece of twentieth-century Dreamtime.

There follows a spectacular display of freestyle skiing. Bond glissades down a tortuous, icy course closely pursued by the leader of the KGB squad who, incredibly, skis without poles and fires his pistol on the go. Out of the turns but still on a steep slope, Bond turns around, skiing backward now, and carefully levels his right ski pole at his pursuer. It is a miniature rocket launcher; the KGB assassin's chest explodes in flame, and down he goes. Before Bond can turn around, he flies over the edge of an embankment. A backward somersault, a twist, and he lands on his skis—

in the midst of the remaining killers. There follows a fancy display of body-blocking and ducking, and Bond is in the clear, but this time going down a really steep slope. And ahead is a cliff!

There is the cliff, and that lone figure on skis is headed right for it. In one heartstopping moment the audience realizes that this is no dummy—not like the ones that took the fall off the log in *King Kong*—and there is no way out. The camera can cut, but our hero will still be hurtling toward his death. This is the real thing. But there is no hint of a splice, and the figure goes over the precipice. The camera is still on, still out there shooting, apparently, from a helicopter. And the skier is falling. His poles go, his skis fly away, and he drops and drops and drops toward a cloud bank. (How high *is* this cliff?) Then the parachute pops open—a gigantic silken Union Jack. A truly remarkable feat.

Cut to Roger Moore swinging lightly in a parachute harness, looking barely mussed. Then back to the figure drifting down through the clouds, into a pair of superimposed, silhouetted feminine hands. The lyrics of Carly Simon's theme song, "Nobody does it better, 'cause, baby, you're the best. . . ," begin. It's time for the credits. As one body, the audience shakes off its tension and settles back in its seat; that was just for openers.

The scene described is only one of a series of dazzling chases that have made the story of Bond a distinctive media myth of our time. Virtually every form of vehicular transport has been explored in these chases. Bond has made cars, planes, boats, motorcycles, and diving gear do things no ordinary, sane person would think of attempting. In *The Spy Who Loved Me* it is, fittingly, a car that is singled out as the piece of *équipement extraordinaire*. Bond's prowess at the wheel reaches its peak when, pursued by a vixen in a helicopter gunship, he roars down a pier and hurtles into the sea. As the car sinks its wheels retract, it sprouts fins, and the dashboard rotates to reveal a submarine control panel. Bond pushes a red button on that panel, and his miniature sub launches a miniature guided missile that takes care of the bothersome helicopter.

Two interrelated questions must be asked of this sensational material if it is to yield any cultural significance: Why should the chase be such a recurrent and compelling theme in Bond films? Why is it so mechanized? It would be inadequate to answer these questions with an appeal to a putatively universal meaning of the chase, for we are not concerned here with the general psychological issue of why the chase has figured in Western literature at least since the time of Homer. Cultural analysis cannot pretend to solve problems of such a universal nature; it should confine itself to a close inspection of particular cultural productions with an eye to discoveries that reveal the appropriateness of those productions to their times. James Bond's duels with several kinds of death at the wheel of his miracle car belong to a particular Dreamtime—our own—and not to a universal psyche. Conversely, a contemporary audience would likely find Achilles' pursuit of Hector around the walls of Ilium a rather tedious affair, definitely not the stuff of supergrossers or even big box office.

The mechanized, gimmicky chase that has become the trademark of the Bond movies is so compelling and timely in part because, as Goffman (1971, 248–52) argues, technology has introduced alarming changes into our perception of the security of space. What Goffman, borrowing from the ethologists, calls our "surround" or area of "flight-distance"—the minimal space we need to maintain between ourselves and a potential predator—is routinely invaded or subverted by weapons that act over great distances and at blinding speed. We have created machines and environments that fill our everyday lives with perfectly justified anxiety: even the servants can become killers. The drunk's car, the sniper's bullet, somebody's finger on the button, all pose mortal dangers that the ordinary individual cannot handle with his ordinary perceptions and reaction time.

Hence part of Bond's appeal as a mythic figure of our culture. He is a kind of advance guard, an agent in fact, sent into the territory of lethal machines to test the possibilities of human survival in a high-tech world. The motorized chase is an ideal dramatic device for creating, through myth, virtual experiences that are scarcely "realistic" in the myth-as-charter sense but that most definitely communicate to us all on a basic level. And while exotic forms of transport come and go in the Bond movies, the car remains as the perennial jousting weapon—an extension of one's personality and thus of the "vehicular units" Goffman describes in analyzing how people handle themselves in public.

Those endless car chases are also cited as grounds for a contemptuous dismissal of Bond movies by the sophisticated: Bond is merely a supercharged adolescent in a juvenile fantasy of fast cars and fast women. But this reaction is too easy, and it short-circuits the necessary cultural analysis that raises the precise question here regarded as trivially obvious: Why should sexuality and aggression be articulated in the context of technological adventure? I would take a very different tack from those who recoil from the Bond movies, and argue that the shallow dialogue and feeble plot of *The Spy Who Loved Me* and other Bond thrillers are admirably suited to telling a fast-paced story without obscuring the fundamental cultural themes that story raises. The car chases and flirtations are simply additional examples of the diffuse aesthetics of myth: myth communicates and grapples with basic issues, but rarely with much style.

Human/Machine, Individual/State: Semiotic Domains in Bond

If Bond thrillers possess that graceless profundity that seems to characterize myth, then just what are the fundamental ideas or cultural themes being explored? I think there are two tightly interwoven themes: the relationship between humans and machines, and the relationship between the individual and the State. To be sure, these are explored in the context of a great deal of gratuitous sex and violence, but it would be a mistake to take that as more than a backdrop for the cultural action in the movies.

Similarities and differences between humans and machines can be explored directly or by reference to a third order of being that shares some of the qualities of both: animals. Bond movies are notable in keeping an animal presence to a minimum and in trafficking in stereotypes of animals. Bond's world is relentlessly high-tech; he inhabits a world of gadgets. Bond uses and abuses the diabolical products of Q's lab—the missile-launching car/submarine, the cigarette lighter/flamethrower, the shoe-string/explosive—in his unending effort to thwart an enemy equally addicted to deadly gadgetry. His enemies are themselves megalomaniac masters of technology—mad scientists, or, more precisely, mad engineers—embarked on a course of global annihilation. In *The Spy Who Loved Me* the archvillain is Stromberg, who plans to retire to an Atlantis he has designed and constructed for himself and a party of the faithful after tricking the United States and the Soviet Union into a nuclear Armageddon. Bond's individual prowess with machines is all that stands in the way of Stromberg's using machines to achieve the unthinkable. And Stromberg, although he apparently loves the sea, is no Earthwatch, Save the Whales wildlife enthusiast; his pleasure comes in engineering the highly technical underwater community that is to become the last refuge of humanity. The animals Stromberg surrounds himself with are complements of himself and his relentless opponent, Bond: the shark and scorpion fish, consummate executioners in their watery domain.

Because the story of Bond is set in the domain of machines and derives much of its dramatic force from exploring the relationship between man and machine, it can be regarded as an epic in a totemism of machines. If totemism as conventionally understood is a body of lore dealing with the relationship between people and animals, then Bond and other cultural heroes of oral and visual folklore who operate on and with machines define a parallel and complementary totemism. Animals have little place in this totemism of machines and hence play minor roles in Bond movies. Stromberg is characteristic of other Bond villains in his fascination with animals that kill; animals appear only as instruments of assassination. There are no clever porpoises, no faithful dogs, no Bambis, not even a lovable little alien with great lambent eyes and a heart of pulsing neon to distract from the spectacle of skilled gladiators contesting to the death with the latest and deadliest products of technology.

The animals Bond confronts are mostly drawn from the nonmammalian orders: snakes, piranha, crocodiles, sharks, and the occasional attack dog all take their turn at taking a piece out of the smartly tailored hide of 007. The Bond movies, like *Jaws,* ascribe an unambiguously hostile meaning to animal life and thereby assert the prominence of that other major category of animate objects: machines.

Bond's hand-to-hand combats also cast him as a clever master of machines rather than a physical superman. He thinks fast and moves fast and relies on his gadgets to defeat physically superior opponents. The contrast is exaggerated by the superhuman, freakish physical powers of these strongarm men. In the early films, slab-sided SMERSH agents, conditioned to the nth degree, took on Bond and fell victim to his cleverness. The first actual freak to go after Bond was Oddjob, Goldfinger's Sumo wrestler bodyguard. Oddjob, deformed by his muscles and inhuman training, mentally dull, obedient as a dog to its master, versus Bond, supple, quick, and flippant toward authority—the contrasts underscore the opposition between physical and mechanical, animal and machine.

A recent Bond heavy, Jaws (played by Richard Kiel), provides an intriguing twist to the physical/mechanical theme. Jaws takes his nickname from some ferocious dental work that enables him to bite through chain metal as if it were soft putty. In his debut in *The Spy Who Loved Me* Jaws is incredibly strong, does not speak and even appears to lack language, and blindly pursues his orders to kill Bond and his lovely companion, Triple-X. Bond is a master of machines, but here he finds himself confronted with a powerful human who is also a machine. Jaws, unlike Bond, has abdicated human control over technology and become its product. He is a kind of spoiled six million dollar man, but without Lee Majors's sex appeal (and when, in *Moonraker,* Jaws meets his lady love she does not resemble Farrah Fawcett).

Bond's deadly encounters with Jaws, as well as developing a semiotic of human/machine relations, illustrate the second major theme of the movie myth: the relationship between the individual and the State. As a secret agent Bond uses the high-tech creations of his state to thwart the evil intentions of other governments or deranged scientists. His missions frequently take him outside his own country to exotic foreign locations where the success of a particular political philosophy depends upon the strength and cleverness of the individual espousing it. The imagery of these locales and the bizzare turns Bond's adventures take serve to unseat one's easy assumptions regarding the civic order: Bond does not file income tax returns, get drafted, pay divorce lawyers, or engage in any of the multitude of daily indignities that bind the individual to a polity. The fantasy and attendant disorientation thus evoked in the reader/viewer of Bond books/movies are necessary conditions to entering the Dreamtime state, where ordinary political reality is suspended and one becomes capable of grasping the essentials of social existence in a global society.

Bond in the Context of American Folklore

Answering the question how Bond movies frame specific statements about the place of the individual in the national state will involve assembling a rather unlikely cast of characters: Wild Bill Hickok, Billy the Kid, John Henry, O. J. Simpson, Mick Jagger, and others. If there is any validity in my claim that Bond movies operate in part on a fundamental cultural level, then it should be possible to establish connections between them and other elements of American folklore and popular culture. If the story of Bond has cultural significance, it did not spring full-blown onto our cultural stage—a happenstance creation of a disillusioned English bureaucrat holed up in his north shore Jamaican retreat. Who/what are the ancestors and cousins of Bond? What are his roots and family?

Bond's roots are readily identified when one recalls the opening minutes of every movie: the silhouette of Bond, seen through a gun barrel, crosses the screen, whirls, and fires directly toward the viewer; the barrel casing framing the figure runs red with blood. First and last, Bond is a gunfighter. The gunfighter is probably the major folk hero of twentieth-century America. To understand the story of Bond, a gunfighter who simply opted for a Beretta automatic over the old Colt .45, it is necessary to understand something of the appeal the gunfighter has exercised in our popular culture. While a thorough study of this subject would be a book in itself, I shall focus on those aspects of the character that develop the two principal themes of this analysis: the human/machine identity complex, and the relationship of the individual to the State.

Although Western cultures have valorized hand-to-hand combat at least since the days of the Colosseum, a significant change in that tradition occurred toward the middle of the nineteenth century, when James Colt introduced a repeating sidearm that was sufficiently light and accurate for an individual to achieve virtuosity in its use. Unlike earlier dueling pistols, which were cumbersome and fired only a single charge, the Colt "peacemaker" could be used outside the elaborate ritual setting of eighteenth-century duels: Gary Cooper needed only to step out into the street at high noon and the gladiatorial event was begun. The repeating pistol thus helped shape a new kind of gladiatorial hero, a man whose mastery consisted in his control over a complex piece of equipment. A gun, unlike a sword, lance, or bow and arrow, is an assemblage of multiple pieces, each of which must be manufactured with great precision. Paradoxically, this complex machine, rather than negating individual differences in skill at arms, actually amplified them. History has not recorded the names of masters of the sixteen-pound cannon, for the very good reason that those weapons were too big, clumsy, and inaccurate and required too many people to operate them. True virtuosity was beyond the design capability of the instrument. But Wild Bill Hickok, Billy the Kid, Wyatt Earp . . . and James Bond are known to one and all as masters of the deadly art of the sidearm. That art consisted in manipulating a machine that could be carried everywhere—strapped on a hip, thrust into a belt, snugged under a pillow—and used at a moment's notice with an accuracy that depended only on the user's competence and cold-bloodedness.

The gunfighter's art inevitably posed problems for him as an individual bound to a State. The legendary killers from Hickok to Bond, besides being masters of machines, share another characteristic: their skill inevitably places them on the fringes of a social group, so that they wind up exercising their deadly art in a no-man's-land between one group and another, or between the law and lawlessness. After Lewis and Clark's expedition, the western mountains beckoned to men who could find no place in the civilized cities and towns of the East and the prairie states. Hunting, trapping, and brawling along the rivers of Colorado, Wyoming, Kansas, Texas, and New Mexico, the mountain men lived their own lives by their own rules. To this unregulated life was added a further upheaval: the Civil War. The war caused many of the mountain men to choose sides and filter back to the border states, where they served as scouts, hunters, and even spies. In the excitement and turbulence of war they found, for a time, an outlet for the lust for adventure that first propelled them into the mountains. And when the war finally ended, they drifted among the social ruins and fragments left in its wake: Springfield, Abilene, Dodge City, Deadwood. In the saloons of these frontier towns and on the dusty streets outside their doors, Yank and Reb refought that traumatic, fratricidal war countless times.

The energies of these restless, deadly men fitted their time and place, and even the more sociopathic among them often found themselves wearing a badge and charged with maintaining a semblance of order in the anarchy of cattle and mining towns (in this regard, witness the Old West's most notorious psychopath, William Bonner—Billy the Kid—who was deputized by the cattle czar Chisholm to enforce his brand of justice west of the Pecos). If group identity, the difference between Us and Them, is a fundamental problem of culture, then it is hard to imagine a more dramatic setting for the operation of that cultural process than the frontier towns that inherited all the confusion and bitterness of the Civil War.

Wild Bill Hickok's career developed in those turbulent war and postwar years and for that reason resembles the career of a later veteran turned agent, James Bond (and is just as much a part of the American Dreamtime, owing to the romanticized, mythologized accounts by which we know not the history, but the *histoire* of Hickok). According to the story of Hickok, he was born and reared near the edge of established society, in La Salle County, Illinois, but at the age of twelve or so was unable to suppress an innate restlessness that made him a runaway. For fifteen years he lived in the mountains, growing strong, developing his woodcraft, and honing an amazing ability as a natural "dead" shot. "I allers shoot well; but I come ter be perfeck in the mountains by shooting at a dime for a mark (from fifty paces) at bets of half a dollar a shot. And then until the war I never drank liquor nor smoked. . . . War is demoralizing, it is" (Nichols 1867, 273–85). With the outbreak of war Hickok joined the Union army and served with distinction as a scout and spy, sometimes donning a Confederate uniform to penetrate Rebel lines and carry back intelligence on troop movements and munitions stores.

The story of Bond is a slice out of this part of Wild Bill's career. Unlike the cold war, the Civil War ended—and Wild Bill did not have to cope with the machinations of a SMERSH. Hickok drifted from town to town, from gunfight to gunfight, until that fateful July day in 1876 when the coward Jim McCann shot him without warning in Carl Mann's saloon in Deadwood, South Dakota. The story of Bond, however, is virtually timeless: he remains an agent in the Secret Service, jousting with the most improbable enemies and permitted by his raconteurs only temperamental and cosmetic changes. Fleming's Bond, for instance, is a morbid cold warrior, continually questioning the rightness of the cause that sends him out to kill his fellowman. But the Bond of the movies, particularly the wisecracking Roger Moore, possesses no conscience, only a stream of glib one-liners. In Bond's recent resurrection by the novelist John Gardner (beginning with *License Renewed*) he retains his former identity but acquires new toys: a Saab turbo replaces the Continental Bentley, a Browning nine millimeter the old Walther PPK. As Gardner continues to produce, the possibility that the movie series will extend into the next century grows more likely.

007 and Wild Bill—James Bond and James Butler Hickok—share the fate of attractive, talented, and unorthodox individuals who must come to terms with the State. Although both possess enough aggressiveness and pride to make them permanent outcasts, oddly they place their deadly talents at the service of the state. If Bond is, like Wild Bill, a gunfighter, Hickok is also, like Bond, an agent of the state in time of war. Ironically, their individuality—the natural gifts and charm they possess—makes them particularly appropriate as a semiotic device to represent the form and boundaries of the state. Although both Bond and Hickok are casual, even flippant, about their responsibilities to the state, they discharge their duties with a remarkable flair that sets them apart from ordinary bureaucrats. And because they serve the state with a distinctive and heroic touch, they provide a rationale or blueprint for merging individual genius with the collective cause. In the very act of rebelling against the hidebound conventions of office they personalize the state, making it seem an amusing, ineffectual old fuddy-duddy (a case being the great fun Bond has with the fat buffoon figure of the southern sheriff in *Live and Let Die*).

As masters of small, maneuverable, and highly sophisticated weapons Bond and Hickok place themselves in impossible circumstances and emerge victorious. One of the major legends in the story of Hickok is the McCanles massacre. David McCanles and nine of his gang, all armed desperados, caught Hickok with only one of his customary two guns and only seven bullets to defend himself. The ten would-be killers cornered him in a tiny cabin and stormed the place. The room filled with gunsmoke and the smell of cordite, knives flashed, fists flew, and when it was over Hickok staggered out of the cabin, bleeding from a dozen wounds and leaving ten dead men behind. After that, so the legend goes, people knew what homicidal rage lay waiting to be kindled beneath the gentle features of the army scout. It was "Wild Bill" Hickok who left that scene of carnage.

The odds Bond faces are even more formidable than the McCanles gang, for he must confront the mercenary armies and massive firepower of one megalomaniac after another: Doctor No, Goldfinger, Katanga, Stromberg, Blofeld. These figures represent the pinnacle of high-tech evil, the power of a complex organization to do mechanized violence in an unjust cause. Doctor No and the others equip themselves with colossal weapons—missiles, nuclear submarines, supertankers outfitted as battleships—and plan crimes on an equally grand scale. In opposing them Bond uses technological products galore, but they are always small, highly personalized devices, often crafted for his express purposes by technicians in Q's lab.

In being so much a man of gadgets and in having so little personal depth (particularly in the movies, Bond's personality consists of little more than a string of atrocious puns), Bond actually personalizes his machines while minimizing his own human character. After all, he is 007, a bureaucratic convenience that need not have any particular name attached to it.

The personality or, as Kidder would have it, "soul" of a machine is an issue of fundamental importance in the kind of identity-building, culture-generating thought distinctive of the human species. It is just that issue that the Bond movies, in however roundabout a way, illuminate. Bond stands in for each of us in our efforts to come to terms with machines in an increasingly mechanized world. And those efforts nearly always involve our individual relationship with the State, for the first and most elemental question we ask ourselves in coming to terms with a particular machine is, "Is it ours or theirs?" Is the machine one of us, or does it belong to some lurking enemy—the compassionless State, the conspiratorial madman—waiting to zap us? Bond's character and actions neatly fix and offer to resolve this lingering dread. Indeed, he seems to say, some machines are evil—those employed by unfeeling totalitarian rulers or psychopathic geniuses—and could easily finish us off were he not there to throw himself between us and the technological menace. And in saving us from mechanized destruction, Bond reveals the other face of the machine world; he jokes and plays with dazzling technological toys while pulling the world back from the brink.

Americans' relations with their machines have a long and complex history, so it is not surprising that their Dreamtime heroes should give mythic expression to that complexity. If Bond and Hickok invest their machines with their own flamboyant personalities and treat them as toys that double as weapons in triumphing against overwhelming odds, the results for other heroes of the American Dreamtime are not so happy. Bond eludes lethal machines that often succeed in destroying his companions, but Dreamtime figures like John Henry and Casey Jones are themselves tragic victims of the products of American technology. These figures thus provide a kind of structural counterpoint to Bond and Hickok in developing the themes of human/machine and individual/state relationships that are central to our culture. Bond and Hickok are winners; even though the latter died by the gun, he was not beaten at his own game. John Henry and Casey Jones are losers, victims of machines they sought to challenge or control.

John Henry provides a neat set of structural oppositions to James Bond: lower class and black versus upper class and white; rural versus urban; manual laborer versus bureaucrat; physically immense and powerful versus mentally quick and supple; master of a simple tool (the sledgehammer) versus master of complicated gadgets; victim of impersonal technology (the company's steam-driven hammer) versus victor over impersonal technology. A perennial criticism of cultural analysis is that it takes insufficient notice of historical processes; in this comparison of John Henry and James Bond we see that myth nicely codifies history, producing folk heroes who represent different modes of relating to an advancing technology in a changing society.

As cultural beings people are continually faced with the task of understanding what their lives are about; even the most complacent and conservative have to make up to their culture as they go along. The business of comprehending ourselves is made particularly difficult by changes in production techniques and products that in turn alter our physical and social environments: from the australopithecine hand ax and the cooking fire to the Walther PPK and the nuclear reactor, our ancestors and ourselves have had to adapt to a world we created. Mythic figures like John Henry and James Bond distill this complex interaction into clear and decisive characters and events. History then assumes the form not so much of a flow of events as a set of stark, stroboscopic images that convey essential information about what it is to be alive in a particular society at a particular time.

Viewed from a contemporary perspective, with the airways filled with ads for personal computers and the streets and malls of our cities humming with the indescribable din of video game arcades, the figure of John Henry evokes acute nostalgia. He represents a (Dream)time when American technology was young enough to take on bare-handed, when a poor black man could still swing his sledge and beat the Company's mechanical monster—even though the struggle would kill him. His death is instructive; it ratifies a transformation in American life from a manual to a machine-based existence. Because John Henry's battle has been fought and the result has been so decisive, it is difficult to imagine a current supergrosser rendition of his story. It belongs to an earlier chapter of the American Dreamtime, one not fully engaged with the problems of the present.

The chapter on John Henry is not closed, however, for his story provides an essential prologue to Bond's. In company with others they form parts of an inseparable corpus: the intertext of American mythology. If

John Henry and Bond are binary opposites in most respects, they are complements in one critical area. Both do battle with vastly superior mechanical adversaries while accepting, even glorying in, the technological world they inhabit. John Henry was that "steel-drivin' man" who was "born with a hammer in his hand" and loved to swing his sixteen-pound sledge with the work crews that fashioned what was at the time perhaps the world's grandest engineering project: the American railway system. Like Bond, John Henry personalizes a technological order too vast and complex to comprehend in detail. And in personalizing it, in touching it with their own charm and dynamism, they rationalize a State that bends the individual to a rather cruel yoke. John Henry, whose attributes could easily be those of the leader of a slave rebellion, spends his enormous energies in the white man's workplace. As an exemplary worker he validates the technological State in the very act of challenging its machine, just as Bond, the exemplary agent, carries out his supervisor's assignment while making light of his instructions. It is another case of the individualist affirming the bonds that tie all ordinary individuals to the State.

The Secret Agent in Popular Culture

If the themes of human/machine identity and individual/state relationships are integral to the structure of our culture, to the American Dreamtime, then the story of Bond and that of John Henry should bear on social institutions other than folklore. It is interesting, for example, to examine how these legendary heroes of folktale and movie are related to living, breathing folk heroes who every weekend dazzle tens of millions of Americans watching them in coliseums and television rooms across the land. Two categories of popular entertainer spring to mind here: football players and rock musicians.

To invoke our Martian anthropologist again, a short time spent watching television or wandering the streets would alert him to the mass appeal and collective hysteria of two distinctively twentieth-century rituals—the football game and the rock concert. The phenomenal numbers of people drawn to those rituals and the intensity of their involvement would indicate that the natives of this peculiar society find them necessary to their enjoyment of life. Inquiring into the cultural significance of football and rock is therefore a means of identifying basic organizing principles in American society (Montague and Morais 1976). If nearly everyone knows something about John Henry, James Bond, Elvis Presley, and O. J. Simpson, it must be because they represent areas of experience that together constitute a vast corpus of myth—the American Dreamtime. But what specifically does James Bond have in common with such diverse personalities as Elvis Presley, Mick Jagger, Jim Morrison, O. J. Simpson, Joe Montana, and Too Tall Jones, to name only a few superstars of field and stage? Clearly all are culture heroes of a sort, but apart from that general affinity how are their several stories specifically linked within a cultural structure?

In "Professional Football: An American Symbol and Ritual" Arens (1976) accounts for the tremendous surge of interest in football over the past quarter-century (it has acquired at least equal prominence with the formerly undisputed "national game" of baseball) by tying the sport to an emergent corporate culture in the postwar United States. Baseball is a pastoral game, played on an irregularly shaped field (any pasture or sandlot will do) by relatively few players, all of whom need to perform several functions well—batting, running, fielding, throwing. This wide-open, bucolic game of summer suited a younger, less complicated America, a compatibility or fit between ritual and society that helps explain the game's exalted status during the first decades of the century, when the Sultan of Swat held court on the diamond. Football, on the other hand, is played on a rectangular grid of unvarying dimensions by players who clump together around the ball (even a wide receiver plays in the middle of a crowd in comparison with a center fielder). And football players have such specialized functions that it is almost incorrect to refer to *the* team at all, since they are divided into offensive, defensive, and special units that take the field at different times. Some veteran team members have never been on the field together during a season, which makes their "team" a rather abstract entity.

The incredible specialization involved in a game that pays men huge sums of money to be full-time nose guards, tight ends, and running backs betokens a transformed and immensely more complex America. In the postwar era corporate giants like General Motors and IBM have expanded to the point that each occupies dozens of skyscrapers in as many cities around the world and employs tens of thousands of workers. And each of those workers is locked into a specialized corporate structure bristling with job description forms—a business climate that would have been difficult to imagine when the Sultan of Swat (who started out as a pitcher) was thrilling the Saturday afternoon crowds at Yankee Stadium.

As a dominant ritual of American culture, football derives its compelling appeal from its ability to organize and choreograph both the nagging complexities of daily life and the elemental dilemmas of existence into a tight, dramatic presentation that can be comprehended as a whole (and ideally in a single sitting, although the notorious "TV time-out" has made a mockery of the sixty-minute football game). The anxiety-ridden junior executive at IBM knows he has to perform in a highly competitive and complex corporate jungle, and yet he usually does not know just how well or how poorly he is doing. How is his work being evaluated on the upper floor? How much damage is that s.o.b. who wants *his* next promotion doing behind his back? Will the Japanese clobber the American computer industry over the next few years and put him in the unemployment lines? These imponderables of corporate life, together with the unnerving certainty that decisions will be and are being taken about one's personal fate, impart an ill ease in corporate America that cries out for resolution and release. And so we watch and, in a way, worship football, particularly the Sunday afternoon NFL professional variety. These games bring all the disguised corporate anxieties out in the open for the world to see, pitting highly paid and trained specialists against one another in a public, television-saturated arena. There are referees, a clock, and a final score; the game unfolds in the compressed temporal and spatial dimensions of ritual and yields a result with a definitiveness that acts as a balm to the frayed corporate psyche of modern America.

The ritual costumes of American sport, particularly football and baseball, are in keeping with its changing role. Even in today's media-saturated big leagues, baseball uniforms remain almost the same casual garments they were a century ago. And the men who wear those uniforms retain their individuality; they are easily recognized by sight and not just by position or number. Television brings the faces of Reggie Jackson, Steve Garvey, and Gary Carter into our living rooms and makes them familiar— makes them personalities. Football is a different story. Players' bodies are grotesquely distorted by their gear: they are padded, helmeted, face-masked and mouthpieced to the point of being unrecognizable even in television close-ups. From the distance of the bleachers, all that signifies on the field is a set of numbers. Like the corporate executive and worker, the football player is virtually faceless; his individuality has been consumed by the voracious demands of his function.

The media finds itself in an odd predicament here. It has hyped a sport in which increasing anonymity is the rule, and yet it needs stars and superstars to continue hyping the game. So Howard Cossell talks (and talks, and talks) about the personal lives of the players and besieges them with uncomfortable questions in sideline or locker-room interviews. The sideline shot of the player off the field and out of his all-obscuring helmet is a favorite supplemental device for imparting personal identity to men who perform their exploits as numbers.

If the football player is a helmeted warrior embodying the self-effacement and competitiveness of corporate America, the rock musician is his antithesis. Glorying in the wildest flights of egotism, the rock star screams for the death of the corporate state. In "Football Games and Rock Concerts: The Ritual Enactment," Montague and Morais (1976) portray these two figures as contradictory models of success in American society. Intriguingly, they suggest that our society does not operate with a single, internally consistent image of success but continuously struggles to embrace mutually incompatible goals. From our earliest years we are inculcated with the value of teamwork and led onto the football fields of childhood. But at the same time we are urged to achieve as individuals in competition with others: report cards, honor rolls, who has more money, who is more attractive are all hierarchical devices that instill in us a strong sense of ourselves as self-determined, driven individuals in a world of other similarly motivated persons.

Paradoxically, the rock star appears to trample on all these social hierarchies and yet achieves for himself a degree of success denied the humdrum multitudes that dutifully pick their way up the social ladder. As a star, he is a kind of individual in the raw, whose appetites and excesses only enhance his reputation as one who drinks life to the dregs. He is part of no institution; his stature is determined solely on the basis of popular appeal: the coliseums fill up and the money pours in. Formal acknowledgment of his stardom appears on television and in the popular press; in the words of Dr. Hook's song, he gets his picture on the cover of *Rolling Stone.*

Given the stylized, idiosyncratic identities of rock star and football player, what possible affinity can either have with James Bond? I believe the answer lies in the power the story of Bond has to bridge or mediate the contradictions generated by the antithetical images of American life embodied in rock star and football player. Bond is obviously neither, but he possesses attributes of both and so serves as a powerful synthesis that knits together incompatible elements of the Dreamtime. The rock star, for instance, is not so independent of the corporate state as his behavior would indicate. Although the embodiment of all that is wild and free in the human spirit, he is inextricably tied to modern technology: his artistic expression—the essence of his public image—requires truckloads of electronic equipment manufactured by large corporations and operated by a small army of technicians. Elvis Presley and Mick Jagger's primal energy would die a few yards from their bodies were it not for the microphones they hold, the banks of amplifiers and speakers, the mixing labs, the television cameras, stations, and sets, the phonograph records and video recordings, the myriad factories where all the equipment is manufactured, and the stores that sell the products.

And like Bond, the rock star's ties to technology are more than a passive dependence. If there is any implement besides the gun and car that permeates popular culture, it is the electric guitar. How many video, photographic and concert images exist of the rock musician on stage, gyrating, howling, and clutching his guitar as the instrument and totem of his identity? The gun and the electric guitar are easily the two most popularized hand-held instruments of American culture, which has somehow managed to impart a similar function to these utterly dissimilar artifacts. The similarity is recognizable at any rock performance, where the guitarist cradles his instrument like an automatic weapon—sometimes doubling also as a penis—and projects his music as though it were a burst of gunfire.

The rock musician uses his instrument as if it were a weapon; Bond uses his weapon with the finesse and precision of a musician. Our culture is virtually obsessed with the human/machine identity conundrum, an obsession given Dreamtime form in the figures of secret agent and rock musician. These cultural heroes posit two modes of the human/machine relationship that alternately oppose and complement one another, a tension whose practice traces patterns across this supremely problematic terrain of our thought. Whether we recognize it or not, we often think in riddles. Because rock musician and secret agent are part and parcel of our everyday consumption/generation of culture, we cannot help framing implicitly the questions: How dissimilar are they? For all their apparent differences, isn't there a haunting resemblance just beneath the surface? I submit that the resemblance lies in their both being masters of machines, virtuosos whose power to fuse flesh and metal or plastic into a dazzling synthesis of form and motion transforms our habitual conception of the machine as something apart, to be picked up and put down and used, in a word, mechanically.

Like Bond, the rock star is a master of machines. But unlike Bond, the rock star in exercising his mastery alienates himself from the state that has provided his equipment. His electric guitar and the lyrics it accompanies are weapons aimed at the heart of the state, an organized mediocrity and sobriety that represent everything his Dionysian spirit opposes. There is an insupportable dilemma here, one of several that make the Dreamtime an unending battleground of ideas. The rock star takes up the sophisticated product of the State, but he continues to fight John Henry's battle against the Company. Although it is far more ambiguous, rock's ties to southern blues are no historical accident, for both confront the perpetually vexing question of how men are to deal with the Man. Bond, of course, deals with the Man by becoming his agent, although as a *secret* agent he has considerably more latitude to express his individuality than the conventional desk-bound office worker. Bond's gun shoots bullets, not musical notes, and is trained at the enemies of his employers. But in taking up the machine in Her Majesty's Secret Service, he personalizes it and demonstrates that mechanical expertise need not be the sole prerogative of an anonymous *apparatchik.*

If Bond is a bit like and a bit unlike the rock star, he is also a bit like and a bit unlike the football player. It is his mediating role between the extremes of individualism versus teamwork and mechanical versus physical identity that gives Bond (and other secret agents who are fast-paced, high-tech replicas of him) his compelling appeal. Like the football player, Bond is a highly trained and specialized team member whose energies are all directed to beating the other side. But unlike the football player, Bond wears no uniform—his number, 007, is invisible—nor does he disguise his personal identity with a helmet, shoulder pads, and the like. Although he retains his civilian appearance, Bond in an evening jacket is every bit as dangerous as a defensive linebacker.

The mediation Bond represents is filled with nuance, for the individual/ State relationship is articulated not by itself but in conjunction with human/mechanical differences. Bond thus provides a dramatic statement of composite identity; he reveals that cultural things are seldom one-dimensional. Football players give up their individuality and rely on their similarly robotic teammates to accomplish feats of physical prowess; the well-oiled human machinery of a professional squad is also a mountain of muscle. Bond mocks the team he serves so well, flaunting his individuality while relying, like the rock star, on state-produced gadgetry to perform his acts of technical wizardry.

Bond's physical attractiveness both complements and opposes the physical might of the football player, which is itself already anomalous: the football player confounds the animal/machine opposition because his superb physical conditioning is the result of monotonous routine. In becoming physically perfect he is forced to abandon a supposedly animal spontaneity in favor of mechanical regulation. This area of tension may help to explain the curious inconsistency in the names of NFL teams, some of which bear traditionally "totemic" animal designations (Dolphins,

Rams, Broncos) while others have function labels that identify them within the other totemism of occupational and ethnic groups (Forty-Niners, Packers, Steelers, Redskins).

Bond's animal nature is signed directly by his sexuality, and his women have become a trademark of both the movies and the novels. His endless flirtations, which strike so many as gratuitous if not contemptible, actually mask a complexity that emerges clearly when one considers the sexuality of his tandem characters, the rock musician and the football player. Both figures are sexual blurs, distortions, juxtapositions of anything that could be construed as a consistent charter of socially endorsed sexuality. The rock musician, a technical wizard at the guitar, indulges every animal appetite. He is expected to run amok; his unrestrained sexuality and drug use are devices that define and reinforce the State in the act of negating it. Note that it would be ludicrous for the media to feature an exposé of drug use by rock musicians, for that excess is theirs by right—it is almost their assigned function in a State that has made them emissaries of an emerging technological culture. Drug use in professional sports, however, attracts tremendous media coverage: those fine, upstanding young athletes should do nothing to impair their magnificent bodies or disciplined training. And the sexual taboos of the locker room are an article of faith from junior high to the NFL; the supremely conditioned animal cannot aspire to the unregulated public sexuality of his opposite number, the rock musician. A six-foot-nine, 275-pound tackle is already so overwhelming a physical force that any further stimulation of his physical nature, whether by drugs or sex, would make it impossible for him to function as a cog in that penultimate Dreamtime machine—the football team. The sexual mediation Bond achieves is to cultivate a flamboyant but cool style that both affirms and denies his animal self; he becomes a technician of passion.

Animal and machine, individual and State are oppositions whose solitary expression is insupportable in any one cultural production. Nothing can be purely animal, for example, without conforming to notions of mechanical regulation that negate its animal status. The very existence of culture depends on a principle of semiosis by displacement: a thing acquires meaning by pointing at what it is not. Our culture heroes exemplify this principle: football players and rock musicians simultaneously establish and destroy stereotypical identities. The secret agent mediates these mediators. James Bond, as the archetypical secret agent, combines and confuses elements of both. It is a generative process, for in combining irreconcilable opposites he licenses the continued practice of those categories in everyday life. There is probably no better term than "agent" to describe Bond's distinctive role—unless we borrow from chemistry the notion of "reagent"—for his presence hastens and amplifies events whose nature is generally obscure outside the Dreamtime setting of our movie theaters. The critics are right in a sense: Bond is empty, devoid of character, no more than a cipher whose mission carries him from situation to situation, woman to woman, group to group, category to category. Essentially devoid of content himself, he can take on that of others in operating in his chosen field—for he is, after everything else, undercover, a spy.

The Story of America

It is all too easy to adopt the refined views of an intelligentsia (Tom Wolfe's cultural mavens) and dismiss football, rock music, and secret agent thrillers as acts in a modern-day Roman circus that the masters of our society put on to amuse and pacify the mob. Too easy and too cynical, for such an attitude rejects the possibility that simple tales and rituals may contain profound meaning and that the mob, lacking in education and sophistication, may still grasp at an intuitive level the vexing dilemmas of human existence. Faced with a tremendous interest in certain cultural productions, the anthropologist—if not the philosopher and literary critic—has no choice but to treat them with the utmost seriousness. When the story of Bond is approached in this manner it yields important clues about how our culture is put together and where it appears to be headed.

In the context of an American Dreamtime the fundamental categories of identity—animal, machine, individual, State—assume stark, dynamic configurations that surely have existed in no other society, ever. Perhaps the most curious feature of our Dreamtime is its simultaneous valorization of the individual and the machine, categories that appear incompatible in principle and that in fact generate considerable antagonism. If our popular culture contains any message that recurs as frequently as the praise we lavish on technology, it is the fear and hatred we voice toward the most notorious avatars of the machine—the computer and the Bomb. That deep-seated ambivalence is expressed repeatedly in the story of Bond: we like to marvel at Q's toys, but we also want to see them destroyed—and see them take other technological horrors with them.

The ultimate signified and puzzle of the American Dreamtime, in which the story of Bond figures so largely, is the concept/myth of America itself. Our movie screens, television sets, and supermarket novels are filled with secret agents and private investigators—James Bond, Sam Spade, Travis McGee, Smiley, Jim Rockford, Harry O., Barnaby Jones, Thomas

Magnum, Rick and A. J. Simon, and many others—because they offer the illusion of discrete, bounded societies and social roles that can be penetrated and set right or wrong. The United States is a land of such sprawling diversity that it can be fashioned into America only through the intercession of a myth-making intelligence that generates culture heroes who appear to confer a uniform meaning on that diversity.

The cultural construction of America is part of a universal process of cultural generativity; citizens of the United States are not alone in their relentless efforts to define themselves and their society. The identities human/machine, individual/State, we/they are not static, known categories but evolving processes of cultural formation. The apparently superficial Fleming narratives and Broccoli movies thus lead into the most profound theoretical questions surrounding the nature of culture. To be human, as to be American, is never naturally (or divinely) to be such-and-such, for what we call "humanity" or "America" is a process through which the symbol-using, myth-making intelligence picks its way back and forth across the category boundaries it has itself erected—animal, machine, our group, their group. On this journey the mind must fashion its own trail markers, which take the form of culture heroes whose characters embody critical juxtapositions or transformations of elemental categories of identity.

These abstract considerations have a highly personal side, for they bear on our individual daily lives. We are all, like it or not, akin to secret agents in that we find ourselves over the course of our lives belonging to diverse, incompatible social units. The family of our childhood memories becomes unrecognizable and disintegrates, peer groups form and reform with different codes as well as different members, loves and marriages occur with sometimes dizzying abruptness, children become if not strangers then at least . . . different. Difference—you and I, we and they—how naturally these terms of belonging, of identity, spring to our lips and yet how artificial and contingent they are. Belonging to a group, being a this rather than a that, is at once critical and problematic; there is simply nothing fixed about this whole enterprise of groupness.

P
A
R
T   Improvising
I I   America
I

Editor's Introduction

Advertising and films stand among the messages most carefully crafted to achieve their impact. As such they can throw only a partial light on the everyday life of the people who live in the United States. The next set of essays comes closer to the experience of struggling with a cultural environment that provides models of the world that appear particularly realistic and yet are always somewhat "off" from what one might want to say or to be known as having said.

The chapters by Singer and by Myerhoff and Mongulla examine what "ethnicity" can do. They raise the well-worn "melting pot" issues in a new way that moves us beyond the old dichotomy. In their essays "ethnicity" does not appear to be a passing stage in American history that full enculturation of all immigrants would make moot. After many generations in the United States, it still makes sense to say that one is of "old Scottish stock," whether or not one can specify genealogical links to Scotland and whatever the amount of intermarriage. Conversely, it seems more and more difficult to argue, as the apologists of the "new ethnicity" affirmed in the 1960s (Glazer and Moynihan 1963; Novak 1971), that ethnicity is persisting as an issue because people in the United States remain "different." While there are undoubtedly pockets of such difference, what is interesting in the political aspects of ethnicity is that it is effective even in the absence of difference. Indeed, Myerhoff and Mongulla suggest that ethnicity becomes an issue precisely when difference is threatened—that is, when the signs of the difference are dissolving, melting away. How can middle-class Jews in a large urban center that does not have a strong Jewish presence establish that they exist? This is the question that Jewish leaders in Los Angeles asked themselves. And by asking this question they also suggested that "the Jews" are not the obvious presence that those arguing for a substantive "ethnicity" affirmed they were. "The Jews" are a set of symbols that must be manipulated if a message is to be sent that one wishes to identify, even only temporarily, with Jewishness. For such a message to be understood it must, like a commercial, make use of a historical, cultural dialect that may be more attuned to its intended audience than to the dialect the speakers use among themselves.

In effect, both essays suggest that, along with motherhood and apple pie, ethnicity is a pillar of American culture. Schneider (1969) led the way toward such an analysis when he showed how formally similar are the domains of kinship, nationality, and ethnicity. Ruskin and Varenne (1983) have tried to recast this argument by showing that ethnicity is also a "discourse," that is, a structured manner of creating a conversation about a topic. As a topic, ethnicity is "different" from religion, political affiliation, or family. As a discourse that makes sense and can convince, it may have the same shape as other discourses about social organization. Families, denominations, clubs and such associations are "groups." So are "ethnics." It is not surprising that they should all be spoken about in similar terms of "substance" and "code for conduct" in Schneider's words—that is, in terms of the substantive characteristics (a property of the individual member) around which is formed a social entity within which certain behaviors are used for identifying purposes.

This analysis should call to mind Beeman's focus on the paradoxes of choice and conformity that he sees unfolding around advertising. Ethnicity, of course, does not seem to be a product one can buy. And yet there is something strikingly effective in a headline used by *Newsweek* magazine for a story on conversion: "Becoming a 'Jew-by-Choice' " (28 January 1985). By the second or third generation, people are rarely simply Irish or Italian. They are probably enough of a mixture that it is difficult to escape the implication that one must make a choice: to affirm oneself as Irish, as Italian, or as nothing. Few things may be more American than the tale of the daughter of a Protestant Scotsman from Northern Ireland and a Catholic woman from Southern Ireland who affirms herself as Catholic Irish while being tempted by liberal Protestant theology, is married to a Frenchman, and lets her children be identified as French.

I write this tale of my wife deliberately to call upon one of the most famous origin myths of America, usually attributed to Crèvecoeur, who wrote in 1782 of a family "whose father was an Englishman, whose wife was Dutch, whose son married a French woman, and whose present four sons have now four wives of different nations. *He* is an American, who leaving behind him all his ancient prejudices and manners, receives new ones from the new mode of life he has embraced. . . . Here individuals of all nations are melted into a new race of men" (as quoted by Glazer and Moynihan 1963, 288). Crèvecoeur, like Glazer and Moynihan, seems to assume that the melting process will—or would if it worked—make ethnic identifications moot. As Sollors has shown (1980), the persistence of the theme throughout the history of America's self-understanding is striking. The theme, however, manifests itself only in dialectical tension with the countertheme of the immorality and unreality of the melting pot. Sollors suggests that Zangwill's play *The Melting Pot* (1911), usually credited with expressing the ideal or concept, can be read as a somewhat underhanded, but definite, celebration of ethnic pluralism that persists even in intermarriage. Conversely, he ironically highlights passages in Glazer and Moynihan, Novak, and others that reinstate the melting pot as a description of the present leading to a new future. Here, for example, is the last sentence of *Beyond the Melting Pot*: "The American nationality is still forming: its processes are mysterious, and the final form, if there is ever to be a final form, is as yet unknown" (Glazer and Moynihan 1963, 315).

What all this suggests is that, whether people in the United States are becoming more or less homogeneous—and there is indication that they are becoming less rather than more—a complex discourse is available to them. In this discourse powerful agents "leave behind," "receive," "embrace" (choose?). Clearly, this discourse requires the construction of alternative modes of life so that they can be chosen. If ethnicity is indeed something around which "choice" is an issue, then we might predict for the future that the more Americans intermarry, the more they become culturally alike, the more ethnic identification becomes a possibility that can be handled more and more "regularly" within the culture.

Singer examines the Americanization of ethnicity through a discussion of Lloyd Warner's analysis of two "Yankee City" ritual occasions: Memorial Day ceremonies and the Tercentenary procession. Both symbolically express aspects of the organization of Yankee City, the former stressing unity and equality through the symbols of nationalism, the latter stressing difference and hierarchy by overemphasizing the symbols of ethnicity. Which is the "real" Yankee City? We can't tell. But we can observe the people manipulating these symbols for political purposes: no wonder the "ethnics" of the thirties were more interested in Memorial Day than in "ethnic" floats controlled by the old Yankees. No wonder, as the "ethnics" came to political and economic power, the relationship of the groups to the symbols changed. More wonderful certainly is the fact that, in the absence of the old Yankees, the new generations that inhabit Yankee City in the seventies continue to express themselves in public rituals so as to affirm both democratic egalitarianism (now expressed in the right all people have to display themselves as "Yankee" in certain rituals) and "ethnic" differentiation (now expressed in the traditional terms of national origin and also in such categories as outsiders/newcomers versus insiders/old-timers).

The emphasis in the essays is on the actual performance and theatrical representation of ethnicity. Both demonstrate the difficulty of constructing events appropriate to the message to be expressed. It is as if we had caught the advertisers in the act of producing an ad. Singer insists on the symbolic character of this message and refers us back to Warner's detailed analysis of the constituent parts of civic rituals. Myerhoff and Mongulla offer a detailed account of the process through which an appropriate ritual is built in the kind of ritual *bricolage* that Lévi-Strauss has placed at the center of all cultural activity (1966). I think of it as a process of "improvisation," for such parades are both performances that are strongly constrained on formal grounds and new statements that use old forms to make effective political statements in new contexts. In parades the distinction between author and audience gets blurred. Parades are special moments, but they are also part of everyday life.

5   The Melting Pot: Symbolic Ritual or Total Social Fact?

Milton Singer

Prologue

The American ideal of the melting pot has in recent years come under a cloud of skepticism and controversy. The persistence of interest in ethnic identity evidenced in "the new ethnicity" of blacks, Hispanics, American Indians, and Orientals, the emergence of ethnic segregation in the suburbs even among "white ethnics," the movements for a more restrictive immigration policy, affirmative action, bilingual education, and prayer in the schools have been interpreted by many observers as a threat to national unity and as a reversal of the melting pot ideal of equality of opportunity and nondiscrimination with respect to race, religion, and national origin.

A series of summer visits I made to a small New England urban community in 1974–81 suggest that these fears of the melting pot's demise may be greatly exaggerated. Since the community in question is "Yankee City," the subject of an intensive and famous field study in 1930–35 by the social anthropologist Lloyd Warner and his staff, it provides a rich data base to compare with present trends as well as some historical perspective on the changes. Warner and his associates published five monographs on "Yankee City" between 1941 and 1959, including one on the nine ethnic groups in the city and another on the sacred and secular symbolic rituals, such as Memorial Day ceremonies and the 1930 Massachusetts Bay Tercentenary Procession. In these and his other monographs, Warner compares the "ethnics" with the native "Yankees."

"Yankee City" may not be as "typical" of American cities as Warner claimed, but his comprehensive and detailed studies allow us to explore the relations of the melting pot ideal to symbolic rituals as well as to social structure. Because Warner himself has generalized from some of these relations in "Yankee City" and from related studies of urban communities in the Deep South, the Midwest, and the Far West, we are able to get a sense of the range and scope of his generalizations.

This chapter does not challenge the validity of Warner's generalizations or his predictions about the eventual assimilation of ethnic groups in American society, although I suggest some qualifications. It focuses rather on an internal ambivalence in the melting pot ideal, the tension between equality and social and cultural hierarchy, and on how the symbolic expression of this ambivalence has changed from the 1930s to the 1970s in the direction of greater equality. In this perspective, the recent expressions of ethnic identity appear not as a threat to the melting pot ideal but as symbolic and often nostalgic reenactments of steps in the realization of an American identity.

From Australian Totemism to Yankee City Myths and Rituals

In 1953 Lloyd Warner published *American Life: Dream and Reality,* which summarized and discussed in nontechnical language the results of the collaborative research on American communities he had launched in 1930. The interest of this book goes well beyond the fact that it encompasses Warner's integrative comparison of the four community studies with which he was closely associated—"Yankee City," "Jonesville," "Deep South," and "Black Metropolis" (for bibliographic data, see References). While it is of course illuminating to read Warner's comparative discussions of the variations and similarities in the social classes and color castes among the different communities, his more significant comparisons are those between the "American dream" and social realities. To be sure, these latter comparisons are often phrased in the supposed popular language of American folk ideology— "the American dream" of a democratic and egalitarian society, "the ideal of the melting pot," and similar expressions. Yet it is precisely because Warner's book incorporates both the presumed American folk idiom of the melting pot and the concepts and methods of social anthropology that it takes on a distinctive importance. A year earlier, in 1952, he had published a version of the book in Great Britain under the title *Structure of American Life*, based on a series of lectures at the University of Edinburgh. The melting pot ideology is practically absent from the British edition of the book; its style and idiom are much closer to those of social anthropology. In revising the book for an American audience, did Warner then relax his value-free stance as a scientific and objective social anthropologist and become an American chauvinist?

The difference between the two editions cannot be explained in this way. Apart from a few references in the revised edition to the American dream of "rags to riches" and to the aspirations of the nation's founders that "are now part of social reality," the social anthropologist's facts about social class and color caste are used to reassess the melting pot ideal and to cast doubt on its reality. Even as a "dream" or an ideal, the ontological status of the "melting pot" ideology remains problematic. The tension between dream and reality in American life is sufficiently great in the revised version of Warner's book to exonerate him from the charge of ethnocentrism. This will become quite clear if we translate the folk idiom into Warner's social anthropological analysis.

Warner's distinction between "dream" and "reality" is not epistemological, a distinction between fantasy and truth. The "dream" of the melting pot is also a component of the "reality" of American life, constituting ideal and aspiration in historically changing relevance to the opportunities that accelerate or retard different degrees of achievement. As Warner writes, "The American Story, both dream and reality, is essentially that of a great democracy trying to remain or become democratic and equalitarian while solving the problems of unifying vast populations and diverse enterprises. The story told here is, therefore, concerned with the values and ideals of democracy and, less pleasantly, with the facts of social class and color caste" (Warner 1953, vii–viii).

In terms of Warner's framework of social anthropological concepts, the "dream" of the melting pot and the democratic and egalitarian ideals belong to the levels of myth and rite, symbol and ceremony. His description and interpretation of Memorial Day in Yankee City as an "American sacred ceremony" probably comes as close as any social anthropologist has come to analyzing the melting pot in terms of a symbolic ritual:[1]

Here we see people who are Protestant, Catholic, Jewish, and Greek Orthodox involved in a common ritual in a graveyard with their common dead. Their sense of separateness was present and expressed in the different ceremonies, but the parade and the unity gained by doing everything at one time emphasized the oneness of the total group. Each ritual also stressed the fact that the war was an experience where everyone sacrificed and some died, not as members of a separate group, but as citizens of a whole community. (1953, 10–11)

The use of Lincoln and the grave of the Unknown Soldier as dominant symbols of egalitarianism adds to the integrating and unifying functions of the Memorial Day ceremonies. "The American Unknown Soldier is everyman; he is the perfect symbol of equalitarianism" (1953, 8). Several older residents of "Yankee City" I interviewed in the 1970s vouched for the accuracy of Warner's description of the Memorial Day ceremonies of the 1930s and also praised his capture of their feeling and spirit. This is an unusual tribute to Warner, considering that he himself acknowledged employing Durkheim's theory of religious symbols as "collective representations which express collective realities" (1953, 22–23). Durkheim had applied the theory to Australian and North American aboriginal religions. Warner had spent three years doing a field study of an Australian tribe before he returned to the United States to study American communities. His explanation of the aptness of Durkheim's theory of collective representations for modern society was that there are "basic similarities between the meanings and functions of American myths and ceremony and those of aboriginal Australia" (1953, ix). He also recognized an analogy between the heightened intensity and social solidarity among the members of a modern society in times of war and Durkheim's belief that the intense social interactions among Australian hunters and gatherers when they assemble periodically during times of plenty cause them to experience an increased awareness of group identity (1953, 16).

The parallels between "primitive" myths and rituals and some aspects of modern society were also noted by other anthropologists, especially Goldenweiser (1910) and Linton (1924). None of these, however, worked out the analogy in such detail as Warner managed in comparing the totemic rituals and symbols of the Murngin with the Memorial Day ceremonies and other rites in Yankee City (Warner 1937, 1959). Not only did he follow Durkheim's lead in linking the increased awareness of social solidarity and of group identity in modern Western wartime with Australian totemism, but he also applied Durkheim's emblem theory of totemism to a modern urban community. Durkheim's analogy between the totem and the flag was reversed in this application: "the totem is the flag of the clan" became "the flag is the totemic emblem of Yankee City." Both totem and flag, in any case, were recognized as concrete, visible emblems of a less visible but permanent form of social association (Singer 1984, chap. 5).

Warner was not so naive as to assume that such comparisons between a "primitive" and a modern community implied there were no important differences between them. On the contrary, he often remarked on the increased size and scale of modern communities, their use of elaborate symbol systems—especially the numerical and statistical forms of computation—and the tendencies of these communities and traits to undergo historical changes as well as to persist. He nevertheless believed that the concepts and methods of social anthropology that he had used in aboriginal Australia, and that other anthropologists had used in the study of other primitive societies, could be applied to the study of modern communities with only a change in the detailed techniques of research. In particular, he saw in the holistic, integrative, and comparative approach of social anthropology an alternative to the then prevailing social science methods of studying contemporary society either through an intensive study of a single institution or through an equally unsatisfactory comprehensive statistical social survey (Warner 1953, chap. 2).

In the late 1920s when Warner was doing his fieldwork in Australia, and in the early 1930s when he was directing the fieldwork in "Yankee City," anthropological theory was developing a functionalist analysis of culture, society, and community as systems of interrelated and interdependent parts. Malinowski, Radcliffe-Brown, Durkheim, and Mauss were among the well-known contributors to the study of functioning social systems and total social facts. Drawing on these sources, and especially upon Radcliffe-Brown, who had supervised his Australian research, Warner adapted the functionalist approach to his study of a modern urban community, as the following paragraph indicates:

The research on Yankee City was not directed toward collecting a mass of separate, atomic social items (or traits) which had only a quantitative relationship with each other. Rather, the investigation viewed the total community as a complex configuration of relations, each relation being a part of the total community and mutually dependent upon all other parts. Yankee City, we assumed, was a "working whole" in which each part had definite functions which had to be performed, or substitutes acquired, if the whole society were to maintain itself. (Warner and Lunt 1941, 14)

One problem confronting Warner at the outset of his American research was that "the total community" of Yankee City was not the total community of the United States, and that he had to justify selecting a small community on the basis of explicit criteria. He explained the selection procedures in two ways. First, "the criteria used were designed to identify communities which are expressions of some of the central tendencies of American society." Using criteria that specified size, industry, agriculture, ethnic and religious composition, civic enterprises and associations, and political, economic, and social hierarchies, he would select a community that was "a microcosmic whole, representing the total American community" and conformed to "a basic type of American community" (1953, 32–34).

This procedure may have been followed by Warner and his staff in selecting the midwestern community of "Jonesville." It could not have been completely followed in the selection of "Yankee City," "Deep South," or "Black Metropolis," by Warner's own testimony. In the first monograph of the Yankee City research (Warner and Lunt 1941, 1–5, 38–41) Warner wrote that when Elton Mayo, the director of the Harvard Western Electric study, accepted Warner's advice and asked him to do a study of the factory workers' relations to the whole community in the Chicago area by the methods of social anthropology, Warner demurred on the grounds that the surrounding communities, Cicero and Chicago, were too disorganized and were undergoing rapid and disruptive change.[2] Instead, Warner proposed to select a community with a well-integrated social organization that had developed gradually over a long period, with a coherent and persisting Puritan tradition, predominantly of an "old American" population that would "assimilate the newer ethnic groups." Such a community, between 10,000 and 20,000 people, could be found only in New England or in the Deep South, according to Warner, and is not a representative microcosm of American communities or an expression of their central tendencies.

"Yankee City" and "Deep South" did fit this community type and contained some admixture of ethnic groups as well as a sufficient agricultural base to give them autonomy and a few industries and factories, in the case of "Yankee City" at least, to make the community study relevant to the Mayo group's original Western Electric research.

Two Kinds of Symbolic Rituals,
Two Kinds of Society?

The criteria and procedures for selecting the communities studied are important not only for the question of how "representative" a particular community may be of American society as a whole, but also for assessing the existence of a "melting pot" in the United States and the manner and rate of ethnic assimilation. In the Yankee City monograph *The Social Systems of American Ethnic Groups,* Warner and Srole conclude as follows: "The American social system is not, strictly speaking, a 'melting pot' which fuses its diverse ethnic elements into a new amalgam, as was once popularly believed, but is rather a system which performs the transmutation of diverse ethnic elements into elements almost homogeneous with its own" (1945, 155).

This conclusion is a bit surprising in view of Warner's interpretation of the integrative functions of Memorial Day ceremonies. Its opaque language about "the transmutation of diverse ethnic elements into elements almost homogeneous with its own" does not suggest any clear image of how the ideals of democracy and equality get realized in ethnic assimilation. One possible solution of the riddle might be to argue that Memorial Day ceremonies are symbolic rituals that express and celebrate democratic ideals once a year, but that everyday realities naturally fall short of the ideals. Such an interpretation would not be consistent with Warner's functionalism, which held that symbolic rituals not only express particular social values but also help to sustain and perpetuate a particular kind of social organization and social structure. On the other hand, it is an interpretation that explains the kinds of obstacles everyday realities interpose to the realization of democratic ideals.

There is another interpretation of the puzzle, suggested by Warner himself, in his description of the Massachusetts Bay Tercentenary Procession held in Yankee City in 1930:

> The conception of the celebration and the pageant had to do with the Puritan ancestors and the flowering of New England culture; the themes of the great ethnic migrations and their assimilation—the melting pot, the Promised Land, and the Goddess of Liberty welcoming them—democracy for all and every kind of race and creed—such themes were nowhere present. Indeed those who conceived and presented the pageant saw themselves as teachers initiating the new peoples into the true significance of the nation. (Warner 1959, 197–98)

Why the omission of melting pot symbolism? It would be plausible to assume that the specific historical period celebrated by the Tercentenary—the founding of the Massachusetts Bay Colony—automatically delimited its themes and characters. Yet the later ethnic groups were represented in the procession, not directly, but in historical roles assigned to them by the organizing committee of the procession, whose members were predominantly from old Yankee families. Warner's closing sentence in the quotation above therefore suggests the deeper meaning of the omission of the melting pot symbolism in the Tercentenary procession—and also of the "transmutation of ethnics"—namely, that the procession was a symbolic ritual that expressed a ranked hierarchy of citizenship status, the status of any particular group being determined by the "distance" of that group's race, religion, and ethnicity, and the historical time of its arrival in the country, from those of the Yankee "old American" first settlers. Each ethnic group's status as Americans was symbolized by the kind of historical role and float in the Tercentenary procession assigned it by the organizing committee. Although representatives of the ethnic groups were consulted, ultimately the assignments depended on the perceived convergence between the symbolism of a particular float and the status and rank within the community of the particular sponsoring group. That the Knights of Columbus, for example, should sponsor the float for Columbus seemed appropriate because of the identity of name, the Catholic religion, and the historical meaning of Columbus as a symbol. But "there was no direct connection of the local association with the person for which the symbol stood, such as the descendants of the first settlers had with the 'landing of the Founders'" (Warner 1959, 199).

This distinction between the Knights of Columbus and the Sons and Daughters of the First Settlers implies a hierarchy of superiority with respect to ethnic group, religion, and racial group that transcends the time of arrival. As "Yankees" and "natives," the First Settlers had a rank superior to that of the "ethnic" Italians, although "Columbus was the 'first' European to land in America and is credited by history with the first beginning of this society, even preceding the Puritans and the Founders" (Warner 1959, 199).

The problem posed by the omission of melting pot symbolism in the Tercentenary procession of 1930 is whether the citizens of "Yankee City" believed at all in the ideal of the melting pot and, if not, what their ideal was. By Warner's account, at least, the "old family" Yankees who predominated among the organizing committees of the procession thought of themselves as the teachers and assimilators of the "ethnics" in the city. The "Yankees," especially the direct descendants of the Puritan first settlers, not only represented their own ancestors in the procession's reenactments, but also assigned proxy American roles for the "ethnics" to reenact and instructed them how to act those roles.

The Tercentenary procession, as a symbolic ritual, presents a striking contrast to the symbolic ritual of Memorial Day, in which each group memorializes its own dead and participates in a series of integrative ceremonies in which equality of sacrifice of the different groups is symbolized by the unknown soldier and national solidarity by the unification of the separate ceremonies at graves into a single set of ceremonies in a single cemetery. The Memorial Day ceremonies symbolized a melting pot ideal of democracy and equality; the Tercentenary procession symbolized a hierarchical society with "old Americans" at the top.[3]

Warner saw that Memorial Day as he and his co-workers observed it was primarily a sacred ceremony, whereas the Tercentenary procession was primarily secular. In his statistical analysis of types of associations in Yankee City, he also found that sacred rituals were more popular with the "lower class" associations than with the "upper classes" (Warner 1953, 206–9). This kind of correlation suggests that the lower classes may have been stronger believers in the melting pot than the upper classes. More direct studies of the beliefs of both kinds of associations, as well as of the wide range of sacred and secular activities, would have been needed to confirm this hypothesis, which Warner never formulated explicitly.

Warner's Social Mobility Theory of Ethnic Assimilation

In her book *And Keep Your Powder Dry* Margaret Mead wrote that "we are all third generation" (1965 [1942], 52–53). She seems to have meant by this not that all or most Americans have a shallow ancestry of two generations in the United States, but that they have a "character structure" that follows a three-generation cycle of acceptance-rejection-moderate acceptance of European and/or parental traditions, no matter how many generations a family has lived in the United States. Her statement, however, that the "odd blending of the future and the past, in which another man's great-grandfather becomes the symbol of one's grandsons' future, is an essential part of American culture" applies more to those Americans who are worshiping not their own ancestors but Washington and Lincoln, Jefferson and Franklin—"the thing for which grandfather left Europe at the risk of his life, and for which father rejected grandfather at the risk of his integrity" (Mead 1965 [1942], 49). Tocqueville reported this ancient vicarious kind of ancestor worship in the 1830s, as Warner and Marquand did in the

1930s. Among some residents of Yankee City in the 1970s, to discover and maintain a historic house's "lineage" was more important than documenting one's own family lineage (Singer 1977, 1984).

If the melting pot is a collective representation in Durkheim's sense, a set of shared beliefs and sentiments expressed in symbolic rituals enacted on special occasions, then Warner's studies of Yankee City in the 1930s document the existence of such a collective representation in Memorial Day ceremonies that symbolize equality of sacrifice and social solidarity in wartime. These same studies, however, also document the existence of another collective representation in the symbolic ritual of the Massachusetts Bay Tercentenary Procession, which symbolized a hierarchy of citizenship status based on birth, religion, ethnicity, and time of arrival. The contrast in meaning between these two kinds of symbolic rituals might be explained by reference to the different historical circumstances in which they originated—for example, the founding of the Massachusetts Bay Colony on the one hand and the deaths in the Civil War on the other. Yet such a historical explanation would not be sufficient to account for the persistence of the contrast as late as the 1930s and beyond, as Warner recognized. He acknowledged Durkheim's analogy between Australian totemism and the effervescent social solidarity generated by modern war fever. And he followed Radcliffe-Brown's extensions of Durkheim's correlations between totemic symbols and differentiated social structures as systems of social status.

It was as hierarchies of social status that Warner analyzed the social classes and castes of American society. This presumably was the hierarchical social reality symbolized by the Tercentenary procession and its later ritual descendants. These do *not* represent the American dream of the melting pot. However, by incorporating *changes* in social status, and social mobility generally, into his scheme, Warner was able to make his empirical studies of Yankee City and other communities relevant to an assessment of the validity of the melting pot ideal. In this way he was able to take account of both the undemocratic hierarchical features of American society and the democratic, egalitarian features. As a system of social classes and color castes the society was, as he perceived it, organized hierarchically into lower and higher status. But the movement of individuals and families within the system from lower to higher status represented upward social mobility, just as the movement from higher to lower status represented downward social mobility (Warner 1953, chap. 5).

Warner's translation of this social mobility model into a representation of "the melting pot" and the "American dream" was based on his assumption that ethnic immigrants entered the system at its lowest levels when they arrived in this country and gradually climbed the ladder of social status as they moved into better neighborhoods, better schools, and better jobs. Upward social mobility thus became a tangible and quantitative index of acculturation, Americanization, and ethnic assimilation. The eventual outcome of this process of upward social mobility, Warner predicted, would be the "disappearance" of the "ethnics" into the mainstream of American life.[4]

There are a number of qualifications and limitations to this social mobility model of the melting pot. Warner recognized some of these explicitly; others have emerged since he made his original study. A relatively minor qualification of the model is that Warner could not find any ethnic group that had climbed beyond the "lower upper" social class, and only the Irish had come that far in Yankee City (Warner 1963, 395). Does this imply that no ethnic group has been completely assimilated? English-speaking Canadians, Scots, English, and North Irish are considered "members of the total population" of Yankee City, according to Warner. However, these "had not formed ethnic groups" (Warner 1963, 418). Does this mean that those who did form ethnic groups and whose "ethnic" ancestry has not yet been forgotten—for example, the South Irish, including the Kennedys—are not yet completely assimilated?

At the other end of the class hierarchy, what about those ethnic groups who were not successful in their efforts to climb the social ladder, or whose social mobility was downward, or who preferred to remain in the old neighborhoods and the old jobs? Warner relates such cases to his social mobility model in two conflicting ways. On the one hand, he correlates the degree of ethnic conservatism with class status: the lower the class level, the more orthodox the ethnic traits. On the other hand, Warner's distribution tables indicate that "natives" and "Yankees" are as well represented among the lower social class levels as are "ethnics," thus raising the question whether a social-structural criterion of ethnicity is necessary or sufficient to define Americanization and assimilation (Warner and Srole 1945, 68–69).

Warner occasionally mentions examples of individuals or ethnic groups who are exceptions to his generalization that ethnic immigrants settle first in the lowest-grade areas of the city and begin their life in America at the bottom of the social ladder. The individual exceptions are usually people who have special knowledge and skills, titles of nobility, or wealth or who have rendered some special service to the country. Exceptional ethnic groups are those who are considered so similar to the native Yankee group in race, ethnicity, or culture that the accident of their foreign birth or accent constitutes no obstacle to their acceptance or to their entering the social system at an upper-class level.

Although the hierarchies of houses, occupations, and social classes are in part based on objective criteria, such as the size and condition of a house, a census kind of occupational hierarchy, and income as a component of social class, the assessment of the status of a house, an occupation, or a social class and the construction of indexes of social mobility in these hierarchies for different groups in Warner's study depends ultimately on the status of present and former occupants of the houses, on occupations, and on social classes. The status of the occupants is determined in turn by the degree of "subordination" of the group to which they belong. To illustrate the kind of comparison now frequently encountered in Yankee City, is the status of a large house in poor repair on a "good" street, occupied by members of an "old family" of early arrivals with a very modest and uncertain income greater than the status of a large house that has been restored, with a good "lineage" of former owners but now occupied by a recently well-to-do ethnic family, only three generations (or less) in the city and in the country? My impression is that the Yankee City calculus of social classes and of social mobility settled such questions by making Yankee "old family" status and a rank order of ethnic and racial "inferiority" or "subordination" the decisive variables.

Warner is aware of this problem in the measurements of social status and acknowledges that the "objective" indicators must be evaluated as "symbols" of status: "For it is not the house, or the job, or the income, or the neighborhood that is being measured so much as the evaluations that are in the backs of all our heads—evaluations placed there by our cultural traditions and our society. From one point of view, the four characteristics—house, occupation, income, and neighborhood—are no more than evaluated symbols which are signs of status telling us the class levels of those who possess the symbols" (quoted in Warner 1953, 66–67; also see Warner and Srole 1945, 68–69).

A Timetable for Assimilation?

These kinds of exceptions to the social mobility theory of ethnic assimilation indicate that there are racial, ethnic, and cultural criteria for social hierarchy that override the criteria of place of birth, size and condition of residence, kind of occupation, and level of education and income. Warner is quite aware of these overriding criteria and himself points out that not all "ethnics" are foreign-born and not all "Yankees" are native-born. In fact, he constructs a "timetable for assimilation" predicting the length of time it will take for various groups to be accepted and assimilated (Warner and Srole 1945, chap. 10; Warner 1963, chap. 14). This timetable is based not only on an extrapolation from the histories of ethnic social mobility in Yankee City and other communities, but also on the assumption that the degree of perceived difference between a given minority group and "old Americans" determines the degree of "subordination" of the ethnic group and its rank of inferior status. "The conceptual scheme which places a subordinate group in its relative rank within our social hierarchy permits us to predict with some degree of success the probable degree of subordination each group will suffer, the strength of the subsystems likely to be developed by it, the kind of rank order it will be assigned, and the approximate period necessary for its assimilation into American life" (Warner 1945, 285).

Applying this scheme, Warner generates a hierarchy of ethnic groups in Yankee City. Using skin color as an index of racial type, language as an index of ethnic type, and religion as an index of cultural type, he constructs his timetable for assimilation. His classification of racial types is based on textbooks in physical anthropology of the period (Warner 1963, 414 n. 1).[5]

When the combined cultural and biological traits are highly divergent from those of white "old Americans," "the subordination of the group will be very great, their subsystem strong, the period of assimilation long, and the processes slow and usually long" (Warner and Strole 1945, 286).

Examples of such groups cited by Warner are Mongoloid peoples, blacks, and racially mixed dark-skinned peoples such as those of India. He believes they form "color castes" in the United States.

A rank order of ethnic and cultural similarities of "old Americans," on the other hand, would follow language and religion, since "the dominant old-American religion is Protestant, and much of our customary behavior is closely integrated with a Protestant outlook on life. Our customary way of life is most like the English, and our language is but one of several English dialects" (Warner and Srole 1945, 287).

English-speaking Protestants would then be ranked as most like "old Americans" (e.g., the Scotch-Irish), non-English-speaking Protestants next (e.g., Protestant Armenians), followed by English-speaking Catholics (e.g., Irish Catholics), non-English-speaking Catholics and other non-Protestants (e.g., the French Canadians), with non-Christians last (e.g., Jews). Warner predicts that light-skinned English and German Jews will assimilate more rapidly, disappearing in five or six generations, than dark-skinned Jews, who will assimilate very slowly.

This general hypothesis about ethnic assimilation was developed, according to Warner, after the fieldwork had been completed in Yankee City and was based on that research as well as on research on black groups in the North and South and on Spanish Americans and Orientals in California (Warner and Srole 1945, 285, 294).

There are three observations to make about this general hypothesis: it adds attitudes toward racial, cultural, and ethnic groups as independent variables in the social mobility theory of assimilation. This addition limits the validity of the social mobility theory both as an index and as a means of assimilation. Second, it gives a much less optimistic interpretation of the "American dream" than the "melting pot" ideal usually connotes, especially for some racial and ethnic groups. Third, by constructing a quantitative timetable that predicts how long it takes for a particular group to assimilate, the theory can be tested by future developments in Yankee City and in other American communities, whatever may have been its validity in the past.

The third point is the most important for testing Warner's social mobility theory of the melting pot. That theory cannot be tested directly by the kind of empirical data provided in Warner's Yankee City studies on the ethnic distribution of houses, occupations, or social classes. None of these data are sufficient to serve as an index of ethnic assimilation because similar distributions, although not identical, hold for "Yankee" and "native" residents of Yankee City. In order to differentiate a measure of social mobility for "ethnics" from "Yankees," therefore, it is necessary to take account of the degrees of "subordination" owing to racial, ethnic, and cultural criteria of inferiority. Such criteria, however, introduce variables that are independent of social mobility, as has been noted. "Good" Yankee families down on their luck may live in poor neighborhoods but still not be "subordinated" as much as ethnic immigrants or blacks living in the same neighborhoods. Successful upwardly mobile "ethnics," on the other hand, who live on good streets do not usually have the prestige of "Yankees" who live on the same streets.

It is of course likely that the kinds of racial, ethnic, and cultural hierarchies of "subordination" that Warner reported in the Yankee City studies were roughly correlated with residential, occupational, and class hierarchies of the 1930s and earlier. There is some evidence in the Warner studies to support such general correlations (Warner 1963, 404–11) and also some independent evidence in the works of Thernstrom (1971 [1964]) and

Marquand (1960). To the extent that the correlations existed, they were not necessarily explained by a social mobility theory of the melting pot. On the contrary, a more plausible explanation for them would be that Warner's original criteria for selecting a community stipulated that it consist of "a social organization which had developed over a long period of time under the domination of a single group with a coherent tradition." The community he selected was a "Yankee City" with a predominantly "old American" population that "ordinarily assimilates the newer ethnic groups" and with "an unshattered Puritan tradition" (Warner 1953, 38–41). That the New England community Warner selected not only met these criteria but also had a reputation of being a conservative and historically "Federalist" city gave assurance that "Yankees" would be in positions of dominance and non-Yankees in positions of subordination. The actual correlations found between an ethnic group's degree of "subordination" and its positions in the status hierarchies of residence, occupation, and social class should therefore occasion no surprise. They were a function of the community's dominant ideology, which, according to Warner, categorized its members into "Yankees" and "ethnics" and rank ordered "ethnics" on a scale of "distance" from the "Yankees" on racial, linguistic, and religious traits. The rank order of any particular ethnic group on such a scale was then used as a basis for predicting the amount of time it would take for the "assimilation" of that particular group.

A rank order of ethnic groups constructed in this manner is not based on an egalitarian melting pot ideal. Neither can it be directly tested by independent data on the statistical distributions of the population in residential, occupational, and class hierarchies, since these distributions may themselves be a product of the degree of "subordination." As Myrdal's *An American Dilemma* pointed out a few years after the Warner studies began to appear, the statistical distributions of people in the social and ecological system depended on a "rank-order of discrimination." Or, as Myrdal also phrased it, the way people are treated is a factor influencing their behavior and social position or achievements (Myrdal 1944).

The Semiotics of the Melting Pot

Warner's social mobility theory of the melting pot, in spite of its initial plausibility, is not easy to put to an empirical test. It is simple enough to find empirical evidence for status distinctions in neighborhoods and houses, in schools and churches, in occupations and social classes. The difficult problem is to establish that these sets of distinctions form unique hierarchies in each domain, that the hierarchies agree in the different domains, and that they correlate with a hierarchy of degrees of "subordination" among ethnic and other minority groups. And even if such correlations can be demonstrated, it remains to be shown whether the hierarchy of "subordination" among ethnic groups is a product of the different status-distinction hierarchies, whether the latter are produced by the former, or whether there is a mutually reinforcing interaction between the status hierarchies and the rank order of discrimination of ethnic groups. From one point of view Warner seems to make the rank order of "inferiority" the determining variable when he constructs a time table for ethnic assimilation based on the explanatory hypothesis that the time required for an ethnic group's assimilation depends on its closeness to the first Yankee settlers in race, language, and religion. This hypothesis also explains, for Warner, why the Massachusetts Bay Tercentenary Procession contained nothing to symbolize the melting pot and the great ethnic immigrations. Ethnic Americans were represented in the procession only by proxy, by being assigned the roles of early arrivals. The only authentic Americans, in this view, were the lineal descendants of the first British settlers, the Society of Sons and Daughters of the First Settlers, for example, who played the roles of their own ancestors in the Tercentenary procession. "In terms of the ultimate identifications and belongingness, the Sons and Daughters of the First Settlers of old Yankee City who sponsored their own ancestors, the first founders, had a collective symbol to represent them to the whole collectivity. . . . It said—and they and the community said—that they completely belonged, and they were so identified" (Warner 1959, 199–200).

In Warner's interpretation of Memorial Day as a "sacred ceremony," a "cult of the dead," there is a closer approximation to the melting pot symbolism. At least the different ethnic groups "represented" themselves and their own war dead before joining with others in a common unifying ceremony in a single cemetery. And though Lincoln, Washington, and other national heroes were invoked on Memorial Day, the message that was stressed is equality of sacrifice in war regardless of race, creed, or national origin. The grave of the unknown soldier is perhaps the most appropriate symbol of the identification and belongingness memorialized by the ceremony. As Peirce observed: "A statue of a soldier on some village monument, in his overcoat with his musket, is for each of a hundred families the image of its uncle, its sacrifice to the Union. That statue then, though it is itself single, represents any one man of whom a certain predicate may be true. It is *objectively* general" (1955 [1940], 263).

The polar opposition between Memorial Day and the Tercentenary procession as symbolic rituals, the former symbolizing a democratic and egal-itarian ideal and the latter a class and caste status hierarchy, does not pre-clude some shared features. Both symbolic rituals expressed, as Warner recognized, a sense of social solidarity that was itself activated and per-petuated by the rituals. This is the famous doctrine of functionalism, associated with Durkheim, Malinowski, and Radcliffe-Brown. Warner placed special emphasis on the thesis that this kind of functionalism was to be found in modern communities as well as in the "primitive" communi-ties of aboriginal Australia. He claimed, in fact, that the general method and concepts he used in his Yankee City study followed those he had used in his Australian research. The explicit parallels Warner drew between Murngin totemism and Yankee City totemism are easy enough to docu-ment in his published books (see, for example, Warner 1959, 116, 227; Singer 1984, 124, 127). Warner's detailed application of the parallel to Yankee City depends on a generalization of Durkheim's emblem theory of totemism. Durkheim's "the totem is a name first of all, and then, . . . an emblem" is generalized by Warner to the flag, graves, and cemeteries, houses and gardens, costumes and rifles, boats and eagles. These objects become sacred or secular emblems in Yankee City's symbol systems (Sin-ger 1984, 122−25).

The result of such an extension of Durkheim's emblem theory of totem-ism is that it becomes possible to incorporate the social and symbolic differentiation of a modern urban community in Warner's functionalist parallel. Of particular significance in the present context is that Warner's extension of the emblem theory opens the way for a semiotic analysis of the melting pot and historical trends of change in it. To summarize the out-come of a preliminary semiotic analysis, we can say that the Yankee City of the late 1970s is a closer approximation to the melting pot ideal symbol-ized in the Memorial Day celebrations than to the hierarchical class-caste society symbolized by the 1930 Tercentenary procession. How the one type of total social fact was transformed into the other can only be lightly sketched by describing the contrast between them in semiotic terms.

To study the historical changes in symbolic rituals and in total social fact it is not necessary to trace the history of discrete individual symbols or of particular social practices. As Warner recognized, by combining a Durkheimian emblem theory of totemism with the functionalism of Malin-owski and Radcliffe-Brown and the symbolic analysis of G. H. Mead and C. W. Morris, of Sapir, Frye, and Levi, of Freud and Jung, he was able to construct a pragmatic and semiotic analysis of symbol systems in changing social and psychological contexts. His emphasis was neither on isolated symbols nor on the purely formal properties of symbol systems, but on how the symbol systems functioned to communicate meanings to particular social groups and individuals in concrete contexts of social interaction (Singer 1984, 102–4).

When my wife and I first started to revisit Yankee City in 1974 we were surprised to find that many symbolic features of the city that Warner attributed to the 1930s were still in evidence. Parades and historical reenactments in eighteenth-century costumes, historical markers on Federalist houses and gardens, flags and heraldic emblems decorating shops and gravestones, ethnic churches, models of clipper ships—gave us the impression that we had entered a Shakespearean world on the North Shore—"a world in which religion, race, ethnicity, social class and rank, occupation, age and sex were all visibly inscribed in dress and speech . . . in the facades of buildings, houses and ships" (Singer 1984, 125).

As we became better acquainted with the community, after several visits, we found that although some of the emblems and symbols were similar to those Warner described, their meanings were changing because the social and cultural structure was changing. The categories of people Warner had identified as "Yankees" and "ethnics," the six social classes, the ecological, occupational, and political hierarchies he had documented were all now difficult to find. In fact the definitions of "Yankees" as authentic Americans and of "ethnics" as foreigners were openly denied, or the usage was changed. The use of ethnic nicknames was disapproved and resisted. Some even insisted on their right to select surnames of their choice for their children and themselves. Not that a sense of ethnic identity had disappeared as Warner predicted it would according to his timetable of assimilation. On the contrary, even those ethnic families who had prospered and moved into Federalist houses retained a consciousness of their ethnic identity and displayed artistic emblems in their houses and gardens that symbolized their Irish, Jewish, Greek, Polish, or East Indian ancestry side by side with emblems of their American identity. Descendants of ethnic families predominated in the city's political offices and in the informal small groups that "ran the city" or organized the major civic celebrations and projects, such as "Yankee Homecoming" and the restoration of Market Square. In their own view these ethnic families no longer are willing to be referred to as "ethnics," "foreigners," or even hyphenated Americans. Some of them call themselves "natives," sometimes "old-timers," or just plain "Americans."

In a series of 1976 editorials and feature stories in the local newspaper, whose editor was a second-generation member of an ethnic family, the success story of the local ethnic groups was described as "a maturation" of the ethnic groups that occurred in the second and third generations, reinforced by the public schools, the baseball diamond, the corner grocery store, and the move to a better neighborhood. A contrast was drawn in these accounts with the confrontational tactics of the famous Irish mayor "Bossy" Gillis. Bossy's dramatic tactics are described by Warner in his last monograph *The Living and the Dead* (1959) using the pseudonym "Biggy Muldoon" (Warner 1959, part 1; 1963, 206–40). Warner plausibly analyzed Muldoon's tactics as essentially an attack on the major emblems of the Puritan Yankee elite way of life—represented by one of their Federalist mansions with its garden and trees, their ancestor worship of cemeteries and gravestones, and their resistance to modern "progress" in the form of plumbing, telephones, and a gasoline station: "the rights of the common [man] against the privileges of the superior, the equality of opportunity and birth against the inequality of inherited wealth and aristocracy" (Warner 1963, 227).

Bossy Gillis started his political career in Yankee City in the 1920s and 1930s. He ran for mayor in sixteen campaigns and was elected six times. His last winning campaign was in 1959, the year Warner published the last Yankee City monograph (Jacobs 1968). Many in Yankee City, including its most famous author, John P. Marquand, looked upon Bossy's gasoline station and rise to political power as the beginning of the collapse of the old social order. Marquand, however, admitted that the outlines of that order were still intact when Warner and his staff came to study Yankee City in the 1930s. It had changed "beyond recognition" in the late 1950s and early 1960s when Marquand published one of his last nonfiction works, *Timothy Dexter Revisited.*

Warner himself, although he devotes the entire first part of his last Yankee City monograph, *The Living and the Dead* (1959), to Biggy Muldoon's career as a political hero, nevertheless portrays Yankee City as still dominated by the Puritan tradition and the old Yankee families in that monograph as well as in his later one-volume summary of the study, *Yankee City* (1963). It is possible that since the fieldwork on the Yankee City research was done between 1930 and 1935 by Warner and his staff, he was like Tristram Shandy trying to catch up in his monographs and reports with the original observations without taking account of the later changes. Such an interpretation would agree with that of the historian Stephan Thernstrom, who criticized Warner for using the timeless method of social anthropology. There is internal evidence in *The Living and the Dead* of revisits to Yankee City in the 1950s and of observations on changes in church liturgy as well as in Biggy Muldoon's later career. Thernstrom does make an exception of that monograph in his general criticism. Warner's monographs on the ethnic groups and on the shoe strike of the late 1930s are additional exceptions, for both contain historical material and attempts to analyze historical processes of change.

A more plausible interpretation of Warner's portrait of Yankee City is that by the early 1950s both American society and Yankee City were beginning to change their "rank order of discrimination." The effects of the Second World War, the Korean and Vietnam wars, and the Supreme Court decision of 1954 were beginning to be felt even in Yankee City. Warner makes some reference to these changes in his book *American Life: Dream and Reality* ("the realities of the present bi-racial situation indicate a continuing change . . . toward equalitarianism and democracy," 1953, 78–79). Their full local significance, however, had not yet become apparent. While introducing his last monograph with the story of Biggy Muldoon as a populist political hero, Warner treated it as the high farce of a well-intentioned clown. Warner also compares Biggy to Huey Long, Al Smith, Senator McCarthy, Franklin Roosevelt, Andrew Jackson, and Abraham Lincoln—a representative of "the common man who challenges the select few and slays the dragon." Biggy's ultimate failure Warner attributes to his "inability to adjust his basic beliefs and values to those that govern American society" (Warner 1959, 100). "Muldoon, the strong man, knowing he was a good man unjustly treated, following the urge of his ego, strove for success using some of the accepted rules of his society; but he, too, violated some of the basic rules of his group" (Warner 1959, 99).

This may be the explanation of Biggy Muldoon's failure. It is not yet, however, the end of the story, for in the 1970s a new bridge across the Merrimac River was dedicated and named for Andrew J. ("Bossy") Gillis. Warner's timetable for ethnic assimilation has been speeded up; the whole idea of a rank order of racial inferiority has been openly challenged by the Supreme Court, and the level of the comman man has become the highest level of Yankee City citizenship. Margaret Mead's generalization that all Americans are third generation in character structure may be correct. In Yankee City, however, the converse generalization is more apparent— that all third-generation "ethnics," including blacks, and many second-generation ones such as Bossy Gillis consider themselves authentic Americans. The "ethnics" have indeed "maturated" and march in "Yankee Homecoming" parades to colonial tunes dressed in the colorful costumes of patriots and rebels once worn by early settlers.

The changes in and weakening of a rank-ordered scale of "subordination" among racial, ethnic, and cultural groups, particularly at the level of civic symbolism, seem to have tipped the balance toward the democratic ideals of the melting pot and away from the kind of Yankee hegemony Warner described. These changes are probably associated with changes in the composition and distribution of the population. Many of the "old families" have moved away and no longer are concentrated on one street. Since the late 1960s at least, young professionals and employees of Boston and North Shore firms have moved into renovated Federalist houses and support the restoration of Market Square and the Waterfront. A contingent of "arts and crafts" people have also discovered the city and adopted it as a haven from big-city life and high rents. These demographic shifts have created some frictions with the "old-timers" over urban renewal policies, zoning, and the future character of the city.

The newer groups are categorized as "newcomers" and "outsiders" and are contrasted with the "natives" and "old-timers." These categories have generated a new kind of melting pot, one not based on race, religion, and ethnicity, and "a transmutation of ethnic elements into an almost American social system." The new melting pot is based on life-style and years of local residence. To become an authentic citizen of Yankee City now requires about two generations of local residence, an acceptable life-style ("workingmen" preferred to "intellectuals"), and participation in civic affairs.

The evidence for this redefinition of Yankee City authentic citizenship was noted in local usage designations such as "native" and "foreign," "old-timer" and "newcomer" as well as in interviews with local officials and members of local families. The redefinition does not imply disappearance of ethnic identity. That persists with the use of ethnic surnames, the living presence or fresh memories of ethnic immigrant grandparents, some continued use of the ethnic language at home, in ethnic newspapers, ethnic schools, and ethnic churches, and use of decorative ethnic memorabilia in the home and ethnic foods and dances at festivals. Genealogical research has become popular but has until recently concentrated on Yankee lineages and houses. The search for *ethnic* roots at home in the attic or abroad has become acceptable at least since Alex Haley's book *Roots* and the television serial based on it. Much of this persistence of ethnic consciousness is symbolic and nostalgic for the grandchildren of ethnic immigrants and does not displace their taken-for-granted sense of American identity.

Regular community wide rituals that symbolize the new kind of melting pot ideal may be emerging. In the meantime, the old ideals—hierarchical and egalitarian—are still cultivated by the local historical and ancestral societies, the Continental Navy of ceremonial paraders, the Memorial Day celebrations, and the firemen's musters in which different companies compete with antique engines to pump the longest stream of water. Some of the newcomers, including transcendental meditators, are being assimilated by receiving civic recognition in the annual Yankee Homecoming parade, a nonhierarchical ceremony that began as a commercial and tourist promotion in the 1950s and has taken on the character of a genuine collective representation reminiscent of the 1930s Tercentenary procession—a ritualization of the past and of the present in which "The Citizens of Yankee City Collectively State What They Believe Themselves to Be" (Warner 1959, 107). If participating in "Yankee Homecoming" does not automatically mature "ethnics" into "Yankees," at least it expresses the belief of newcomers in a "no-fault" Yankee City citizenship that does not exclude or penalize anyone because of skin color, creed, surname, age, and gender or because of residence, occupation, and income.

6 The Los Angeles Jews' "Walk for Solidarity": Parade, Festival, Pilgrimage

Barbara Myerhoff
and Stephen Mongulla

The large, complex, and immensely varied collectivity of Jews in Los Angeles is for the most part a loose aggregate that rarely comes into being as an interactive body or community, except briefly and then usually during emergencies or crises. After all, how often can huge numbers of people assemble in any city, overcoming diversity and separation like that included in the category "Jews"? Los Angeles Jewry can easily be segmented into many parts: Jews can be Orthodox, Reform, or Conservative; affiliated or nonaffiliated; Hasidic, Sephardic, Ashkenazic, or "Yordic"; there are new and old immigrants from dozens of countries. Shades of religious preference, national difference, and linguistic categories are legion, not to mention the standard sociological variations of age, sex, occupation, and social class. Cultural preferences and organizations of all kinds make for a bewildering spectrum. The variety of political opinion and involvement in philanthropic, social, and secular activities is just as bewildering. Jews in the city gather across all these divisions for only one day each year. On that day, the participants simultaneously experience and display in a public place their commonality despite their radical pluralism, and that is the event we will examine here: the "Walk Festival."

We approach this event from the two angles that, together, organized what could be done to affirm this commonality. On the one hand, the Walk Festival must be understood as the product of the historical situation of Jews in Los Angeles. This situation provides various settings and models for possible symbolic expression. It suggests lines of interpretation and offers "appropriate" symbols. On the other hand, the Walk Festival must be understood as an improvisation in uncertainty. At every stage, the organizers and the participants have to worry that their performance is not doing what they want it to do. Here is the tragedy of human life. In fact, the Walk Festival may accomplish more than is intended. In this lies the glory of human life. In any event, both tragedy and glory are possibilities that must focus our attention on process.

Ritual as Improvised Process

The Walk Festival is a march through "Fairfax," a section of Los Angeles that is generally known throughout the city as a prototypically "Jewish" neighborhood. The Walk coincides with, and is presented as supporting, Israel's celebration of its national independence. As a "march," it is an American popular performance that is now well established and can be used effectively for such varied goals as raising money for medical research ("the March of Dimes") or protesting any number of political decisions. It is related to, though distinct from, the "parades" that have an even longer history in the United States. As an event that involves making a large number of persons move together for ideological expression, the Walk is also related to the processions, pilgrimages, and other such religious rituals that are found in most cultures and have become of interest to many anthropologists (K. Turner 1980; V. Turner 1979).

The Walk is especially interesting in the context of American urban life, where assemblages that cross so many categories are often highly problematic and ineffectual. Los Angeles is one of the more challenging places in which a presentation of unity can be claimed across the mosaic of social worlds that constitute the city. Folk humor is accurate—Los Angeles is "a collection of suburbs in search of a city," described more recently as not even a city, but "a posturban process." The Los Angeles Centennial struggled heroically with the problem of bringing together its fluid, untidy fragments into a unity to celebrate itself and experience an awareness of mutual membership. In the view of many, it was not successful. It may be that belonging to the city is most powerful when ethnicity and locality coincide, but only rarely are these units able to overcome their indifference to others and mount a sense of ceremony or cohesion or to establish sufficient organization for common action.

Los Angeles is, of course, only a perfection of a long process in the development of American social forms. It is the ultimate frontier town—the town that stays on the frontier. By the same token, the ritual forms that model these social forms are themselves rooted in a long American history. The parades and ceremonies of Yankee City that so fascinated Warner (1959) and that Singer brought back to our attention (chap. 5), the "community services" that bring together various denominations for an afternoon in a small town, are variations on the well-worn themes of "unity in difference," *e pluribus unum.* These remained available—and became perhaps even more pregnant with meaning—during the various travels of those who have come to the United States and then to Los Angeles from the many "old countries" of the five continents. The paradoxes of individualism and community, separation and integration must be continually reenacted, resolved, and reaffirmed.

The Eighth Annual Jewish Walk Festival was particularly successful in this task. How symbolic and ritual forms were manipulated to make this possible is our focus in this discussion. A critical ingredient in this success, we maintain, is its form as movement. The joining of bodies with a territory, demarcated by procession, provided the richest and strongest metaphor for the walk, with some unplanned symbolic statements that described the meaning and directionality of the movement. The march defined the boundaries of a community, concentrated awareness of membership, and transformed the spaces involved in several ways. More than that, movement was perhaps the only metaphor that could succeed in carrying off this event, in this city—in this country indeed—where social life takes the form of rapid movement over great distances. Motion is one of the best symbols for activity, success, life. In Los Angeles the truly disfranchised are the sedentary; the truly disprivileged or noncitizens are those without cars. Ceremonially and socially, movement provides linkages between places and between people. Movement not only is display and performance, it is also highly motivating. Solidarity is built into its very form. One moves *toward.* A common goal or destination underlies processions, and this was one of the key symbolic messages planned for the Walk.

The Walk was not an established, traditional event. The forms, background myths, and symbols for it were not "given." The organizers could not rely either on the kind of absolute prescriptions that rule Catholic masses, for example, or on strong customary framings that suggest the form of something like a Christmas pageant. The planners had to choose among available symbols, make decisions, and then reconcile discordant needs and themes. This put them at some risk. In secular urban rituals the truths to be presented are more provisional and temporary, less naturally convincing, inevitably more diffuse, and usually therefore in some danger of being tepid. The final event not only may fail to arouse the effervescence that Durkheim considered the point of such events but, worse, may call into question the very messages it was designed to demonstrate. Cynicism and self-consciousness may replace fervor and revitalization, personally and collectively; witnesses and participants may depart feeling more unsure and unmoored than before they began the undertaking.

We are dealing here with secular ceremonies that require innovation, persuasion, and metaphoric usages that are not fully institutionalized. The data we have on this event cover the planning stages of the Walk in various segments of the groups and associations involved. These data permit us to see the symbolic resources available to planners and what choices they had to make. We can thus see not only the "ritual process" (Turner 1969) that transports the participants, but also the creative process that produced the ritual. This focus on the process of improvisation allows us to highlight the way mythical forms, once they are embodied in ritual—that is, once they have been externalized as an event available to further interpretation—enrich themselves with possibly unintended meaning. The "master of ceremonies," and the organizing committee behind him, had very clearly stated intentions regarding the high truths that the Walk, through its staging and design, was supposed to express. All this, however, was an overlay to another statement. It is as if a concurrent performance was held—not explicitly planned, but nevertheless an accurate and spontaneous reenactment of some historical facts about the Jewish community in Los Angeles. The problem set before us, then, is a complex one, but it cannot be omitted from any study of ritual or ceremony, for such events work on both psychological and social levels at once. We must consider how the intentional, conscious messages interact with the unintentional, unconscious social historical ones.

The Los Angeles Jews

The geographical focus of the Walk Festival is the neighborhood of Fairfax. Fairfax embraces but is not exclusive to the most religious members of the community. It is an ethnic neighborhood heavily marked as "Jewish" by the restaurants and small stores found there, by the services offered, and by a general reputation. There are numerous synagogues, delicatessens, bakeries, cultural and recreational centers, and ethnic, religious, and social institutions that mark it as a specialized social world. The Fairfax area is an area that presents itself and is known as homogeneously Jewish, though this "homogeneity" embraces a staggering internal diversity. Fairfax is not systematically blended into mainstream American life, though within it of course live a great many assimilated Jews. It is a living, vigorous neighborhood, clearly identified with Jewry by insiders and outsiders, and its Jewish character exists as a daily, normal feature.

Fairfax is also the area that many Los Angeles Jews have moved away from over a period of several generations in the predictable process of assimilation. They have traveled to the west of the city as they have ascended the social ladder, shedding the markers of their ethnicity or religion to become Americans first, then Jews. In several western parts of Los Angeles, Judaism is a strong element but not recognizable as a concrete entity. Outside Fairfax, Jewishness is more subtly manifested, marking no streets with signs in languages other than English.

Like other ethnic groups whose success led them to the suburbs, Jews paid a price for their move out of Fairfax with its clear ethnic markers. What could be measured in added affluence was lost in flavor; the richness of the Jewish experience was missing in the suburbs and was replaced by a different kind of security. The ethnic infrastructures were not there. Extended families became nuclear, and the continuity of Jewish life-style was endangered. Temples established as urban Jewish nodes did not compensate for the loss of culture bound by an ecological enclave such as Fairfax. The construction of a symbolic enclave to provide social comfort was no substitute for holistic Jewish socialization. In the absence of such intense socialization and in the presence of a pluralistic society, a Jewish identity had to be more consciously sought and was more difficult to maintain. In these symbolic enclaves (temples, secular organizations, etc.) of suburban Jewish nodes, voluntary associations replace socialization as the vehicle for ethnicity. Such associations can link individuals by emphasizing some commonality, but in the context of the many other voluntary associations that compete for the attention of the people, even the specifically Jewish ones transform the Jewish identity that may be recreated. In the suburbs Jewishness, like Catholicism and, earlier, Protestantism, becomes a matter of choice among alternatives in a neutralized environment. However many Jews may be residing in a suburban neighborhood, the neighborhood itself is always marked as being "mixed." Indeed, it is estimated that, by now, fewer than 20 percent of Jewish families live in all-Jewish neighborhoods.

As Jews move toward such suburban enclaves, their cultural interests shift—from language, institutions, and religion to social, economic, and, now, properly labeled "ethnic" concerns. The ties between Jews cease to be ties of socioeconomic dependency. They are now always mediated by non-Jewish institutions and modern technology. The Jews drive cars to temple services and call their mothers on the telephone. It is easier, less time-consuming, and "the next best thing to being there."

More important perhaps, the process of assimilation has also entailed further differentiation along new lines. It is not that fewer people now claim the label "Jew." Rather, it is that those who do so are differentiated in ways that they do not control in quite the same fashion.[1] Relationships between Jewish groups are now organized along class and way-of-life lines that place them in different relationships with non-Jewish groups. The American Jewish Committee raises money for research at dinners and cocktail parties but normally will not come out for a protest march. B'nai B'rith organizes and demonstrates in protest marches but generally is not invited to dinners. This specialization and compartmentalization of tasks is quite natural in a bureaucratic society. But it has the effect of preventing any group, or any locality inhabited by the group, from being granted the right to *represent* Judaism. The new Jewish groups relate together somewhat like Protestant denominations, none of which can claim to speak for Protestantism. This leaves them all with the problem of finding new ways of expressing their commonality.

And yet there is still a sense that Jews in their fragmentation, which is not unlike that experienced by liberal Protestants or evangelical churches, have something in common that must be expressed in new symbolic forms. From this perspective it is easy to understand how the Fairfax zone would take on added historical and symbolic importance. From a neighborhood of Jews, it has been transformed into the symbolic center of Los Angeles Jewry and its origin. Fairfax is the neighborhood in which all Jews are one.

The Walk Festival

On 3 May 1981, fifteen thousand Los Angeles Jews assembled to participate in the Eighth Annual Walk Festival, to celebrate Israel's thirty-three years of independence as a state and one hundred years of *aliyah* (pilgrimage or immigration to the Holy Land). "We are one" was the festival slogan. It was "a day of Jewish solidarity around the world." The explicit purpose of the event was to demonstrate support for Israel, to experience and display Jewish solidarity in the city, to celebrate this common membership, to raise money for Jewish causes here and in Israel, and to enjoy a Jewish ethnic/cultural festival. The Walk consisted of a procession through the traditional Jewish areas of the city, a circuit of eighteen kilometers, that began at 8:00 A.M. and ended about 3:00 P.M. The gathering started and finished at a city park on the perimeter of the traditional Jewish section of the city, situated between the older, denser, less affluent community known as Fairfax to the east and the more recently settled, wealthy, dispersed neighborhood of Jews sprinkled through a larger region to the west. In the park a picnic was held for the returning marchers.

At the midpoint of the circuit, in Fairfax, another kind of festival was held, different in feeling and tone from that of the park simply because it required no artificial transformation of the neighborhood. The marchers' arrival here was in fact the major point of fulfillment and satisfaction, not structurally but emotionally.

Festival walkers had to enroll for the march beforehand; they lined up sponsors who promised to pay a fixed amount of money for each kilometer a participant walked. Walkers stopped at a set of checkpoints where their "passports" or "walk validation cards" were signed, allowing them to redeem their pledges. The checkpoints and "additional points of interest" along the circuit covered a great variety of Jewish institutions: synagogues, the mikvah, social service centers, Chabad (an orthodox outreach organization), a Center for Holocaust Studies, a Holocaust Museum, schools and yeshivas.

The Walk, therefore, was a back-and-forth movement between a public park where it began and ended and Fairfax through which it moved, making the neighborhood the symbol both of origin and of the lost past. As the shofar was blown signaling the commencement of the Walk, the point of departure was a desolate, secular, neutral ground with only the bare bones of the many booths and tables that would later become a place of abundant food, music, and festivity to greet the travelers upon the completion of their metaphoric journey through time to the territory of origin, Fairfax.

Clearly Fairfax was the true destination of the procession. Here the walkers had returned to the center of the Jewish area of the city and for a short time blended informally with the native inhabitants, to talk, eat, sing, and rest before returning to the park. The procession from west to east was made mostly by young people who were going back to a region dominated by older people, thus making a symbolic return to a point of origin. The grandchildren were here retracing the route of assimilation taken by their elders away from the Jewish center over several generations. It was an unintentional but symbolically significant return to their beginnings. The model for pilgrimages suggested by Victor Turner (1979) is apt; one leaves from a mundane secular center and goes to a sacred periphery that then becomes a center for the individual, an *axis mundi* of his faith.

The Re-creation of Judaism

The Walk carnival is largely a secular festival. It is also a unique opportunity with great appeal to special-purpose groups who want to use its symbolic power to advance their causes. By being involved at a time when Los Angeles Jews state that they are assembled in their totality, these groups can claim an extensiveness and generality not ordinarily available. The occasion has a natural appeal to politicians, promoters, leaders, factions, and alliances, all wishing to signify their distinctiveness and commonality, to show that they are the parts that stand for the whole and that the whole is greater than the parts. Separations must be maintained but transcended, and this requires considerable preparation and interactive as well as symbolic work.

The problem for the organizers was to mark it unmistakably as a *Jewish* festival for both the participants and their non-Jewish audience (onlookers, media, etc.). Ceremonies, amusements, food, educational exhibits, and displays all had to make the statement. This had to be carefully planned, and well before the march, committees of various kinds were very active. One of their earliest tasks was an informal patching up of old wounds. The official planners had lunch with various representatives of particular elements in the city and negotiated the shape of each group's participation. Eventually, close to fifty different dimensions of Jewish life were represented, all symbolically demonstrating their distinctive features and their common membership.

The major problem the planners of the Walk Festival had to deal with is a common one in secular rituals: it was necessary to mount an assemblage of disparate ideas, purposes, and people, then literally parade them as unity. The motto of the event was "We are one," so as to publicly demonstrate unity. Yet it was necessary to allow the separate ingredients to remain intact, symbolically and experientially. This is of course a paradox—the simultaneous announcement of universalism and particularism, distinction and fusion—but like all true paradoxes it is fundamentally unresolvable. It is only through ritual, through performance, that the event could succeed at all, making the paradox into a simpler experienced reality, enacted rather than rationalized or explained. An unsystematized, loose, basic, vague, but emotionally powerful statement of commonality—"We are all Jews"—was indeed mobilized for one day and then, like the park setting in which the event began and ended, was dismantled for another year.

The planned (as opposed to unintended) aspects of the event presented some interesting ritual and symbolic difficulties of a practical nature distinguishable from the unpredictable ones in secular ceremonies. The planners were quite conscious of these difficulties. How could the event be used simultaneously to, as they put it, "unite people, educate people, raise money, and entertain"? The first goal, unification, was perhaps the simplest: people moving together, publicly demonstrating their solidarity, can be counted on to produce at least a visual appearance of oneness, particularly as they travel through public streets that are not exclusively theirs. The demonstration to a witnessing world of outsiders that they "stand and move together" creates a temporary but very clear solidarity. Moreover, it would be naive to overlook the double meaning in the phrase "educate people." The event was designed to do more than promote consciousness among Jews that "they are one"; it was hinted (though not emphasized) that non-Jews should be reminded that though the Jews' religious/ethnic identity was irrelevant or in eclipse in many contexts, it nonetheless remained basic. It could be mobilized. It was a source of pride and pleasure.

The second, less explicit goal of the planners had to do with the display of the variety that was brought together. The picnic area in the western park accomplished some of this organizational and ceremonial work by accommodating the materials designed to inform and educate the assemblage. The area was primarily a place for celebration rather than solemn emotional purpose. The park, for this day, became a temporary Jewish zone, just as a fair or a circus moves into a neutral space and is later struck. As in all such cases, the transformation was hasty, ad hoc, partial, and transparent, for the park belonged to no one ethnic, religious, or cultural group.

At another level, the Walk was also a fund-raiser. This presented a complicated problem. How the money raised would be allocated had been established during earlier marches. It would go to a mixture of local, national, and international Jewish charities and causes, with a specific amount marked for Israel. But the need to raise money was sometimes at variance with the establishment of unity and the demonstration of solidarity that imply social equality. At one point, for example, it was proposed

that the presidents of all the community organizations walk together ceremonially for the last mile of the march, and that the organizations they represented each contribute one hundred dollars to permit the presidents to
parade in this fashion. A lengthy discussion ensued in the planning committee. One group argued that many organizations that had given much
more than a hundred dollars were being "taxed" to participate. Moreover,
was not their contribution being underestimated, equated with those who
had given only one hundred dollars? And what about those who could not
afford to contribute money at all but who gave support in nonmonetary
form? The organization presidents, it turned out, were offended and might
not take part. It became apparent that unity and fund-raising issues could
not be reconciled. The focus had to be changed: unity over funds. "We
cannot accept money without the presidents' participation. Besides,
everyone knows that Jews give to take care of their own. Thus there's no
need to show that."

This statement by the planning committee made a resolution rather
easy: two opposing values had presented themselves. Both were affirmed;
their opposition was glossed over and a ceremonial solution provided. The
presidents would be invited to donate any amount they wished anony-
mously; all were to participate in the march in any case. The leaders'
physical presence was to be a sufficient statement of their community support. The financial and symbolic elements were separated and both norms
salvaged with a private reference to a piece of self-definition so clear and
so fundamental that it need not be stated in public: "Jews take of their
own" was self-evident.

A variation on the "funds versus solidarity" conflict surfaced in regard
to the participation of young people. In the early days of the Walk Festival,
involvement of youth had been particularly heavy. Then, its celebratory,
carnivallike flavor was especially pertinent. But as the event became more
popular and drew attention to itself as having "additional possibilities" for
fund-raising, it was taken over by more formal organizations, official committees, and the like, and youthful participation diminished. Now the
planning committee faced the dilemma of bringing the young back in,
reintroducing the element of festivity while holding on to the financial benefits. A special group attempted to include youth in the planning, and since
young people would be likely to walk farthest, they could raise the most
money and could be especially honored and rewarded. The inclusion of
raffles, prizes, food, and music that would appeal to youth became particularly important concerns. But it was soon apparent that prizes, fun, and
rewards were not universally appealing to all segments of the community.

It was suggested, for example, that a carnivallike atmosphere would be provided by including balloon rides at the park. But what was Jewish about a balloon ride? The rides would attract younger people but violate the thematic basis of the festival. Somehow a Jewish characteristic had to be found—this was, after all, not a secular or universal event. But, the committee learned, the balloon was being donated free, which increased the pressure to include it. It was agreed that a huge banner would be hung on the balloon, carrying the Walk logo. Money could be charged for the ride; the youthful element would be delighted. And so the balloon was made Jewish, hence appropriate to the day's theme.

A similar dilemma arose concerning suitability of prizes. One suggestion was that dinner with the prime minister of Israel be the major prize for the person who won a raffle or gathered the most money. But this, the committee pointed out, would not appeal to the young. Someone suggested a crystal menorah as a prize, but this was not appealing to anyone who was single or without a household. Finally a set of the *Jewish Encyclopedia* was selected: proper to the theme, and suitable to people of any age or religious bent. Other items available were watches, radios, and television sets—highly valued by people of all ages, ideal as raffle prizes. But the problem again was that they were not Jewish. However, these items too were donations and could hardly be refused. The solution: the first prizes would be trips to Jewish camps in Israel; the secular gifts would be "lower" in value, given to "runners-up," less conspicuous but still alluring, possibly desecularized by their association with the genuinely and more conspicuously mentioned "Jewish" prizes.

The planning of entertainment for small children presented interesting parallel problems. Camel rides were ideal, evoking images of ancient Israel and delighting the kiddies. Elephants too were to be brought in: donated free, they were very popular but as awkward symbolically as they were physically. Ultimately the elephants defied the symbolic imagination of the planning committee. They remained simply elephants, incompletely assimilated ingredients that marked the liminal nature of the festival— partly ethnic celebration, partly designed to generate an air of festivity, a circuslike abandonment of reality of a kind American Jewish youth grow to expect as "fun" in a secular society, required for any "successful" entertainment.

Another interesting choice presented itself to the planning committee: for an event of this kind publicity was essential. The event was, however, a recurrent one. When the media were approached, they were not willing to provide "promo" for something that was seen as routine. They would cover the event only if the planners could "come up with a different angle." It quickly became clear that that meant finding something controversial. The planning committee discussion turned to recent anti-Semitic events in the city and, in that context, the need for considerable security measures during the march. After much talk the committee resolved to forgo publicity rather than exploit or heighten the fear of anti-Semitism or let themselves appear to be "running scared." "We have our own security monitors, we are taking care of the situation," was their resolution. Losing publicity meant losing funding, but this was set aside in favor of the presentation of their basic symbolic message: "We are one," stressing elements of pride and festivity rather than fear and sensationalism.

The "We are one" symbolic message was stretched for one case only. Contact had been maintained through a Black/Jewish Dialogue Committee throughout the march planning. The Youth Outreach Committee recommended that green ribbons be supplied to marchers in recognition of the death of black children in Atlanta, "to show Jewish caring for neighbors in trouble." This was generally supported, but the problem arose, What about the other minorities and suppressed groups we are not including? What about the Falasha and Soviet Jews? How should their oppression be signified? The resolution was exquisitely symbolic, hence ambiguous and multireferential. Since it was spring, near Passover, a time of renewal and the rebirth of Israel, green was the right color. It would refer to all these and also to the murdered Atlanta children.

Eventually all these matters were resolved in ways that satisfied the organizers. All except one that threatened the very foundation of the event: the Walk was to be pan-Jewish and to celebrate Zionism and Israel as the ultimate symbol of the difference and unity of Jews within America. And yet there was no way to hide the presence of immense numbers of Israeli immigrants to the United States, which caused some embarrassment. Indeed, one of the officials opening the event publicly lamented the presence of so many Israelis in America during a ceremony celebrating Zionism. Most Israelis picnicked and played in the park with family and friends; perhaps they were unable to stay away, but they often seemed as puzzled and pained by their presence in America on this occasion as were the leaders of the festival. Paradoxically, the Israeli immigrants were most fully members of the Jewish world being celebrated and were also a class of traitors: at a festival celebrating one hundred years of immigration to Israel, these people were emigrants from Israel—Yordim, betrayers of Zionism. Their presence could not be celebrated—it could only be ignored.

Experiencing American Judaism

The day of the Walk arrived. The power of the event, however, may not have sprung from quite the elements the organizers had most carefully planned. Rather, its symbolic power sprang from what was taken for granted in the conscious understanding: the Walk involved *movement*, an apt metaphor for any display in this particularly dispersed and autocentric city. More important perhaps, the Walk recreated dramatically the journey the participants and their families had taken to arrive at their present status in the middle-class suburbs of Los Angeles.

The marchers were above all the young, the symbols of what Margaret Mead thought of as the "third generation" (1965 [1942], chap. 3). They were the American ones, and they depicted—backward first and then forward, as it were—the population movement of the Jews as they migrated into the United States over the past seventy years and then into Los Angeles over the past three decades. Young people were walking back to the old part of the city, the neighborhood of their grandparents; they returned to the symbolically less American world of immigrant Jews who were left behind when their children, then grandchildren, became absorbed into mainstream society, jettisoning the markers of ethnicity and religion that had set them apart. The social mobility and assimilation achieved by the younger generation had a corresponding spatial form as a movement away from the more eastern, denser, poorer, older Jewish section of the city. There is here the symbolic spatialization of a social process, a physical movement of return that dramatically restates a parallel temporal and social movement. The disintegration of the old world and the world of the old people, its dispersion outward over space and time was transcended and bridged as the younger generations marched back into the ghetto for this celebration of Jewishness.

The return to the roots was from a conspicuously artificial, temporary, symbolically tenuous festival of Jewishness, existing for a short time in a neutral, secular zone—a public park, in which no one actually lives. The park, with its booths, rides, and other entertainments that had to be so consciously planned to express Jewishness, was thus a re-creation of the suburban present of the participants, with their specifically marked "Jewish" voluntary associations in the neutral see of middle-class America. From there, the marchers returned to an organic, vital neighborhood occupying a genuinely inhabited space in the Fairfax region. There all symbols of Jewishness were indigenous and permanent, casual but powerful and convincing. They carried the sacrality of daily use and cultural embeddedness, recalling the historical/cultural circumstances when being a Jew was not an episodic, vague social identity—voluntary, partial, ebbing and flowing in intensity, depending on context and circumstances as it is among assimilated people. The marchers returned to a place that retained elements of a previous all-encompassing experience of social/religious identity. In Fairfax, Jewishness did not have to be consciously performed as a separate, special event. It was unmarked.

Two points are of particular interest here: first, the recapitulation of the movement of Jews from the eastern to the western parts of the city in a pilgrimage form was not an intended and fully comprehended ingredient in the festival (judging from all we know through attending the many formal and informal planning sessions). Indeed, Fairfax as the "midpoint" was meant to be only a designated resting place. The official sites along the pilgrimage route were elsewhere—the significant religious and social institutions, museums, schools, and synagogues, important and prestigious places that represented major structures of the Jewish community. One might say these stations constitute a political/economic map of the formal dimensions of the community—the public, conspicuous sites of power and prestige. They were strongly marked. In contrast, the main street of Fairfax specialized in what we might call the ethnic/informal/cultural foci of the community. These were the backdrop that became foreground precisely because they represented the mundane and ordinary and displayed the distinctive domestic features of Jewish life in concentrated form. The authority of the familiar worked to make this alleged "midpoint" the true destination of the march, transforming a secular ritual into a quasi-sacred one.

The elements of intention in ritual and unconsciousness in symbolic messages are intriguing, essential questions of considerable complexity. They cannot be resolved here, but they are worth mentioning. All secular rituals must to some degree overcome a public's awareness of its intentions; all symbols must have unconscious dimensions to move us emotionally as well as merely inform us. Success in ritual proceedings comes by degrees; this particular ritual succeeded beyond its explicit purposes and in ways not anticipated—by arousing a yearning for the lost, fuller world of Judaism of an earlier day and, for a short time, by allowing younger people to taste that half-imagined, half-felt paradisiacal state of wholeness that humans long for so regularly and persistently and that they so diligently seek in pilgrimages of all kinds and to all places.

A second interesting issue we can only mention here involves movement per se as a symbolic form: the peregrination was made to a sacred center by a set of strangers for collective and personal regeneration. Differences were overcome; an experience of unity was achieved, and this was publicly proclaimed, experienced as shared in a voluntary, temporary ordeal that is in some way part of God's purpose. These are some of the features of pilgrimage in terms of which we have discussed the Walk Festival. Of course it partook of many other forms—a political demonstration; a display of disparate parts presented as unified; a secular parade where social, political, and legal institutions were publicly acknowledged and included; and a protest march, hinting to critics or enemies that a strong, united community was well and alert—all were reverberations of this event. As a ritual, the festival had a transformative element, but equally it was a confirmatory ceremony of simple display.

Pilgrimages and Cultural Expression

The event had features that are strikingly similar to the classical, perhaps universal markers of pilgrimages everywhere: pilgrims move from a secular periphery to a sacred center and, in the course of that, experience a physical ordeal that is nonetheless joyous. They are united and equal in this achievement and experience a return "home." Structural and worldly markers are absorbed in the pilgrims' camaraderie; they were strangers when the day began and would be strangers again when it was over. The space traveled was emotional as well as physical; messages and ideals— of unity and belonging, return and reversal—transformed from banners, emblems, and T-shirts were symbolic messages that became experienced personal verities. What was planned, cognitive, and merely desired blossomed from public desiderata into emotional individual desire and belief; precisely what Susanne Langer (1942) meant when she used the term "symbolic transformation"—a fusion between symbols and their referents. It is that capacity that distinguishes symbols from signals and signs, thus empowering them to function cognitively, emotionally, and imaginatively at the same time.

A recent volume (Turner 1980) does much to advance our understanding of the symbolism of processions, particularly the article by Kay Turner on an Italian-American procession in Brooklyn. She suggests a model for the study of procession that is as useful as the pilgrimage image. In considering this event she stresses that procession is a boundary-maintaining and defining form, marking the outer perimeter of a community, encouraging all those within its ambience to become aware that they live in that place. Such movements extend the "power field" of a holy region to a profane realm, usually by displaying a sacred icon through the streets of a neighborhood. Such procession eases transitions between profane and holy zones, confirms their integrity, and transforms them into "special places." Because walking, stopping, and going are part of procession, departing in a circular movement, ending up where one began "simultaneously proclaims . . . cohesion and transitional incorporation and distinction; homogeneity and hierarchy" (1980, 18). One ends up where one began: life and death are suggested as part of this set. Processional movement, Turner goes on, breaks down the barriers between secular and sacred, "then proceeds symbolically to exemplify through transitional and transactional motion a flow between fixed points which symbolically as well as physically threads together the various structural elements of the community. . . . The fixed points imply static condition, order, hierarchy, norms, structural hegemony, but the procession flows on, so participants see and feel the transactions between contexts. This movement is a physical intensification, a 'walking metaphor,' a 'transaction between contexts'" (1980, 19–20). Unlike elements are united and opposites joined, individual moving bodies themselves serving as the connection between disparate realms.

In the Walk Festival, the structural points were indeed joined by the walkers. The presidents of major organizations paraded with their rivals and even their enemies, amid the anonymous and unimportant whom they usually led or controlled. The stations visited represented hierarchy and the formed, ordered elements of the Jewish community; it was these people who stamped the "passports" of the walkers that would allow them to collect their sponsors' pledges. But then the walkers continued. The deepening of the emotions involved in the procession—the genuinely religious moment, transformational as well as confirmatory—occurred with the marchers' arrival in Fairfax, where the young rejoined the old. Biologically, chronologically, and historically, the history of the city was reiterated by the life cycle, American immigration and ethnic history fusing and linking it all. Of course the linkage was momentary, as such intensifications must be. After arriving and resting, the young people departed in no special order, at a rambling and relaxed pace, returning to the park for simple obvious pleasures at the contrived Jewish zone of ethnic celebration before leaving at the end of the day. The leaving was individualized. When they left they were as when they came—Jewish situationally and intermittently—but we may assume something was genuinely rekindled by the festival. An immensely complicated event with a set of ambitious and somewhat conflicting aims was managed, and on this day all were one.

They did assemble a vast crowd that would otherwise not be brought together in normal circumstances. They educated themselves and others to the variety and range of Jewish secular, religious, and social organizations and interests in the city. Moreover, they raised seventy-five thousand dollars in the course of the day's work. For an ethnic/religious group so diverse, scattered, untidy, and multiform, both socially and geographically, this was no easy triumph.

P
A
R   Resolving
T   America

I
V

Editor's Introduction

Parades, like movies and commercials, are crafted products, rhetorical performances addressed to a specific audience for a specific purpose. Some parades are in fact quite as carefully crafted as artistic or pseudoartistic performances. Conversely, the kind of temporary resolutions of difficult dilemmas the next two chapters examine are themselves the result of complex improvisations. By separating the preceding set of essays from the others I have tried to suggest the usefulness of looking at certain types of cultural manifestations as somewhat under the control of apparent authors.

Parades, in this sense, are only a particularly striking example of a large set of everyday occurrences in which we specifically display something that is meaningful within the culture. In ethnic parades and in myriad other settings, we are specifically in the business of "doing ethnicity." Ruskin and Varenne (1983) showed how ethnicity is done in interviews "about" ethnic difference. Ethnicity can also be done in schools (what should a kindergarten teacher do on Columbus Day?), in cafeterias (green tablecloths on Saint Patrick's Day), and in churches ("Today our Jewish friends are celebrating the great feast of Yom Kippur. This should remind us . . ."—a sermon in a liberal Protestant church might begin). Ethnicity, like a host of other major symbols ("family," "love," "America," "religion," "education"), is an explicit theme. For a performance to be recognized as "ethnic," certain things must be mentioned ("difference," "values," "blood ties to a country outside the United States," etc.), and others must stay in the background. From then on things are loose; we are free to improvise. Indeed, the themes are so well worn, the myths so well known, that the quality of the performance can affirm itself. People in the United

States soon learn to "read" a float in a parade as, in our case, an "ethnic" float designed to recognize the "contribution of those who came from Poland." But some floats are "good" and others are not so good. Ray Charles's rendering of "America the Beautiful" may be offensive to some. To others it may have the power of putting back into a dead expression of trite nationalism the symbolic force that overuse has killed. And this power can of course be employed for ulterior motives: those who decided to use this rendering during the 1984 Republican convention knew very well what they were doing.

Such improvisations on a theme are part of everyday life. Foreigners and children may not learn for a long time, if ever, the "true meaning of ethnicity," but they are soon taught to distinguish an ethnic performance from a nonethnic one. On Columbus Day in New York one must deal with the fact that the discovery of the Americas symbolically "belongs" to Italy (and not to Spain, Portugal, or Denmark) because it has been agreed that, in the scramble for appropriate totems for the various groups, Christopher Columbus and his odyssey were granted to the Italians (just as the color green was granted the Irish, corn was granted the native Americans, etc.).

Writing the minutes of a Southern Baptist association and planning a floor party in a dorm are also improvisations on well-worn themes. But the emphasis in the next two chapters is put on the historical process that leads to the need to improvise. Like minutes and parties, parades are also answers to problems. Both Singer and Myerhoff and Mongulla mentioned the problems that were addressed. Greenhouse and Moffatt trace in more detail how the need to resolve a paradox arises. They detail the conversations that lead to a pattern for future events (Greenhouse) or to the single event (Moffatt) that answers, and perhaps lays to rest, difficult questions put to the groups involved.

In the chapter by Moffatt (chap. 8) we see black and white late adolescents try to deal with an altogether impossible situation. Both blacks and whites know that they are "doing" ethnicity and racism or rather, they hope, ethnicity and specifically *not* racism. They know that anything they do in relation to each other can be used as an example in any conversation about ethnicity and racism. This is all the more stark since they are part of a deliberate experiment in racial and gender integration designed to demonstrate the open character of a bureaucracy—Rutgers University. To the administration of the college, they are rhetorical proof that policies are color- and gender-blind. To a campus newspaper editor, they are proof of the failure of this policy. To us, they are an example of the way people in the United States deal with certain symbols.

To themselves, however, the students were a puzzle. They wanted to brush their teeth in peace, but they also knew that every time they walked into the bathroom they would also have to improvise on the themes of ethnicity and racism. And they were not so naive as not to know that such performances are never politically benign. Moffatt suggests that they also knew, though in a different way that they might not be able to articulate fully, that the symbolic framework being offered them, far from offering easy solutions, instead presented new difficulties. To address these difficulties they gave a party designed to demonstrate their unity as against accusations of mutual animosity. The party may have expressed some of their values. But the occasion and form of this expression was a rhetorical statement, an answer to the reporter's rebuke, framed within a general conversation the students did not control.

The chapter by Greenhouse (chap. 7) traces the historical development of the apparent resolution of another classic American puzzle. When and where are free speech and the affirmation of one's personal conviction (and interests) appropriate? Where are unanimity and consensus needed? Here again the symbols that signal whether a statement is framed as either "free speech" or "consensus" are clear. But there are no mechanisms that prescribe which symbols are to be used at any one time. The "time" in Greenhouse's essay consists of the historical minutes of a Southern Baptist association. Should such minutes reflect the variety of opinion on matters of doctrine and politics among and within the congregations belonging to the association or should they, as symbolic displays of the insiders to themselves and to outsiders, present a united, consensual front? Greenhouse shows how the association moved from the first to the second resolution of the question. She also emphasizes that such a resolution is necessarily a fragile thing. The display of consensus is not based on the absence of conflict. On the contrary, perhaps.

What is important is that, to this day, consensus remains an important symbol among church members. They know about conflict; they know about the institutional means at their disposal to deal with conflict. They can talk about it. However, their traditional answers to difficult questions about the response that must be given at times of conflict precludes their participation in both formal and informal displays of conflict (disputing and litigation) available institutionally.

7　History, Faith, and Avoidance

Carol Greenhouse

Introduction

Tocqueville's journey did not take him to the hilly backwoods of Georgia, but—as this chapter suggests—he would not have been surprised by that frontier. In the 1830s, north-central Georgia formed an uneasy border between the United States and the Cherokee Nation, and Tocqueville already understood that the Cherokees and the other indigenous nations would be defeated by arms and the law—and saw why. The issue of states' rights was a rampant crisis, but Tocqueville understood Americans' profound ambivalence toward authority. He would have found deep yet volatile allegiances, but he comprehended the ahistoricism that gives American families and communities their peculiar character. He knew that slavery would not last. He knew that American politicians would never be philosophers. On the other hand, Americans' spiritual life was apparently so shadowy a realm that it was easily extinguished by the glare of practical concerns. Tocqueville's discussion of American religion is a scant two pages of commentary on "a sort of fanatical spiritualism" that exists "here and there" in American society (Tocqueville 1969 [1848], 534–35); the society he witnessed was profoundly secular. "The recollection of the shortness of life is a constant spur" to what Tocqueville calls the "bootless chace" in pursuit of prosperity and "felicity" (Tocqueville 1969 [1848], 536–37)—that is, commerce.

One is tempted today to hail Tocqueville as a prophet, but he was not one. Modern Americans' sense of being on familiar ground in *Democracy in America* is the result of Tocqueville's insight, not foresight. Where he lacked a ready-made method, he developed one; where the language lacked the vocabulary for his conclusions, he invented it;[1] the very framework of his study brought to the public new, cutting-edge usages of the term "democracy" (see Williams 1958). The word "culture" had not yet been generally adopted by scholars to refer to human experience,[2] yet in attaching Americans' symbolism to the "logic" of the Revolution, Tocqueville managed a cultural analysis of the United States of unparalleled grandeur. His achievement was the perception and explication of a coherent and unified symbolic system, born in revolution of British and Continental parents. The three cornerstones of this symbolic system were equality, democracy, and individualism. Each is embedded in the other two, and all three are the consequence of the Revolution's having irrevocably erased all historical bases of authority from the American cultural vocabulary. Family, inherited property, nobility—these are silenced. In the aftershocks of 1776, only free elections, the free market, and the public good remain as acceptable idioms of authority and control.

This essay presents evidence that the transformation of America's cultural discourse was widely felt and that it generated some practical problems in the organization of public life, even at very local levels of society. The data come from a small religious organization, an "association" of Baptist churches, in north-central Georgia. The relationship of these data to the larger study of which they form one part is explained in the next section. Their significance is in their implication that the American ambivalence toward authority makes conflict, particularly overt dispute, very problematic. Authoritative intervention is allowed only on very narrow grounds (as the cases below will show), and unless a group can rely on consensus, disputes may escalate very rapidly to social fission. This may seem an odd point to make about a society that perceives itself to be excessively litigious (falsely, as it turns out; see Galanter 1983). Although litigiousness is a popular concern, that concern ignores the fact that the domi-

nant mode of dispute settlement in the United States is nonconfrontation-
al—"lumping it," or resignation. Resignation and litigation are two routes
to avoidance relationships (see Merry 1979), and part of my concern here
is to interpret the silence that avoidance represents.

In developing the evidence and the argument, I draw on themes raised
by other authors in this volume. On the one hand, Beeman (chap. 3), Moffatt (chap. 8), and Myerhoff and Mongulla (chap. 6) raise substantive issues
that are relevant here. Beeman's discussion of advertising suggests that
though advertisers do not know if ads "work" to increase consumption,
ads do teach consumers how to interpret their own consumption in terms
of particular categories. Principal among these is a political category, freedom. Advertisers assume that sales increase when consumers are convinced of their own freedom to choose among competing alternatives.
One can readily imagine applications of this principle in other domains—
foreign affairs, for example—and conclude that Americans find a certain
social appetite in their relish for adversarial relationships. In the data to follow, the church association is deeply concerned to sharpen the categories
of orthodoxy and heterodoxy and to monopolize the interpretations of that
distinction—meanwhile insisting on worshipers' freedom and compelling
them to choose. Moffatt's essay shows a group of students struggling to
form a community and failing largely because their symbolic categories
make a parody of their politeness. Their politeness, interestingly, entails a
kind of ahistoricism, a refusal to acknowledge the historical and experien-
tial sources of black and white identities in the United States. The church
association more successfully managed to silence the past by progressively
extinguishing every forum for controversy. Myerhoff and Mongulla's chapter, like Beeman's, is about a problem of interpretation and about the demands for flexibility in a symbolic system faced with interpretive challenges. The Baptists, too, scrambled—over twenty or thirty years—to
defend their sacred categories against the predations of secular affairs.

On the other hand, this essay also resonates to themes of analysis and
interpretation raised by Varenne (chap. 10) and Drummond (chap. 4).
Drummond's choice of the national scale as his cultural domain hardly
needs more convincing validation than the media analysis of the 1984
presidential elections—a "supergrosser" par excellence. The early Baptists successfully packaged their positions as revolutionary, sacred, or
southern, depending on the audience—that is, they evoked images and
self-images with wide, uncharted appeal. Varenne's essays point to the
armature of such appeals in "friendliness" and "community." "Friendliness" appears to be companionship without biography; "community"

seems to refer to groups who can forget (or forgo) their histories. These symbolic assertions amount to a denial of the possibility of analysis of American experience on the part of the native-born; indeed, a widespread popular belief holds that America no longer has a culture, now that "traditional" values have been "lost." This belief provides some of the exotic fascination of the subject of American culture, even to anthropologists. It also returns us to Tocqueville, who disbelieved Americans' professed resistance to cultural analysis in their dogged pragmatism. *Democracy in America* makes it possible for us to understand pragmatism as a deficit, a silenced discourse of history, philosophy, faith, and power. In that light, let us now turn to "Hopewell," Georgia.

Avoidance in Hopewell

Hopewell is the seat of a metropolitan suburban county on the outskirts of a major southern city. When I began my research there in 1973, the most recent census placed the town's population at four thousand; the county had just touched one hundred thousand. Recent developments included the "four-laning" of the local stretch of county road to accommodate the new interstate that had cut across one end of the county. A few new restaurants and businesses, a new hotel, and a movie theater were still novelties in 1973. Ten years later, the development that was new then has quickened its pace; the few miles of vacant meadows that separated the city from Hopewell are now filled with shopping malls, subdivisions, and businesses. When I went to Hopewell in 1973, it was in anticipation of this process.[3] My particular interest was the community's response to interpersonal conflict and its assessment of its own remedial needs. I intended to study patterns of interaction in and around the court; I expected that tensions between long-term residents and newcomers would be played out there.

I found no such thing. Instead, local people expressed a strong aversion to going to court. Further, local Baptists maintained that not only litigation, but any disputing was to be avoided. Since this view seemed so contrary to both the popular and the academic images of "litigious Americans," I decided to explore it ethnographically and historically. Let me stress that my work was limited to a single major congregation of Southern Baptists in a single town.

Local Baptists present their rationale against overt conflict entirely in scriptural terms—for example, Matt. 5:38–40:[4] "You have heard that it was said, 'An eye for an eye, and a tooth for a tooth.' But I now tell you: do not take revenge on someone who does you wrong. . . . If anyone slaps you on the right cheek, let him slap your left cheek too. And if someone takes you to court to sue you for your shirt, let him have your coat as well." The conviction that Jesus is both the author and the sole judge of human affairs exempts believers from pressing their own interests in confrontational settings; indeed, to do so would imply a lack of faith. Ideally, local Baptists say, one need not plead one's own cause even in prayer. God already knows and responds to every individual's needs. (Is it only in America that Protestants proclaim in conversation and in advertising: "You have a friend in Jesus"?)

While modern Baptists' explanations of their attitudes toward disputing and secular law are undeniable, they are not inevitable. The historical record—on which the rest of this chapter is based—shows that Hopewell Baptists were once all too ready to join issue in adversarial contests, and that the church itself was once a forum for voicing and resolving disputes. Doctrine and Scripture provided the idiom of those contests, just as today they form the idiom of restraint and silence. Here I examine the development of this transformation, which saw the end of the local church's active role as a third party and as an arena for dispute. The transformation centers on an issue of authority. The church once asserted its own authority to define and defend orthodoxy; it now asserts that doctrine precludes the legitimacy of any human authority. Why authority should have been the central issue is a question as large and as old as the Reformation, and—to put it another way—as current and immediate as the criteria of control and submission that Canaan finds in the sexual politics of modern American teenagers (chap. 9). My concluding argument is that it is this question of authority that marks the Baptists' struggle with conflict as an American cultural debate, both for the terms in which it was played out and for its consequences. The meanings of contemporary cultural categories among Hopewell's Baptists preserve the relationship between the possibilities they accepted and the ones they rejected—hence my longitudinal perspective.

My major source is the minutes of the church association to which the Hopewell Baptist Church has belonged since its founding in 1824. Copies of the minutes were distributed to all church members every year. The association's jurisdiction consisted of about thirty churches in the few counties around Hopewell, including the one of which Hopewell is the seat. Thus it defines a small geographic area with multiple internal ties—marriage, commerce, electoral politics, and so on. The Hopewell Baptist church was active in the leadership of the association, whose delegates met each fall to discuss business and to pray. This church was also often singled out for its high or low levels of religious participation. Indeed, membership in the local church appears to have had wide swings as local and regional issues distracted its members from their spiritual concerns.

The issues that divided the Hopewell church over the years were the same issues that divided the nation: Cherokee removal, slavery, secession, and finally, war. Local people were particularly divided in the Jacksonian and later antebellum period, as loyalties cross-cut. The issue of "benevolent associations" (which dominates portions of the minutes) concerned whether Baptist church funds should be spent to missionize among the Cherokee, who still lived in north-central Georgia. The Baptists were officially promission; for this reason, Jacksonians perceived the order to be pro-Cherokee. This left the Baptists on the losing side of a profound and volatile conflict in this pro-Jackson, anti-Cherokee region. At the same time, proslavery elements used the benevolent association issue to accuse Baptists of being abolitionists—the charge would have carried the clear innuendo of antisouthern, in addition to antislaveholding, sentiment. This county was not a strong slaveholding county; however, nationally, the Southern Baptists seceded from the national order to protect their autonomy on the slavery question. (See Phillips 1968 [1902] for an excellent discussion of Georgia politics during this period.) The local Baptist church had a difficult time surviving these controversies institutionally for three reasons. First, as the only established church in the county, its members appear to have had quite diverse opinions along the political spectrum. Second, local Baptists were particularly divided by these issues, since the order nationally (i.e., in the South) stood for aristocratic interests, whereas the local members were fervent populists. Finally, local divisions were increasingly overridden by "southern" issues, as we shall see. The local minister wrote in his diary in the early 1850s that it was often difficult to induce a congregation to cease its political debate long enough to enter the church for worship.

A studied harmony—rooted in symbols of religion and southern identity—eventually assured the church's survival, and this essay is about the process through which harmony emerged as a key symbol for local Baptists. Today's Baptists in Hopewell resist any suggestion that these data "explain" their contemporary emphasis on harmony. That explanation is self-evident in Scripture, they say. Other townspeople are actively engaged in historical preservation, genealogies, and historical reenactments (see Singer 1977 for a comparable situation in the North), but Baptists tend not to participate in these affairs. For them, the past is done; Jesus promises eternal life, that is, an eternal *now* that is the essence of the Baptists' contemporary modernity. They do not see their faith as the heritage of anything old.

My argument, through these data, is that the modern Baptists' avoidance of confrontation and their ahistoricism are two faces of the heritage of their cultural past. For many local Baptists, it is not even "their" past, since they are recent newcomers who have joined the church. Yet by their very participation in the ethos of harmony and modernity, they join a cultural tradition that is a distinctly local voice in a dialogue that had and continues to have national and global proportions.

Developing Christian Harmony

The first published minutes of the White River Association appeared in 1825. They contained a "circular address"—a regular feature of subsequent reports—describing the establishment of the new organization. The association was formed with "so much harmony and brotherly affection as to amount (in our view) to a demonstrative evidence of Divine approbation to this step in your Christian procedure" (1825a, 8).[5] The association had three purposes: (1) maintaining the Gospel in a state of "purity"; (2) "settling of the Churches upon the Apostolic plan" and (3) maintaining a pure and "unblamable" ministry. These functions entailed a degree of authority over member churches that the founders apparently felt compelled to justify: "We would [not] exercise authority over you, but . . . experience has proven that something of this kind is necessary" (1825a, 8). Indeed, the triple agenda of the association in rationalizing the churches of what was then the frontier inevitably entailed playing an active role as third party in disputes within and between churches. Eventually, the association rejected that role in favor of less controversial forms of participation. Baptists seem to have felt some tension between interventions of human authority in personal affairs and religious doctrine concerning God's supremacy and omniscience.

The first few years of the association were at least superficially harmonious, although the minutes make clear reference to conflicts outside the association that threaten the group with "schism and division" (1825b, 3). This appearance of unity vanished in a dispute over alleged heterodoxy in a member church. In typical style, the association's report does not explain the source of the conflict that divided the church but only mentions "unfavorable reports" (1829, item 32). When the association sent a committee to investigate the church in 1829, its moderator, Benjamin H. Wilson, denied them seats. Wilson must have been a colorful character, at one point declaring that he would rather be "burnt at the stake" than to have "any . . . set of men under Heaven" intervene in his church. Eventually this church divided: Wilson's heterodox (and majority) faction was expelled from the association; the orthodox minority remained. Church divisions quickly became a pattern and, just as quickly, so did ambivalence over the association's authority to examine member churches for doctrinal purity. In response to numerous letters of protest, the association reinterpreted its action at Wilson's church (1830, 7):

> the contentions and divisions, which unfortunately crept into some few of our Churches; the Association had to pass upon those heart rending circumstances, by *withdrawing herself from refractory members* [my emphasis], in consequence of their having apostatized from the original faith of the orthodox Baptist. . . . We have great reason to believe that the Association in withdrawing herself from the refractory part of a church, was done in the spirit and meekness of Christ.
>
> DEAR BRETHREN, pray for us—pray that order and Christian love may be fully restored to the bosom of our Churches; and that we may be found discharging all our duties as consistent Christians; so that we may have it to say for a truth, that we have been with Jesus.

Presenting exclusion as withdrawal was strategic in that it replaced the offensive idea of intervention with an inoffensive one, avoidance and maintenance of purity. But this statement by the association was fundamentally important because it was the first articulation of the idea that conflict is itself unchristian. Earlier statements had stressed the antithesis of Christian and unchristian ways of life (and interests) without making this equation that was to become so vitally important in structuring the relations of the Baptist church to its community, even today.

The defense of its own "spirit of meekness" was insufficient as a means of preventing other disputes from escalating within the association, and its leadership began to take further steps to contain conflict outside the organization. In 1831 the association asked the member churches to take special care not to send unnecessary queries: "Send no query to the Association until [you] have first endeavoured to answer it, and failed, and secondly, have called upon the sister churches for aid, and have failed; unless it be a matter of general interest; which does not properly come under the jurisdiction of a Church."

Nevertheless, letters of protest continued to haunt the association over its intervention in the growing number of church schisms. Significantly, the protests did not address in any way that I can detect the reason for the schisms, but dealt only with the association's use of authority. In 1832 two sister associations delivered a complaint making clear reference to abuses of power by the association. This is an interesting watershed in that it raises issues that were to arise again and again: the legitimacy of a minority group, the concept of representation (the association's "speaking for" its own committee), the validity of any decision that is not unanimous. While the association apparently used the ballot to avoid such unconcealed applications of authority as appointment of officers, the complaint insisted that consensus was the only permissible basis of a decision.[6] The tension between Baptist doctrine and all forms of human authority became and remained critical for many years, as the number and severity of disputes within the organization increased. Pleas for forbearance went unheeded. The extent of the acrimony within the association is suggested in a circular letter (1833, 10–12): "The churches composing this body, by their returns [i.e., membership statistics], prove most conclusively that a sad decline in matters of religion has taken place." (Indeed the Hopewell church had only ten baptisms in the period 1828–33, compared with fifty-eight during 1824–27.)

In the following years the minutes are exceptionally uninformative. The 1835 circular letter expresses relief at the peace within the association, though it also complains of "languidness" with the churches (1835, 7). In 1836, too, the association correspondent complains of "coldness" in the churches (1836, 2). The bulk of the minutes is devoted to publication of "the decorum," or rules of procedure, for the association, reprinted at intervals and eventually annually.

A resolution at the end of the 1836 minutes (pp. 2–3) suggests that the churches may have been preoccupied with a major regional issue, tolerance and support of "benevolent associations." The resolution objected to benevolent associations on the grounds that they were "unscriptural"— "inventions of man"—and declared "nonfellowship" with them. The benevolent associations listed in the resolution were Bible, missionary, temperance, Sunday school, and tract societies, all of which made appeals for monetary support from their congregations. The resolution urges withdrawal from these societies on doctrinal grounds, arguing that they blur the scripturally demanded separation between members of the church and "the world." In other contexts, Baptists objected to salaries for ministers on the same grounds, that a church did not have the authority to demand worldly goods of its members for any purpose (clergy during this period lived by voluntary contributions from their congregations). In this case, however, doctrine may have been a pretext, since the antiabolitionist groups, as benevolent associations, would benefit from church-sponsored support. The whole issue brought the already diminished churches to the brink of a major schism.

The association defended benevolent associations on the grounds that "freemen" ought to have the right to dispose of their "names or money" as they chose (1838, 5):

> The Baptist denomination have always boasted of the freedom of con-
> science, which is allowed them in supporting the Gospel in the way
> which each member might feel inclined to do—Therefore, none are
> compelled to give or not to give, even to their own Pastors, but the
> case is left between them and their God, to be governed by his
> word. . . . our forefathers might as well have submitted to a grievous
> taxation, without a fair Representation, for Baptists now to yield up the
> rights of conscience to the domineering spirit of ecclesiastical usurpa-
> tion. . . . Pure religion is better understood by being felt, than it can
> be by being defined.

This is a rich passage, since it invokes prior idioms of debate in new ways. First, the idiom of authority—or rather its abuse—is central. While the charge against the church association was its use of authority in supporting benevolent associations, its reply was that it was in no way involved in their support and, further, that taking an official stand would be an intolerable breach of believers' freedom. Second, the theme of freedom rings with American connotations; in the symbolism of the passage, freedom of association within the denomination is represented as direct descendant of Americans' freedom from the British. The implicit reference may have been to political issues then current in the secular sphere. Indeed, at this time slavery and states' rights were both volatile issues. In context, the circular letter contrasted freedom of association, or individual freedom, with political stands that appealed to secular forms of identity—southernness, for example, or party politics. The contradiction between the two (sacred and secular forms of identity) was mitigated by the statement that religion resists definition.

The construction of a symbolic opposition between individualism and collective forms of identity is not new in the minutes, but its salience was very clear in 1838. The Flint River association had suffered a series of schisms in which it consistently sided with minority factions of churches, and now almost half the member churches had withdrawn over the issue of benevolent associations. The Baptist church, at least locally, appears to have been increasingly thwarted by its own strategies. Whereas earlier its applications of authority were attempts to enforce ideological consensus within the group, now a refusal to apply authority left it with the appearance of being antisouthern, or traitorous. Essentially, the association was strangling on its conception of politics and religion: in politics, it invoked freedom; in religion, it defended its own authority.

In a new strategy, the association sought to minimize its vulnerability to conflict by (again) increasing its remoteness as an arena for dispute. The earlier effort had been a request to refrain from letters of inquiry except as a last resort. This time the effort was aimed at the church congregations themselves, urging them to refrain from bringing disputes to church at all, except as a last resort (1843, 8–9).

> It has been and still is a custom too widely practised among you, to bring all offenses, which are called public in their character, whether facts or reports, immediately before the Church, without that treatment which is pointed out in the word of the Lord, being first attended to. This is often if not always wrong, and connives at the direction of the word of the Lord which provides a sufficient rule in all cases of difficulty. This practice is wrong, because it fosters neglect of duty, as well as want of brotherly love and christian care; and it encourages *tale bearing* and the *sowing of discord* among brethren, on which subject we would have you remember that the apostle that said, "If ye bite and devour one another, take heed that ye be not consumed, one of the other." Gal., 5th chapter, 15th verse. (Emphasis in original)

Whereas earlier statements describing the association's commitment centered on active leadership in the prevention of error, the new voice of the church was abstract, symbolic, and devoid of overt implications concerning its own authority—a statement entirely consistent with the exhortation to feel, rather than define, religion (1843, 9): "Now it is written that men do not light a candle and put it under a bed or bushel, but on a candlestick, that it may give light to all that are in the house; and the Church is called the candlestick."

The association's new tone of conciliation, withdrawal from conflict, and leadership by example was reflected in two instructions to ministers: first, that they become the friends of sinners, and second, that they not participate in politics. The circular letter in 1844 dwelt upon politics in a way that suggests what the relationship between preachers and their secular communities might have been in those days (1844, 10):

> And how he is rebuked, who by profession a preacher of righteousness, becomes a "noisy dabbler in party politics"? And what, we would ask, does such a minister gain? He may become popular, but his is the populatity, not of the *preacher,* but of the *partizan,* and the

homage which he receives is paid, not to his *piety,* but to his *political*
zeal. And worse than all, his time is wasted, his spirituality destroyed,
his feelings embittered, his usefulness diminished, and the success of
his labors sinfully obstructed. (Emphasis in original)

It is difficult to know how the author of this passage intended the reference
to wasted time to be understood, but that is certainly the theme that has
endured to the present day. The modern construction is that since all secular life is relatively ephemeral in the face of judgment, politics is vanity.
Some of this meaning might have been suggested in this case, although the
burden of the exhortation seems to have been, instead, on the distractions
of politics. But these two interpretations differ only in degree, and a transformation in the imagery of the church soon emerged to unite them.

Meanwhile, national events provided a solution to a dilemma that had
earlier proved a trial for the church—that is, the tension between sectarian
doctrine and southern loyalty. The resolution came in the national schism
of the Baptists into Northern and Southern Baptist Conventions, over the
issue of slavery. The Northern Baptists had introduced a motion at the
national convention to abolish slavery, a motion the southerners would
not tolerate on principle, no matter what their private views. In fact, as I
have said, the region that formed the association was not a major
slaveholding area, but it was very solidary on the question of states' rights
and the unacceptability of the state's authority in private affairs. Even the
association, then, welcomed the division in print and, its southern identity
now secure, boldly referred to the issue of benevolent associations for the
first time in several years (1845, 7):

We report the necessity of separating from our Northern Brethren, but
highly approve the action of the late meeting in August, which organized the Southern Baptist Convention, and earnestly recommend our
churches and brethren to support this institution with their liberal benevolent contributions, and highly approve of the recommendation of
the Baptist State Convention desiring the Southern Baptist Convention
to establish a publication Board to supply the Southern Churches.

The establishment of the new Southern Baptist Convention initiated a sort
of rebirth for the association. It once again preached on such benign (but
highly significant) themes as "My kingdom is not of this world" (John
18:36; 1846, 1). And once again the circular letter drew the old equation
between church government and God's will on earth. Its central discussion
referred to the great variety in church practice in such matters as the extension of fellowship to prospects, the granting of letters of dismission, the
conduct of meetings, the election of pastors, and so on. The letter did not

refer to the doctrinal and political schisms that produced this variety, but instead averred that uniformity of practice was essential to overall church discipline. The letter concludes by exhorting all churches to adopt the same rules of "decorum," that is, rules of order.

The plan for developing rules of decorum—a task that would have been fruitless only a few years before—began with the *premise* that there had never been conflict over matters of faith and that, therefore, abstracting principles of faith would not be a problem. In fact, the premise of consensus had always been considered a safe one even during the years of conflict that are under discussion here; dissent was always glossed as heterodoxy, not controversy. The general strategy of the plan was to equate consensus in matters of faith with consensus in matters of practice and, less overtly, to make practice the proof of faith.

The general effort of the association during the years following the explosive benevolent association issue was in rebuilding the organization on somewhat new, or rather renewed, principles. The minutes were increasingly devoted to circular letters, which grew in length and indirectness. Whereas the association's earliest response to conflict was to allow churches to divide, its next response was to bring the excluded factions back into fellowship, and now the association attempted to regularize the group along its original purposes and principles.

The activity of the association, correspondingly, was increasingly directed at projects outside the organization itself that would unify the group, particularly in the area of missions, education, and temperance. The association's churches soon had missionaries in Brazil, Africa, and China in addition to American missions for the establishment of new churches both in Indian territory and locally. All of these required support through donations by church members.

Queries in the mid-1840s dealt almost exclusively with treatment of heterodox Baptists, and the association assiduously recorded unanimous votes. Circular letters, took, reflected the new tone. They began to stress the ideal of separation from the world to a greater degree than before; however, the implicit reference to politics remained clear. For example, in a circular letter exhorting Christians to refrain from drink and common social vices, the author included the following (1848, 6–7): "many others [i.e., self-proclaimed Baptists] are to be seen in the streets talking politics—telling their social jests or conversing about subjects which should be considered beneath the dignity of the children of God. . . . This is not yielding fruit to the glory of God." Subsequent letters, too, stressed the need to abandon "undue attachment to the world" (1849, 7), the importance of evangelism (1851, 7) and, once again, the need for uniform principles of practice, or decorum (1850, 9). Finally, the circular letters ceased entirely in 1852; they were replaced by the reports of the committees that performed an increasing amount of the business of the association.

In the midst of this era of consolidation and renewal, conflict occasionally reared its head. The most serious dispute arose over the association's publication of articles of faith and practice, which were hotly protested. The record of that dispute shows that the association had strengthened its policy of intolerance—avoidance—considerably over the previous ten or fifteen years, but that its rejection of dispute as a legitimate form of discourse continued to require enforcement. The issue of benevolent associations once more (by calculation, perhaps) emerged in 1861, producing another minor wave of ideological housecleaning. In both cases the price of consensus was antithesis, as dissent became associated with "unchristian" attitudes.

By the time of the fall meeting in 1861, other matters had arisen to preoccupy the association. Although that year's minutes read as usual, a new committee was added to file an annual report—the Committee on the State of the Country. The South had seceded in January 1861, and the four committee reports of the war years were tokens of the region's declining hope. Only the first of these reports (1861, 11) acknowledged the potential contradiction of a church association's offering a statement on political events: "Although this is an assembly of Christians, we are desirous to express our feelings on the state of the Country, because, as Christians and citizens, its affairs are near and dear to our hearts." But the overriding concern was southern identity and solidarity, which the association expressed in the form of resolutions.

In responding to the war first as southerners and second as Baptists, the association experienced a new form of unity. Earlier rallying points had been internal disputes; however, the war provided the organization with a purpose beyond its own administration and mobilization. The minutes during the war years consist of reports from the missions—and finally commentary on their absence as communication was severed by battle—reaffirmation of the purpose of the war, and exhortations to courage and unity. In 1862 weekly prayer meetings were begun "for special prayer for our suffering country, and for the protection and safety of our dear soldiers" (1862, 4); these replace the formerly frequent descriptions of exemplary Christian lives. The war accomplished something that the association had not been able to accomplish on its own: the conclusive equation of harmony, Christianity, and southernness. In the new spirit of union through common suffering, some of the divisions over doctrinal questions and issues of authority were resolved, others were not. Conflict never again crossed the pages of the minutes.

Throughout the war and the painful years of Reconstruction, the association never failed to meet, although the minutes—always cryptic—became increasingly skeletal and uninformative as they continued. The years after 1865 are primarily concerned with activities of the association in the church communities—for example, temperance, the establishment of prayer meetings, Sunday schools, and the reiteration of the rules of decorum (now reprinted in every annual report) and the articles of faith. In 1868 advertisements began to appear for consumer goods (clothes, shoes, etc.), and these continued. Dancing was unanimously ruled disorderly in 1870 and sanctioned with withdrawal by the association. From 1866 until the available minutes ceased in 1911, there are no signs of the questions of divisions that troubled the White River Baptist Association during the first forty years of its existence, in spite of severe regional divisions over other questions. Through the years of Reconstruction, depression, and Populism, the church was silent. In a sense this silence was a triumph. The war had achieved a unity of identity and purpose that had long been the goal of the association leadership, and the last minutes reflect the association's new role as the facilitator of sectarian business.

The Silence of Modernity

Unable to achieve any effective means of exerting control over conflict without simultaneously escalating it, the church association developed its policy of avoidance ("withdrawal") in a sequence of distinct phases. In the earliest years of its existence, the association was willing to serve as an active third party in church disputes and even in interpersonal disputes, although avoidance was already included in its remedial repertoire. The next stage consisted of concerted efforts to distance itself from conflict, although the tendency of the association to justify its interventions in print produced further crises. In this stage the association capitalized on secular solidarity as war loomed to insist on and enforce doctrinal consensus. Finally, issues beyond the local community intruded, with the result that the triple equation of Christianity, harmony, and southern identity was completed. This triad remains today as the heart of local Baptists' ideology of conflict, although the historical referents have been lost from memory.

Although the rejection of adversarial conflict, so important to local Baptists as a central emblem of their identity, is not important—or important in the same way—to Baptists everywhere, the link between avoidance of legal authority and fundamentalist Christianity has a long history in the United States. Konig reports that "many people . . . regarded the legal system as unchristian" in the first half of the seventeenth century (Konig 1979, 136) and refers to "the polarization . . . between those who relied upon strict legal forms to regulate society and those who opposed the law as unchristian" (p. 137). Strout draws a connection between the "weakening [of] the legitimacy of an established religious order" and republicanism (Strout 1974, 49) in the eighteenth century and cautiously suggests a link between "evengelical popular Protestantism" and Jacksonian politics in the early nineteenth (p. 113). Miller (1965, 103) also draws the connection between the "antilegalism of the early nineteenth century" and Jackson's partisans, but in an exceptionally interesting passage (p. 104) he argues that the one does not explain the other.

> By 1790 or 1800 . . . , the distrust had become basically suspicion of the law as by its very nature sophisticated, whereas the American people are natural, reasonable, equitable. A last echo of this legal pietism persisted as late as 1846 in the claim that the Gospel forbids brother to use brother; "therefore all matters of difference in a profoundly religious community should be settled by moral law." . . . [this possibility, although it occasionally had support in the Revival [of the late 1850s], became daily less and less tenable.

In this passage Miller illuminates the American cultural premise that "distinguishes between the dignity of sublime Nature" and "the constricting efforts of the intellect and of intellect's vice-regent, the law" (1965, 104). At issue in that distinction is human authority and the grounds of its legitimacy. Hopewell's Baptists interpreted and continued to interpret the maintenance of that distinction as the fundamental task of religion. Other Americans maintain the distinction in their strong preference for self-regulation. In Perin's words (1977, 106), Americans "resort to spite fences because . . . they are accustomed to using walls but not rules."[7]

Hopewell today is the seat of a burgeoning suburban county that doubles in population every ten years. Hopewell itself is teeming with newcomers; the church is very much their place. The new members quickly learn the vocabulary that divides the damned from the saved. It is a vocabulary that draws heavily on larger American cultural concerns: authority, individualism, freedom, and union. In the vocabulary of their faith, Hopewell Baptists perpetuate the fundamental triad of Christianity, harmony, and local identity that was forged in the harrowing days of slavery and Cherokee removal. Today's Baptists do not see their faith as the heritage of those days; in fact, the Baptists I knew in Hopewell were distinctly uninterested in history. In their view, history explains nothing; life reflects God's current plan. Indeed, they explain their rejection of adversarial conflict as the corollary of their devotion to God. It has been my aim in this chapter to show that devotion conceived in these terms also compels a rejection of history. The early Baptists' transformation of all adversarial issues into issues of Christian doctrine made it possible for them to survive the conflicts of their day without either justifying them or resolving them. Silence and consensus thus "stood in" for the stuff of history. The experience of their descendants suggests that history—that is, a silenced history—is one price that harmony can exact; harmony built on avoidance lacks a structural form in which historical controversy can remain viable. Thus the very contemporaneity of the suburbanites in Hopewell should not deceive us as to the nature of their "community," which has long cultural roots in the past. The ideology of conflict perfected a century and a half ago is very much alive in the dramatically different social environment of today, but the past—whose heritage is a harmonious silence in the face of conflict—is at the heart of the contemporary Baptists' insistence on both their modernity and their faith.

8 The Discourse of The Dorm: Race, Friendship, and "Culture" among College Youth

Michael Moffatt

Racism and Individualism

There are two basic positions on the ideological relation of racism to other American values such as individualism and egalitarianism: Gunnar Myrdal's assertion that racism is a violation of the American "value premise," an archaic, castelike residue of something more primitive (Myrdal 1944), and Louis Dumont's suggestion that racism is a specific ideological corollary of individualism and egalitarianism (Dumont 1980a [1961]). Western ideology, Dumont argues, largely ignores social causation and vigorously denies hierarchy. Therefore perceived inequalities cannot be located in the social, in the *inter*individual; they must be due to things *in* the individual, and they must be physical. The inequality of allegedly subordinate races does not violate individualistic egalitarian values with respect to "humans," for racism specifically states that these races are not quite human. The question of a close logical link between racism and social definitions Americans value in other contexts is not an idle one, for given such a connection, racism or racist inclinations may be less easy to eliminate than if they are an irrational archaicism.

For one year, 1978–79, I was a participant observer one day a week on the third floor of "Erehwon" residence hall, a dormitory in the school where I teach—Rutgers College.[1] About half the residents on the floor were black, members of a black "special interest" section; the others were mostly white, a random selection from the generally white student body. This essay is about race relations on the floor and about students' attempts to interpret race—the discourse of race—mostly from the white residents' point of view, as I was able to listen to them and observe them during that year of research.

In interesting ways, both Dumont and Myrdal were right. The white students applied to the blacks the same fundamental individualism, largely asociological and ahistorical, that they applied to every other social relation (and my data on the blacks, though thinner, suggest a similar if not identical ethnosociology); and such a folk theory led them ineluctably in a certain direction: there must be something wrong with people who do not act appropriately—something wrong inside them as individuals. However, the white students also knew that the outcome of this logic was somehow illegitimate in an interracial context, and when thinking of blacks they did not follow it through. They brought into play a different construct, "culture"—people act differently because they have different values. Yet this secondary explanation was less than fully satisfying to them, in ways I will try to specify below.

However, the discourse was also more complex than this synopsis suggests. For one thing, it was carried on in many different contexts and at many different levels of seriousness and intensity—in joking allusions, in casual remarks embedded in daily life, in more self-conscious attempts at explanation, problem solving, and self-justification, and in collective situations of crisis. It is often hard in evaluating the discourse to say whether statements at these various levels were comparable, were really about the same thing. Second, it was located in history—it was "about" larger societal problems in the late 1970s, and it may be about new social facts in the mid-1980s. Third, it was embedded in complex actions on the part of its pseakers, actions that sometimes appeared to transcend its logical limits strictly construed (e.g., the party described below).

Thus this chapter has two somewhat contrasting main points: the relatively impoverished logical limits of American folk individualism in an interracial context, and the human, interactional complexities within which such an individualistic discourse can function. It is also intended to contribute to the understanding of a macroscopic American societal issue by examining its cultural phenomenology at a microscopic level. What happens in the dorm is an example of how Americans think and act out race, individualism, and egalitarianism in their daily lives. And all this is very close to home, for not only do these young Americans operate with concepts borrowed from the social sciences, but "we" social scientists are often also "Americans," and the ways we live out these issues may be closely connected to the ways we think them out at more general, formal, and abstract levels.

The Floor as Community

Erehwon residence hall was built in the 1950s, when Rutgers was an all-male and virtually all-white college. Its architecture is undistinguished utilitarian modern—boxy brick and glass. Each floor of the dorm is similarly structured: two "sections" of fourteen rooms each divided by an elevator shaft and fire doors, a mixture of double and triple rooms; one common bathroom on each side (each clearly marked by its urinals—still in place in 1984—as a men's room); and a "lounge" on each side, expressly designed to foster sociability among the students in the section. In response to the nationwide youth revolt in the late 1960s, the college first began admitting significant numbers of black (and other minority) students in the late 1960s. Almost immediately, black student spokesmen called for separate living spaces in which black students could support one another in the new, unfamiliar collegiate environment and in which "black cultural" awareness could be fostered. Collegiate authorities initially balked at the apparently counterintegrational implications of the proposals (no doubt also fearing the potentially "disruptive" effects of residentially concentrated blacks), but they finally gave in to the well-organized black demands by redefining the black section as another type of "special interest" group. Just as students whose particular interest in—for instance—creative writing might be fostered by allowing them to live in concentrated groups, so too black students might be permitted to live in a "special interest" section. Black identity, seen by many blacks as fundamental and ascriptive, was thus recategorized less problematically by the college as a matter of "choice"—officially, it was assimilated to the general pluralistic ideal of mid-twentieth-century American liberal education.

By the late 1970s, the single black special interest section in the college, the Paul Robeson section (named after perhaps the most illustrious alumnus in Rutgers's history, black or white) had been on the third floor of Erehwon dorm for a number of years. Its thirty black residents[2] constituted the only black concentration in the Rutgers College student body; many of the remaining six-hundred or so black students at Rutgers (7 percent of the total student body) were "integrated," scattered in the white dorms (others lived at a separate, minority-centered college across the river). Members of the Robeson section were there by "choice": first-year residents had been recruited over the summer by older members, who promised them black solidarity in a mostly white school and guaranteed housing in a central, favored campus location. Robeson members thus expected to be a community, and at one level, the structure of the floor "said" they were, for the section was a bounded, almost self-contained living space complete with its own semiprivate lounge.

But in other ways the structure of the floor denied the communal autonomy of the Robeson section, for the floor contained *two* sections. The other side was mostly white. Its residents had not chosen to be in it in quite the same way as the Robeson members. First-year residents (the most numerous on both sides, about one-third of the floor population) had been assigned to their rooms and to their roommates by a computer; upperclassmen had had some degree of choice, depending on their position in a lottery; third-floor Erehwon had filled up relatively late, owing to known problems on the floor. Despite this history, most of the white students expected the entire floor to form a community.

Why was this? Why couldn't the two sections simply go their own ways as two distinct groups of noninteracting youths? First, because that was not how all other floors in the college were set up (with the exception of spatially different living units, arranged vertically around stairwell clusters or segmented into apartments). Other floors—and the third floor of Erehwon as well—had a single student authority or "preceptor." Other floors, like this one, were expected to be "friendly" groups of people who knew one another, held regular meetings and made decisions in common, held common programs, and partied together; from the beginning of the year, the floor and the dorm were established in most people's minds as the only place in the highly bureaucratized college environment where individuals and individual identities mattered. Other floors, like this one, were supposed to police themselves in many ways; informal collectivities of students who knew one another personally kept order, spotting outsiders and to a degree guarding the group against them. And clearly the college expected third-floor Erehwon to be the same sort of community; otherwise its official liberal ideals might be cast into doubt.

There was a second, seemingly contingent reason the two sections were not entirely self-sufficient: residentially, gender cut across race, and the old male bathrooms had not been subdivided. Both sections of third-floor Erehwon were "coed by alternating room," the most popular of the coed dorm setups at Rutgers (and coed dorms dominated generally). Gender integration developed at Rutgers about the same time as racial integration, also an outcome of the 1960s—in this case linked to the eclipse of in loco parentis, to the women's movement's emphasis on females as persons rather than sex objects, and probably to more earthy student interests in male-female sociability. Generally, gender integration was less problematic than racial integration; students took it for granted and said it made male-female relations more like those in the "real world" than they had been uder traditional collegiate arrangements. But gender integration did not extend to bathroom integration, on third-floor Erehwon or elsewhere. As on other floors, one section's bathroom was declared the women's room one semester and the other section's bathroom the men's room, and vice versa the following semester. Thus, in the first semester white females had to troop over to the Robeson section, where they first started saying "hi" to Robeson members, to bathe and perform other intimate functions with black females, while black males went to the other section. At one of the most intimate daily levels, integration was a fact.

Nevertheless, initially the floor did not work as a community in the way the white students and the authorities expected it to. Whether by design or unconsciously, the Robeson section made a dramatic ritual statement of its lack of interest in floor solidarity in the first floor meeting of the year. An anxious and poorly prepared white preceptor suggested floor parties; an impressive, large black male spokesman from the Robeson side indicated that "our" musical tastes are not the same as "yours," so how can "we" have a party together? Common programming was suggested. Canoeing? White nervousness was discernible, and the meeting broke up with no positive agenda agreed upon between the sections.

Though I was aware (through private interviewing of the blacks) that not everyone on the Robeson side necessarily agreed with this ritual statement of preferential segregation (or even knew about it)—that not everyone on the Robeson side intended to deny floor "friendliness"—most members of the white section saw the meeting as a unanimous collective statement by the blacks on the floor. In the next few weeks, many white residents expressed their fear and resentment of the Robeson section's denial of community, sentiments that were expressed in the language of a simple folk theory of sociability centering on the individual, choice, and friendship.

The theory is familiar to analysts of American culture (c. f. Tocqueville 1969 [1848]; Riesman 1955; Hsu 1972; Lukes 1973; Varenne 1977; Spindler and Spindler 1983; Quinn, n.d.). It was presupposed by virtually all whites' statements on the interracial situation on the floor, and (though my access to black discourse—especially its informal modes—was much poorer) its basic logic was apparently supposed by the blacks as well.

Race and the Logic of Friendship

In this apparently widely shared American folk ethnosociology articulated by the students, individuals were evaluatively and conceptually primary and chose to enter into associations with other individuals with common interests. No one was supposed to force anyone else into common group activity, and groups that existed for other reasons—status-conscious "cliques," self-interested political coalitions—were generally illegitimate or suspect. One apparent exception to this proposition, acted out in the case of the newspaper attack discussed below, seemed to be: if an outside agency attacked a collectivity as a group, it was legitimate for the collectivity to respond as a group (alternatively, the fundamental logic might assert, this is no exception, for outside attack *gives* a collectivity a common interest—self-defense).

Furthermore, though different persons were expected to have different interests—in fact they ought to, for diversity was also valued—interaction between different persons ought to follow certain commonsense principles; people of goodwill ought to act "friendly" toward one another even if they were not actually friends. There was something wrong with persons who violated these assumptions—who formed groups illegitimately, who interacted inappropriately. That wrong had to be *inside* them, since the folk logic rarely admitted to social causation or historical causation (though it referred occasionally to people's past experiences and learning): the inappropriate actions had to be due to a moral, intellectual, or physical flaw. This conclusion was applied both to individuals and to sets of individuals believed to be similar in their behavior.

"Friendship" had a key role in this system of meaning. In many ways it was the ideal social relationship, since it was based strictly on personal choice—as opposed to other relationships that were externally imposed or influenced. All the students, black and white, gave virtually identical formal definitions of a "friend." A friend was someone you liked, someone who shared your interests, someone you had fun with, someone you could trust with your confidences, and someone who would go out of the way for you. Other parts of the definition of "friend" came out in conversation or behavior. Friends said "hi" to each other and talked to each other for a while when they met. Friends ate together. Friends filled each other's needs, but they were not friends only *because* of needs ("she only acts like a friend when she needs something"). Friends were required to share confidences (I flunked in early interactions with student friends while initially pretending to be another incoming student, because I didn't talk about home, family, girl friends, etc., in exchange for such confidences from other students). Friendships, being based on personal choice and individual interest, changed as persons changed, "matured," "grew." Friendship could not be forced; friends also had to respect one's privacy and autonomy ("she acts like my mother, not like my friend").

Since friendship was the purest relationship by the assumptions of student ethnosociology (being most voluntary), it was the coin of sociability in the dorm. From the very first day, students continually rated each other on their "friendliness." "Friendliness" minimally meant saying "hi." (I was glared at for not speaking to a freshman girl on the floor, at the main door downstairs, after one week.) Residents of the floor were expected to say "Hi [first name, abbreviated (i.e., "Mike," not "Michael"), or nickname]." Being first-named by someone whose name you did not know generated embarrassment. Being "friendly" was the minimal expectation of fellow floor members — it established the possibility of the relationship of "friends." That relationship, of course, was a matter of mutual choice and was most clearly marked externally by eating together and spending time together.[3] Deception was always possible, of course; when I circulated a confidential "friendship questionnaire" in the middle of the year, students sounded me out on whether I would break confidences and reveal whether X, whom they'd privately named as "close friend," had so named them. "Friendship" was a scalar or multivaried relationship; my questionnaire was criticized by some for having too few categories ("acquaintance," "friend," "close friend").[4]

Within this pervasive set of assumptions, linked in white minds to a basic mapping of "normal" friendly behavior in the dorm and especially on the floor, the Robeson section's apparent denial of community was especially scandalous. Other, half-perceived factors were known to divide black and white residents — what both whites and blacks called the "stereotypes" that were the residue of the unhappy history of American race relations. To varying degrees, residents of both sides knew the interracial past. To varying degrees (depending on the racial balance in their home high schools), residents had had personal interracial experiences.

And to varying degrees, they knew that the floor itself had a history, not an entirely easy one. They feared each other, and at a certain level of consciousness they knew an easy, relaxed relationship like "friendship" was unlikely to flourish in an atmosphere of fear. They knew they were from different backgrounds, and they defined one another—again, to varying degrees—as belonging to different cultures or subcultures. My own private interviews suggested some subcultural differences on the matter of friendship itself. Though blacks' and whites' *definitions* of friendship were virtually identical, friendly *styles* varied slightly; a cooler or less effusive initial interactive style was favored by blacks than by whites, especially among the males. Also, in my very small sample, there was a difference in willingness to extend friendship among blacks compared with whites— some blacks said it took a good deal longer to know who you could really "trust" than what most white students said, and two black males were the only informants to say they had no "real" friends (one said his only friend was his mother). Blacks were also more likely to see "friendship" on the model of "kinship"—using a kin term like "brother" or "sister" for a friend; in certain ways friendship was a more serious, less ephemeral relationship (or was thought of as such) among blacks than among whites. Thus, in an initial encounter, a white male and a black male might seriously misinterpret one another's friendship cues: to the black male, the white male might seem suspiciously interactive, trying to be "friendly" too soon; to the white male, the black male might seem initially hostile and basically "unfriendly."

Given all these known and sensed differences, if the blacks had not apparently denied community, the whites might still have had a hard time—in their own terms—being "friendly" with the blacks; and they certainly would have had a hard time being their "friends." That would have been something to feel bad about, for good Americans are "friendly people." But since the blacks *had* apparently denied community, the whites could ignore these contingent factors and stress the central value system: people of the same age, in the same college circumstances, living on the same floor, *ought* to be friendly.[5] And they ought to be friendly in immediately discernible ways. If they were not, there was something wrong with them; *they* were the bad people. And complaints about lack of friendliness were the whites' dominant grievance. In a set of interviews I did privately with most first-year students in the first month and a half of the term, ten of the thirteen whites said there were or had been problems between blacks and whites ("I try to be friendly, but it doesn't work"; "I tried to be friendly, but I've stopped"; "people don't say 'hi' ").

Black opinions, however, were evidently different. They felt they *were* friendly. Maybe not as friendly as the whites wanted, perhaps because the blacks did not really expect to become "friends" of the whites, perhaps because "friendly" was signaled in different ways by the blacks. At the beginning of the year, four out of six blacks I interviewed said there were no problems with the white side—that they had encountered prejudice on the outside, in the university or in the town, but not on the floor—and two said there were "minor" problems (one mentioned "funny looks" when she went to the white side). To the blacks, "whites" were the whole society, not just "those people over there, who aren't bad." And some blacks, though they may not have expected the whites on the other side to be real friends, did see the coresident whites as "friendly" in their own (urban black) sense of the term; they were friendlier than the whites back home, and they also had a common interest (the minimum basis of sociability in the folk ethnosociology) with the blacks:

Interviewer: What would you tell people at home that people at Rutgers are like?

Black student: Well, I'd tell them at . . . Rutgers, there's a lot of Caucasians, there's a few blacks, but everyone here, you know, is here for one reason—to try to learn, to try to make something of himself. But everyone's . . . friendly, you know . . . they're not hostile up here. It's a break [from what it's like home in the city].[6]

Friendship questionnaires that I circulated in the middle of the year confirmed the lack of interracial relationships. Only three of thirty-three reciprocated "close friendships" were interracial (one was between interracial roommates who had been paired by the lottery); only 5 percent of the larger number of reciprocated "friendships" were interracial. There were quite a few more friendships than this between the sections, some which turned out to be monoracial relationships involving the few black students who had wound up on the white side—indicating that the section division did not entirely determine friendship patterns.

White attitudes toward the blacks in the first few months ranged from fear and hostility through apathy to a desire to "understand" and improve things. Among the most reactionary students were two white males. One came into the dorm at the beginning of the year with an oversized baseball bat labeled "NBC," which he told me privately meant "nigger be cool"; and in the first few months he made a series of remarks in my hearing and the hearing of other white residents, just out of earshot of the blacks, ranging from the "joke" (on seeing one of the larger black males emerge from the men's room), "these guys could eat a poor little white boy like me for breakfast . . . honkey on toast, cheese honkey"; to the "analysis," "They're overdoing the hostility business . . . they're trying to make up for two hundred years of hostility in two semesters, and they're pushing it." Note the reference to historical context here, albeit a dismissive one. Another male told a small group of white friends that he had been visiting another college the previous night when five or six "niggers" (he looked over his shoulder when he said the word) jumped out of a car and came toward him: " 'Shit! This is it!' I said to my buddy, but they went right by us—they were going to a party!"

A white female's answer to the question, "Do you have any problems with blacks on the floor?" is interesting both for its near racism and for its ambivalence:

Yes! . . . I went to school with them, and . . . the population was 30 [percent black and] 70 [percent white], and they're, how do I put it? They're always trying to do something. Like this morning . . . [narrates incident the same morning, involving a misunderstanding with a black female over a bottle of shampoo]. . . . a couple of them are real nice. I say hello, I always say hello . . . but just some of them are real bastards! Yuck. [Interviewer: "Are the nice ones guys or girls?"] That I can't even . . . See, I don't even really get close to them . . . I try to be friendly, but then . . . I went to a [high] school and I guess I wasn't stuck with college people, and they were very uncivilized, very rowdy and gangy and, you know, saying they, you say one thing wrong, and forget it! You had fifty of them on your back after school! So I came in with a very bad attitude about them and it's just not getting any better . . . [The ones here are] a lot nicer than just regular ones, cause I guess they're smarter and they know a lot more.

The terms in which blacks are condemned in this statement are consistent with those traditional in American racism: "uncivilized," "rowdy," "gangy." They are inappropriately given to group aggression ("fifty of them on your back"). Yet even this student, who was the most openly anti-black person on the white side, and who described herself defiantly at another time as "prejudiced," was not unconflicted in her attitudes. Note the statement again: she can't stand to be near blacks, but some of them are "nice"; they're all the same (first few lines), yet the ones at Rutgers are "nicer" and "smarter" than "regular ones." She even hedges on her personal responsibility for her perspective, indicating she does not quite approve of it in herself: bad experiences in high school *caused* her to have a "bad attitude," which experiences in college aren't changing—somehow without involving the active "she."

Other white statements on the floor at the beginning of the year were also conflicted, but less fearful:

I don't really know anyone in the other section. Because, you know, you'll say hello to them, but they don't even say anything. I don't know, it's not that I'm an overfriendly person, but I think it's just snobbish when you walk past someone not to say hello. . . . I just figure that color and race didn't make any difference, that people would still basically, you know, be the same. The only problem is . . . is just the music, like I don't like disco music at all.

Two problems are referred to here: lack of friendliness, closely linked to a disproof of the supposition that people are "basically" the same, and music. The salient life-style difference cited by whites with reference to blacks was musical taste. (White resident who lived in the black section, early fall):

They're really nice. They're just different, totally different. They have different interests. They're totally into music—disco—they've never heard of the Grateful Dead! They have a different ethnic identity.

I did not ask enough of the right questions to determine why music was so crucial within this system of interpersonal definitions, but some points seem clear. Music was loud and public. Musical taste was considered a matter of personal individual expression, linked somehow to one's essence, a free choice, like friendship; yet against this was the disturbing percept that musical tastes correlated closely with racial identity. Music was closely connected in adolescent age-culture with differentiation from adults. There is an apparent affinity between this distinctive feature and classical racist definitions of blacks as "naturally musical," but no white ever articulated this in my hearing, and it would have contradicted their own self-definitions; whites also saw themselves as fundamentally involved in music, though their own tastes may have seemed less "ethnically" determined to them.

Race and "Culture"

The preceding quotation also mentions "ethnic identity," and this explanation of difference was the one most commonly used by liberals among the whites:

Yeah, we got to do something about the conga [drum] section. They're not friendly; they're not interacting. I guess they have different cultural values.

"Culture"[7] was a way of going to another level of analysis, one with apparent group reference. But "culture" also covered another set of ambivalences implicit in the individualistic, voluntaristic ideology that obtained elsewhere. Positively construed, "culture" was something like individual subjectivism writ large: of course, just as any individual has a right to his or her own opinions, so too did any group. It also accorded with a simple folk psychology that has been articulated once or twice above: our experiences *do* influence the way we think and feel (thus the "bad attitude" of the reactionary woman quoted above resulted from her bad experiences in high school), so different "cultural" backgrounds might cause different groups of people to make systematically different choices in music and in other areas of personal taste. Yet the realm in which this was allowed to operate was tacitly very narrow; people had the right to different *opinions,* but in everyday behavior (e.g., in ways of being friendly), all normal human beings ought to act similarly, for these behaviors were "natural." A thoughtful white sophomore woman on the floor who had heard me lecture on symbolic anthropology the year before asked me one day, "What are you doing here [on the floor]? There's nothing symbolic about this." I expressed my anthropological belief that all realities were equally constructed and arbitrary. She asked, "But aren't some more natural than others?"[8]

In accord with assumptions like this one, most students were very uneasy when "different culture" was strongly manifested in behavior. A sophomore woman was defensive about her Lebanese boyfriend, apologized for his Islamic name, and said he was "really nice"—he was an exception to other "Arabs" she had met; they were "*really* different." Several white males told me, half-jokingly, about an East Indian who had behaved inexplicably in the dining room the year before, eating alone, fastidiously, "with his hands." They had watched him with amusement all year and nicknamed him "Pow-wow." From their descriptions I was fairly sure he had been a southern Indian eating in traditional fashion, with his right hand; silverware is considered unclean because it has been used by so many strangers. I explained this to them one evening and gave them a demonstration; they were polite and amused, but also embarrassed and slightly disgusted watching me. In other contexts, students criticized stereotypic statements. A freshman male described one woman's hometown boyfriend as a "wimp" and as "typically Jewish." A non-Jewish interlocutor protested against "typically Jewish" (but not against "wimp"); the teller said there was nothing wrong with such a characterization, that he himself would not mind being called "typically Catholic" or "typically Irish." A sophomore male got upset and told them both to shut up. Another time, the same sophomore male said of the friend, "Y gestures with his hands. He can't help it; he's Italian." Y replied, "I'll breaka your legs. I can't help it; Ima Italian."

Given these reservations, the student's working concept of "culture"—for use in an interracial context—was not especially deep or sophisticated. Notably missing was the idea that culture can fundamentally determine habitual modes of thought and deeply affect behavior, or that it is relativistic in any sense more profound than one person's having a taste for one leisure activity and another for another.

Interviewer: What are the different types of people you've met at Rutgers?

Student: Well, I've noticed a lot of people here are into frisbee. Is that what you mean?

Rituals of Separatism and Integration

Periodically through the year, the floor had collective moments—they could be called "performances" or "secular rituals" (cf. Myerhoff and Mongulla, chap. 6)—in which its problems were either expressed, exacerbated, or ameliorated. These collective actions were another way students could live through, and attempt to define, the complex realities of race and friendship. The initial floor meeting was one such occasion, "stating" the problem of disunity—at least from the white point of view. The floor's inability to hold a floor party was another. On other floors, floor parties were simple rituals of integration, valued periods of collective sociability; but Erehwon third floor could not pull one off for over half the year, because a party meant music, and no musical tastes were felt to be shared between the two sections.

A third failed ritual was Secret Santa. Secret Santa took place on every floor at the end of the first semester. It involved the exchange of gifts, and challenges to do personally embarrassing stunts, between males and females on a floor. It was widely felt to be "fun," and it was widely considered to enhance floor sociability at a time when the beginning-of-year friendliness had petered out. The Robeson section declined to hold Secret Santa together with the white section, however, and conducted its own instead.

Toward the end of the fall, some younger males from the Robeson side engaged in minor depredations on both sides of the floor, common and generally unsanctioned freshman and sophomore activities in student culture. In this case, however, there was great hostility from the white side, for these activities were allowed only between friends, and the Robeson section was not friendly. Several floor meetings were held to discuss "tensions," and a few people on each side made efforts to talk to one another. Personal fears on the white side declined as the floor became a familar, routinized location; but by February the floor had had no success as a unit of sociability. Floor members talked about the problems among themselves, but their official position to outsiders tended to be: "We all get along; there's nothing going on here we can't handle."

In early March, this posture became no longer tenable. A black student reporter visited the floor a couple of times, talked to residents on both sides, picked up evidence of problems, and wrote a front-page story in the campus newspaper describing the lack of community on the floor. He was especially critical of the "two cultures" explanation and specifically blamed the black section for acting in ways that kept old "stereotypes" alive. His article aroused tremendous hostility on the floor, from both sides, and brought about the first genuine cooperative actions by members of both sections: several effective meetings, a floor letter of response to the newspaper "attack," and a floor party.

In the first, well-attended floor meeting, residents from both sides (who had been quoted by name in the article) apologized to the other side for things they had said, generally claiming their statements had been taken out of context; all personal apologies were apparently accepted. Representatives of a campuswide black student organization attended a second meeting and told residents that the floor was being unfairly blamed simply for reflecting a racist society. Students from both sides explained to one another that "special interest" sections always tended to become noninteractive. And everyone agreed that the reporter was the real villain and that a jointly written, jointly signed letter to the campus paper was in order. A subcommittee of residents from both sides wrote the letter, which simply denied almost everything in the article; it was circulated and signed by most members of both sections, and it eventually appeared in the paper.

The written and oral discourse of this crisis period referred to "culture" with some frequency, suggesting both its explanatory salience and its limited legitimacy. In the original newspaper article, a white resident was quoted as saying, "Some whites on the floor probably resent members of the [black] section because they are so far into their own culture. I think culture may be a big part of the problem." A black was quoted as saying, "Many blacks on the floor have personal preferences of being with their own kind, sharing their cultural heritage, and maintaining their identity." Neither speaker in these responses takes personal responsibility for the attitude in question. Similar ambivalence came out in the later letter by the black organization in defense of the floor. The residents of the floor, it said, were being unfairly accused of "the unforgivable crime of preferring their own culture. . . . We're not saying that this situation is the most desirable, but preference is a God-given right, [and] who is [the reporter] to question it?"

A few days after the letter appeared, the floor held the first and only floor party of the year, a shaky but successful ritual creation of something that had not existed before: floor sociability. The residence counselor, a black female graduate student who lived downstairs, worked together with the preceptor and with representatives of both sections, and a plan was formulated to overcome the lack of musical consensus. The floor agreed that alternate records would be chosen by the Paul Robeson section and the white section. A subcommittee consisting of the residence counselor and one male resident of each side would oversee the arrangement during the party. And the party would be held on the white side, to encourage persons from other floors (mostly all white, and still afraid of the situation on the floor) to attend.

The party was not as large as most floor parties, but it did work. For most of the evening, members of both sections sat together in friendly interracial groups, though the dancing was generally monoracial. I watched one popular black male ask three or four white females in a row to dance, and all turned him down (probably saying they didn't know disco dancing). He didn't seem surprised, and he stayed at the party. When the music chosen by the black section was played, the blacks got up and danced an almost choreographed disco with tight group coordination; when music chosen by the white section was played, the blacks all sat down and the whites stood up and danced in diverse styles, in separate couples, mostly non-touch dancing. Students occasionally drifted off into rooms together, mostly monoracially, once or twice interracially, for quieter talks, other music, drinks, or smokes. Five or six people from other floors were present at a time, generally watching rather than participating. To me, at least, the party had seemed a collective demonstration as much for the benefit and reassurance of those on the floor—that things were not as bad as reported in the paper—as for any outside observer. For a week or two afterward, residents of both sides agreed that the party had been a success and told residents who had not come what they had missed. But the party was not repeated during the year.

In the end, I felt the students were holding their fundamental logic of friendship firmly under control when the subject of race came up. Several times during the year I privately asked all the first-year residents if they felt any antagonism toward other students on the floor. Many referred to the lack of friendship between the two sections, and some labeled the two sections different "cliques," but no one said anything personally nasty about a person of another race—"apathy" was the most negative emotion mentioned. Nor did the white residents say anything negative about one another, in a context where I knew at least two cliques were operating. Similar questions on another, all-white floor revealed five major cliques and five minor ones, marked by strong, willingly expressed personal antagonisms: "unsociable," "inconsiderate," "loud," "snob," "stuck-up," "pushy," "wimp," "burnout," "asshole," "snot-face," "strange person," "smells," "thinks that her crap doesn't stink," "obnoxious Jew" [said by another Jewish student]. The judgments are the normal negative pole of the logic of friendship; the persons in question were personally flawed because they lacked the skills to be properly friendly, or they were innately unworthy of friendship. Such judgments could not be rendered between interracial nonfriends on the floor where I was working, however, for the judger would reveal himself or herself to be a racist. And the lack of such expressible sentiments interracially apparently also damped "normal" interpersonal evaluation within the whites.

But the effort hurt. Being on the floor was hard work, and a floor, unlike the rest of college, should not be hard work—it should be a domain of easy, friendly sociability and of choice. Though the fears noted above on the white side declined through the year, though some acquaintanceships developed, though many of the whites said they had learned a lot during the year—that it had been a "good experience" to live on the floor—hardly anyone wanted to remain there the following year.[9] Their opportunities for social life were restricted, several white students stated; they could not meet as many "people" there as on other floors. Blacks had the same complaint; social life at Rutgers was thin because there were so few of "us" here.

Racism in the Dorms?

Are these students racists? In most cases no. At some very fundamental level, most of them agree with Myrdal's sense that categorical racism is somehow antithetical to the American "value premise" (and even the most openly "prejudiced" are defensive about their racial attitudes). Are they untroubled by race? Again no. American racism has left a historical legacy of fear and perceived difference whose causes are generally outside the discourse of the dorm. These differences cannot be handled within the simple folk sociology of friendship that dominates the students' categories (and evidently most American folk categories); as Dumont suggests, the students' egalitarian constructs have no place for legitimate "difference." In the individualistic logic of friendship, someone else's unwillingness to be "friendly" in a taken-for-granted way is referred to character defects in the other (all the epithets mentioned above). Such a logic cannot be applied to racially correlated differences, however, for everyone in the dorm feels uneasy with the apparently racist connotations of such an explanation. Technically speaking, the explanation would not be racist; technically a racist explanation would go one step further and locate character flaws in the genetic makeup of the stigmatized other. Student ethnosociology does not directly refer to questions of heredity versus environment, but in referring instead to "culture"—an environmentalist notion—it alludes to the distinction and takes the conventional liberal position on it: "they" are not to blame; you have to understand "their" "cultural" background.

In all likelihood, "culture" as the students use it derives historically from Franz Boas's use of the term in his early twentieth-century critique of scientific racism. Compared with Boas's rich and complex culture concept (see Stocking 1968), the student concept not only lacks genuine relativism and a notion of "behavioral determinism," it also contains no suggestion that the students imagine there is anything fundamentally important or positive to be learned from the interracial cultural differences. And there is the additional paradox that both blacks and whites appear to follow a similar logic in accounting for apparent group differences between one another of "culture" by referring them to "cultural" differences; their culture may be identical. Nevertheless, the students are certainly better off with "culture" than they would be without it; it gives them a semilegitimate (or perhaps "mediating") explanation of difference in an instance where otherwise only racism might be rhetorically possible.[10] And in other contexts, students see "cultural difference" more positively; they are at least theoretically interested in what they might have to learn from anthropology, for example, or travel—from the different cultures of the world.

Race, Gender, and Recent Developments

There are interesting parallels and contrasts in student concepts of race and gender. On the one hand, the white students—like the college—would be most comfortable with racial integration in housing, as they are with gender integration (up to a point at least: male/female roommate pairs are not yet encouraged, just as "integrated" black students still tend to have black roommates, though white/black pairs also occur). Even more systematically than they denied racist feelings, the male students denied—at a formal level—any "sexist" inclinations (though they said they "kidded around" with the females a lot; and a few of the females perceived sexism in the dorms). The males also generally denied that a girl as "friend" was different from a boy as "friend"; both were "persons," in the same way as people of different races *should* just be "persons" to one another. ("They're just people whose skins happen to be black!") And friendship statistics bore them out on females as persons; as many people mentioned "friendships" with members of the opposite sex (clearly distinguishing these from romantic involvements) as with members of the same sex.

On the other hand, gender difference may actually be more strongly rooted in nature for these students than racial difference—an apparent meaning of the racial integration of the bathrooms compared with their gender segregation. Stated more precisely, the "natural" differences of gender remain, in student logic, more fundamental than the "natural" differences of race: one determines salient features such as sexuality, the other superficial differences such as skin color (almost everyone denies believing in a link between either sort of natural difference and moral worth, intelligence, etc.). And research in 1984 indicated that the increasingly visible gay community was a more profound challenge to the ideological liberalism or relativism of college students than was the black community, for with homosexuality, gender and sexuality become unhooked in ways profoundly disturbing to young people still establishing their own sexual identities. With homosexuality as with race, students deny naturalistic explanations at a formal level; most students say they do not think homosexuality is "genetic." But in this context they then turn not to "culture" but to folk Freudianism; they generally root homosexuality in traumatic early childhood family dynamics. Homosexuality is thus abnormal and, for some heterosexual respondents, "unnatural." Being black may be unfortunate from the white students' point of view, a cross to bear, an attribute to be ignored among the liberals; being gay, on the other hand, is a disease.

There are signs that race relations among the students are far from fixed—that the interactive pragmatics of Erehwon third floor can vary from year to year. In 1984, six years after the original research for this chapter was done, the situation on the Robeson floor was apparently quite different. Black and white residents alike mentioned "no problems" and no incidents between the sections. Observed friendly interactions were much easier than they were in 1978–79; there was at least one interracial romance across the sections; and several white residents of the Robeson section (students who wound up on that side by accident) joined the Robeson club and by all accounts participated enthusiastically in black cultural activities. The original myth that membership in the section was a matter of "choice"—unrelated to racial background—had been actualized. Floor parties were held successfully, in part because of an evolution in musical stereotypes; blacks and whites were still held to have generally different musical tastes, but they were also now said to share a liking for a "gray zone" or "crossover" performers (e.g., Prince, Michael Jackson)—and this was the music emphasized in interracial parties on the floor, which were apparently held with less difficulty than in the late 1970s ("crossover" music also existed in 1978–79, of course, but it was not used as a solution to sectional problems).

It is hard to say whether this is a long-term change or the result of some lucky situational factors in 1984: an accomplished, well-trained black female preceptor living on the white side; more experienced, less interracially threatened students on the white side (a remarkable side effect of the floor's success this year is the report—both from the white section and from members of the gay association—that a gay student who "came out" on the white side recently had been treated more tolerantly than was the rule in other dorms); a predominance of females over males on the Robeson side; and a higher incidence of middle-class residents on the Robeson side, from predominantly white home communities (one Robeson leader this year said he chose the floor in order to experience living in a mostly black group for the first time). What had not changed, as far as I can see, is the fundamental discourse. Why shouldn't things be working out on the floor? the students seemed to suggest in 1984; we're all just people. Fair enough, as long as things go well. When they do not, however, American ethnosociology continues to give its natives an elemental individualistic rhetoric that is if anything becoming more simplistic. Its terms are folk paradoxes: uneasy racism or uneasy tolerance, denied nature or uncomfortable nurture, individual choice or "culture." With this simple set of terms, American natives—these college students are only one example—must continue to struggle to understand, and to live through, far more complex social realities than the terms themselves identify.

PART
V

Doing
America

Editor's Introduction

All the chapters in the volume stress action in culture—that is, action constructed in response to certain traditional problems and as statements within an ongoing conversation. As we have moved from advertisements and movies to parades and then to minutes and parties, we have also moved to situations when the response of the audience is more and more closely tied to the statements that came before and to those that follow. While it has been argued that the great "themes" of American culture are more than simply "made explicit" in such texts as advertisements and movies, it would be easy to think of them as detached statements with little relevance to action. Parades are acted out, but they are too clearly collective (theatrical) representations to point out to us where an emphasis on action in culture is leading.

The next two chapters move us further in this direction by looking at ways of handling everyday life: in the first (Canaan, chap. 9) through an analysis of various statements or texts about it, and in the second (Varenne, chap. 10) through an analysis of a brief exchange between a man and a woman one day in a Manhattan park. Both essays emphasize the role of the traditional themes (of love, sex, individualism, hospitality, community), the confusion of the actors, and their deliberate, active efforts to build something that satisfies the often contradictory needs to express experience, make it make sense, and place the audience in a position where its legitimate responses will not be too destructive. Both essays show how, in this ambiguous and, in these cases, rather unsatisfactory process, the culture is reproduced as a condition for further exchanges and yet perhaps subtly subverted.

These chapters should make explicit how the collective effort of the authors of this volume differs from the work done in old-style culture and personality or recent cognitive science. In our perspective, the analytical task goes beyond elucidating the knowledge participants must have to decipher the messages addressed to them or to produce behaviors that will be effective locally. We are not simply looking for the formal rules one must know to offer hospitality in America. Neither are we looking for the pragmatic rules one must use to refuse a sexual advance or an invitation to drop in. Rather, we are assuming uncertain, resistant, ambiguously knowledgeable informants who easily lapse into inarticulateness as they find themselves in situations they did not produce and in which they are made to suffer. The young women of Canaan's paper are not yet able to produce the kind of articulate statement that, one can imagine, they may learn to make after a few more years of growing up, reading, attending college, and so forth. They are not fully knowledgeable informants. And yet they may know more than the culture forms at their disposal will ever easily let them express. Who knows but that several years of college will limit rather than expand their consciousness by training them more thoroughly in certain rhetorical forms? As for the actors in Varenne's essay, they are actually silenced as they never utter the words with which they are struggling.

Culture is not knowledge. It is not "character" or "personality." It is the context of action that makes itself through us. Although there is pattern in this context, and though we are placed in the position of reproducing it, we are not, singly, responsible for it. By ourselves, or in a small isolated group, or in the many niches where mass cultures do not reach us, we move cultural patterns until the old models look radically foreign. We do not apply rules to form our behavior. We create our behavior by handling what is given to us and then by responding to the continual responses that greet our behaviors.

All the texts presented by Canaan and Varenne should therefore be seen as utterances within ongoing conversations and thus dependent in their constitution on the same principles of coherence, trust, and collusion that have been identified by those who study face-to-face discourse. The stories of kinky and normal sex, rape, and love told by Canaan's high-school "kids" are contexts to each other. They do not tell us "what" the kids know or believe. As we will see, what they seem to know or believe is altogether unformed and contradictory. The kids, however, have to handle their sexual experiences, and the totality of their texts—only some of which they can individually perform—constitutes a cultural system within which their own statements fit as one voice in a large chorus. Varenne looks both at a set of texts that respond to each other by presenting different possible ways of handling sincerity in the offering of friendship ("meaning a greeting") and at a set of closely linked utterances in a brief tape-recorded conversation. The latter analysis is intended as a final argument for the need to separate the individual participant from the cultural structure within which he acts and which he thereby reproduces.

Good girls don't, but I do.

The Knack

What is at issue, briefly, is the over-all "discursive fact," the way in which sex is "put
into discourse." Hence, . . . my main concern will be to locate the forms of power, the
channels it takes, the discourses it permeates in order to reach the most tenuous and individual modes of behavior, the paths that give it access to the rare or scarcely perceiv-
able forms of desire, how it penetrates and controls everyday pleasure.

Michel Foucault 1978, 11

9 Why a "Slut"
Is a "Slut":
Cautionary Tales
of Middle-Class
Teenage Girls'
Morality
Joyce Canaan

Introduction

Sexuality is perhaps the most fundamental, problematic, and contradictory set of actions or practices with which American suburban middle-
class teenagers—or kids, as they call themselves[1]—today construct themselves as individuals and group members. Teenagers are not the only
contemporary Americans or Westerners to so emphasize sexuality in self
and group construction. Foucault's (1978) analysis suggests that, since the
Middle Ages at least, Western sexuality has increasingly been represented
as providing the key to the innermost and truest part of the self. This part is
revealed and concealed in discourses of power hierarchically relating the
person with others.

In contemporary American culture, sexuality is intimately related to
love (Schneider 1980 [1968]). The values with which the process of love is
constructed provide the basis for group formation more generally (Varenne

1977). The values operating in the discursive process of love specifically represent intimate relations with others, although these same values can be appropriated in less intimate, less highly charged relations as well. Although the discourse of love contains a marked set of practices for persons of all ages, the power of these values is particularly evident in the discourse of those moving toward adulthood—that is, toward gender-specific completion or fulfillment. Adulthood is demarcated in part by its conferring the right to express and explore sexuality and to experience intimate relations beyond the family. Examining statements and silences with which teenagers construct sexuality and love contributes to the more comprehensive understanding of this transition as well as the meaning of sexuality and love in America.

This chapter focuses only on teenage girls' discourses about sexuality and love. To this extent it is incomplete. Understanding teenagers' practices concerning sexuality and love requires the conjoint examination of both genders' practices.[2] However, because girls are invisible and silent in most analyses (McRobbie and Garber 1976), examining only their practices provides insight into ways members of this less visible and audible gender represent themselves.

After a description of the theoretical position motivating and underlying this analysis, I will turn to the community of "Sheepshead,"[3] where I conducted fifteen months of field research among middle- and high-school teenagers. I will focus particularly on two contrasting "texts" involving what informants consider the "kinky sex" of "Debbie" and the more "normal" heterosexual activities of "Melissa." Relationships between these texts will be delineated, showing how their conjunction provides insight into teenage girls' construction of their sexual practices today.

Sexuality and Love: Practicing a Discourse

Foucault suggests that the notion that sexuality has been repressed in the West at least since the beginning of industrial capitalism hides the underlying deployment of discourses on sexuality. Focusing on these underlying discourses, Foucault indicates that they speak to and elaborate progressively more complex means of "policing" the person (1978, 25). As a result, sexuality has become increasingly comprehensive: "It is no longer a question simply of saying what was done—the sexual act—and how it was done, but of reconstructing, in and around the act, the thoughts that recapitulated it, the obsessions that accompanied it, the images, desires, modulations, and quality of the pleasure that animated it" (1978, 63).

Sites of sexuality have become increasingly pervasive in Western cultures. The person is represented as containing a sexually constituted internality that must be known and spoken. Sexuality is increasingly legislated in and through external social institutions. It has become a system of power and knowledge enabling the regulation and articulation of individuals' internal motives and external practices. This socially constituted system of surveillance is not naturally or biologically determined; it takes different forms in different cultures and at different periods of time in the same culture.

Despite its social and historical localization, Foucault's insistence that sexuality always involves relations of power that change infinitely and infinitesimally is static. Baudrillard (1984) infuses Foucault's notion of power with dynamism by suggesting it be viewed in an encompassing framework of symbolic exchange: "Power has to be seen as something which exchanges. Not in the economic sense, but in the sense that power accomplishes itself according to a reversible cycle of seduction, of defiance and ruse (neither axis nor relay to infinity, but a cycle). . . . Power seduces . . . by this reversibility that haunts it, and on which is installed a minimal symbolic cycle" (1984, 202–3). Baudrillard represents power as a process that can be defied at any moment. Defiances stop prior representations in their limited tracks of meaning and force their repositioning in discourse.

The following analysis rests on this perspective. It posits that teenage girls represent their positions as subjects in discourses of romantic love with limited cultural values that they take for granted and whose limitations they cannot quite articulate. This fixing of meaning provides a coherent discourse of limited representations that cannot account for contradictions in lived experience. Limited representations blur or diminish rather than articulate contradictory components (Coward and Ellis 1977; Williams 1977).

This essay focuses on sexual practices of teenagers, in the various senses of the word "practice." In part it examines what (some) teenagers do by considering the discourse of romantic love with which they interpret their actions or practices. It also centers on ways teenagers practice how to act in sexual situations where they are not yet fully competent and must confront difficulties the discourse at their disposal cannot quite handle.

As Schneider (1980 [1968]) observes, in contemporary American culture sexuality expresses love, and love is the process with which the most fundamental American group, the family, is formed, transformed, and affirmed. American kinship is in part a classificatory system based on sexual intercourse. It specifies relations of "blood," or whatever substance kin share that acknowledges their relatedness, and actualizes relations of law that rest on the legal bond of marriage tying kin together. Sexual intercourse signifying love links these two kinds of relations in a single powerful practice. Marital partners legally bound together engage in sexual intercourse, a physical act of love affirming and instantiating spiritual closeness. Sexual intercourse simultaneously provides the basis for the bond of blood. Children formed from their parents' conjoined substance during intercourse affirm the parental legal bond, carrying it into the future in a new form: "Sexual intercourse is an act in which and through which love is expressed; it is often called 'making love,' and love is an explicit cultural symbol in American kinship. . . . As a symbol of unity, or oneness, love is the union of the flesh, of opposites, male and female, man and woman. The unity of opposites is not only affirmed in the embrace, but also in the outcome of that union, the unity of blood, the child" (Schneider 1980 . [1968], 38, 39).

In America this system is used strategically to relate—or not relate—the self to others, including some who are not kin and excluding some who are, depending on personal feelings about them. Varenne builds on Schneider's analysis to show that components of American kinship constitute virtually all social relations:

Love is the total giving away of oneself to somebody else who must answer in kind and equally. . . . There is no love if it is not shared. . . . Differences have to be minimal in all aspects of behavior, though the only relevant domains are considered to be those pertaining to the psychology of the person. . . . One-mindedness and the stress on the psyche as defining the nature of a man are direct concomitants of the reciprocal and individualistic implications in the idea of love. Insofar as true humanity lies in the full psychological realization of a choice, it is believed that communication through exchange, on which small groups are based, demands full psychological—that is, in fact, ideological—similarity inside it. (1977, 204)

Love is the process in and through which two persons exchange as equals. Equals are viewed as persons *like* oneself—that is, with similar psychological characteristics. Actors affirm their similar internal motivations and their equality by reciprocally exchanging—that is, mutually giving to and receiving from each other. Since groups are supposed to be formed by common internal motivations of actors mutually exchanging as equals, the same principles organizing the love relationship coordinate the formation of wider groups. The present emphasis on components of love as contributing to the construction of all relationships contrasts dramatically with the initial emphasis on love during the Middle Ages. Medieval love logically ended in death; as such it differed from other relations and was the least social of all relationships (de Rougemont 1956). Today components of the love relationship are central not just to the family but to the formation of all American groups, and love has become the most social of relationships (Varenne 1977).

The love relationship is also seen, in contemporary America, as essentially unstable, and thus the stability of all relationships is always uncertain. The principles of the constitution of American groups are fundamentally contradictory, since they insist that groups are formed from transient and transformable subjective feelings of individual persons. The factors used to explain what motivates the formation of any group are the same as those used to explain its dissolution. Participants are thus led to consider the possibly incipient destruction of the group they have constructed. Their fears lead them to expend much effort in affirming group solidarity (Varenne 1977).

In contemporary American culture, where satisfaction of personal desires or the pursuit of pleasure is preeminent (Lasch 1977; Mercer 1983; Zaretsky 1976) and where sexuality increasingly provides the center with which the person is constructed (Foucault 1978; Heath 1984), sexuality is defined as the primary desire requiring satisfaction and is separated from its prior relationship with marriage and the family. The progressive disjunction of sexuality from the family and procreation opens up sexual practices toward greater variety than mere sexual intercourse between two different-gendered persons (Coulson 1980; DuBois and Gordon 1984; Foucault 1978; Heath 1984). The sexual domain is no longer a Pandora's box opened hesitantly by gender- and class specific groups; it is an area of desires and gratifications many Americans readily explore.

Among adults, sexual pleasure in and of itself is emphasized while the model of sexual intercourse for procreative purposes is deemphasized — but not ignored. This reproduces in a new way the American — and, more generally, Western — mind/body dualism (Dumont 1980b [1966]). The fusion of physical and spiritual aspects of the self in sexual intercourse previously provided a moment when these dual aspects of the self were conjoined with those of another in a procreative context. Now that such a conjunction is no longer seen as necessary, sexuality can be engaged in to satisfy bodily desires alone, for bodily satisfaction in combination with love, or for procreation alone. Previously fused parts of the self can be separated.

Whereas adults are reconstituting the sexual domain, American teen-agers experimenting with sexuality are aware that the contours and components of this domain are unclear. They struggle with the need to construct the sexual domain without clear-cut guidelines. They constitute themselves using components from an increasingly complex domain. It is perhaps for this reason that most stories I heard during fieldwork spoke of sexuality. These stories very clearly capture the ambiguities and contradictions with which teenagers articulate the sexual domain.

This essay examines lived experiences of teenage sexuality giving rise to stories of this kind. These stories will be evaluated for their expression of teenagers' struggles as they tell each other about sexual acts, psychological motivations, and love. The teenage construction of sexuality can be discerned in a reading of these stories. This analysis of texts is guided by Marcus's suggestion that, given the current disarray of theory in anthropology, analyses today should provide a rhetorical background for the world and speak through fragments that have "the self-conscious aim of achieving an effect which disturbs the reader. [Such analyses] shift focus to dialogic and the reciprocity of perspectives involved in any ethnographic project. They want to say something about the modern world as much, if not more, by self-conscious attention to the form of the ethnographic text as by direct attention to the bounded life world of the ethnographic subject" (1986).

Here I focus on textual fragments that teenage girls produce to position themselves in their sexual practices. By speaking through such fragments, I seek to articulate dissonances in the representations of sexual practices of contemporary American teenage girls—and perhaps of other contemporary Americans as well. Before turning to these texts, I first will describe the community of Sheepshead, where research was conducted, and then will discuss briefly the significance of representations in texts of Debbie's and Melissa's sexual practices.

The Community of Sheepshead

Sheepshead is an upper-middle-class community of thirteen thousand near a major American city on the eastern seaboard. Single-family dwellings constructed largely since the end of World War II are interspersed with undeveloped wooded tracts covering 14 percent of the community's six square miles. Through the center of town runs Main Street, lined with retail and service-oriented stores as well as offices of doctors, lawyers, and den-tists. Two shopping centers with chains of primarily working-class department stores lie on the community's outskirts. Ten miles away a cluster of shopping malls with middle-class department stores allows residents to buy virtually any commodity they want. Sheepshead is 97 percent white and 3 percent Asian, Hispanic, and black. There are eight houses of worship, with which two-thirds of the community's members are affiliated. These include a Roman Catholic church, a Ukrainian Catholic church, five Protestant churches, and a Jewish synagogue. Per capita income is third highest in the state, and 73 percent of the community's work force hold white-collar jobs. Per-capita funding for the community's five public schools is third highest in the state.

Of the 2,624 students in public schools, 937 attend three elementary schools (kindergarten through fifth grade), 634 attend middle school (sixth through eighth grades), and 1,053 attend high school (grades nine through twelve).[4]

Debbie, Melissa, and Mythical Texts

The stories of sexual practices most embellished during and after my fieldwork were about one girl, "Debbie." I heard about Debbie from boys and girls, from popular and not very popular kids, from kids close to her, and from those who knew her by name only. But I never spoke with Debbie about these stories or anything else. I talked only with kids who chose to speak to me. I was tempted, after I began hearing these stories, to figure out a way to get to know Debbie, but such an opportunity never arose. Even if it had, I was unsure how to gracefully discuss these stories without her thinking I only wanted to talk with her about these stories—which would have been true. Although my reasons for not talking with Debbie were motivated by my peculiar position vis-à-vis her and her high-school peers, very few people telling these stories had talked with her either. For them as well as me, Debbie was distinguished from others by what we heard and told others about her. She was a mythical character about whom grandiose tales were told, and telling these tales made Debbie and her exploits into events in which all participated with relish.

Whereas girls freely and gleefully talked about Debbie's exploits, they were neither free nor gleeful in talking about their own sexual experiences.[5] Only near the end of fieldwork did I begin talking comfortably with informants about sexuality—and then only with those I felt closest to. Even then I sometimes found myself in difficult situations, especially with boys who disconcerted me during such discussions by playing upon and reconstructing between themselves and me our gender-differentiated roles. I attribute these disconcerting situations and my discomfort to my sharing with informants American assumptions that sexuality appropriately belongs and is discussed in the most private of private spheres (Coulson 1980) and, most commonly, within intragender groups.

The contrast between informants' free and easy talk about Debbie and the constraints on their discussions about their own sexuality struck me as significant. To understand why kids freely discuss Debbie's sexuality but not their own and how this difference contributes to their construction of the sexual domain, the analysis of texts of Debbie's sexuality will be followed by an evaluation of texts that Melissa—a student to whom no exploits were attributed and whom I could talk with—constructed about her own sexuality. As I compare these representations, the teenage creation of the sexual domain will be articulated.

The following analyses focus on *texts* about persons, motivations, and events rather than on actual persons, motivations, and events. I do not know what Debbie did, experienced internally, or thought while she lived the experiences she told about, or even while she was telling me her experiences. I do know, however, how kids like Melissa express themselves and thereby interpret, construct, or reconstruct the events, people, and motivations represented in the texts produced for me.

My knowledge of boys' positions in these texts is even more distant. Because this analysis focuses on girls' representations of their own and boys' positions in sexual encounters, it does not examine texts boys produce about such encounters and thus does not provide insight into their actions, feelings, or thoughts. Boys enter the following analyses only through girls' representations of them in texts. Consequently, when I say below that girls assume boys do *x* or *y*, I do not mean boys actually do *x* or *y* but that girls construct boys as doing so. In short, although boys are historically, socially, and culturally constituted beings, here they are known only as mythical figures in girls' morality tales.

Stories of Debbie

"Debbie" is a high-school student in Sheepshead. Her peers describe her as very pretty, with a nice figure and good taste in clothes, and as popular. As one informant observed, Debbie "comes across to anyone that just meets her for the first time as a real innocent, sweet kid; I mean, like, harmless to anybody. But the story behind her is like a really disgusting one. The kid's into like a lot of kinky things." Stories about Debbie circulate among almost all informal student groups, leading many to say that Debbie is a slut, "the whore of Sheepshead high."[6]

The first and most frequently repeated story I heard about Debbie had to do with french fries. Debbie and her boyfriend Jack went to Burger King, bought several packages of french fries, and went to Jack's house, where he dipped them in her vagina and then ate them. This was the only story I heard about Debbie during the first fifteen months of my fieldwork. I heard it repeatedly in informal contexts, from the same and different girls and boys in almost all social groups. When I briefly returned to the field seven months later, another story had been added. On the previous Saint Patrick's Day Debbie was gang-raped by six local boys—some in high school, some who had already graduated. The boys were very drunk, came across Debbie, and decided to have intercourse with her. It was said she protested with the first one or two boys and then began enjoying it. Some informants had heard that Debbie might press charges against the boys.

A few months later when I spoke with Melissa about these stories, she told me several more. One night Debbie and Jack were at his house when his parents were out. He tied her to his parents' bed, and they began having sexual intercourse. His mother walked into the room and said nothing— though later both his and her parents forbade them to see each other. Debbie and Jack defied this prohibition by sneaking out of their houses in the middle of the night and spending time together. After a while they broke up, but Debbie kept up and expanded her kinky practices with new partners. Melissa once had double-dated with Debbie. The two couples went to Burger King, where Debbie and her date—not Jack, but a new boyfriend—bought several packages of french fries and ended the double date early to find a place to engage in her renowned kinky practices. Melissa also mentioned that Debbie had begun similar actions with Cool Whip and Chicken McNuggets and put ice cubes in her mouth when engaging in fellatio.

Stories of Sex

All stories about Debbie share one feature; they tell stories about "kinky" sex. As such, they implicitly contrast with nonkinky sex. First I will deconstruct the stories to elucidate contrasts between kinds of sexuality and their underlying similarities. This deconstruction illustrates how kids make sense of these stories *after* they have entered discourse. Then I will briefly examine these texts in the order of their temporal production, suggesting motivations for this temporal ordering of texts.

In all the stories save the one about rape, Debbie and her partners engage in sexual activities using objects in addition to their bodies. While each addition is a permutation of nonkinky or straight sexuality, these variations are presented as together constituting a domain known as "kinky sex." As one informant noted, "it's out of the normal for me. . . . it's gross. . . I look at these people . . . and I, you know, it makes me want to throw up. There's something wrong there." This statement represents kinky sex as abnormal or unnatural, repugnant and immoral. By implication, nonkinky sex is normal or natural, appealing, and moral. This opposition reproduces the general American proclivity to "draw and maintain an imaginary line between good and bad sex. . . . Most of the discourses on sex . . . delimit a very small portion of human sexual capacity [as good]. . . . The 'line' distinguishes these from all other erotic behaviors, which are understood to be dangerous. . . . The line appears to stand between sexual order and chaos. It expresses the fear that if anything is permitted to cross this erotic DMZ, the barrier against scary sex will crumble and something unspeakable will skitter across" (Rubin 1984, 282).

Melissa, whose texts on sexual practices will be evaluated below, implicitly makes the same point about the need to draw lines so she can delimit spheres of practices she feels comfortable with. She observed that "There's a cut off point there. I think if you go to bed with somebody because its love and you're going out with a guy for awhile, I think then its all right. But, um, people who just go to bed with other people just for, uh, something to do, you know, like, uh, on a date or something, that's a whore." Drawing a line is critical to the construction of sexual—and other—practices. It enables kids to specify components comprising the restricted domain of "all right" sexual practices that should further provide them with a means of proceeding in sexual situations. As will be seen below, the process of drawing the line is highly problematic. The only thing that is clear is that a line must be drawn.

All stories of Debbie's kinky sex except the rape use mass-produced and heavily advertised food products. In a culture where distinctions between persons emerge during production and producers mask such differences by shifting workers' attention from the process of production to products for consumption, advertisements rely heavily on this shift toward self-definition with commodities (Ewen 1976; Williamson 1978). Although advertisements frequently link commodities with sexuality to enhance their desirability, Debbie's practices invert this logic. Using food to enhance sex expresses her resistance to this logic. Debbie's relatively tame and middle-class kinky sex may be seen as an exploration and transformation of conventional power relations in capitalist cultures that, however, generally reproduces or embellishes rather than transforms traditional sexual roles and their implicit power relations (*Z/G* 1980). The recent proliferation of fellatio and cunnilingus as "normal" sexual practices suggests that a predisposition to conjoin oral and genital desires and organs motivates an association of food and sex. Moreover, all the foods Debbie uses are considered "junk food," that is, food with little nutritional value. Since, as I discovered during fieldwork, teenagers eat junk food in excess when not constrained by adults to eat "properly," such food encodes one form of resistance against adult norms. Debbie's appropriation of such food in sexual practices compounds this form of resistance.

Advertising slogans may also contribute to her practices. Debbie's first and most renowned kinky practice was with french fries from Burger King, whose slogan is "Have it your way." Weren't Debbie and her partner doing just what the ad said? Her later use of Chicken McNuggets, a product introduced after my fieldwork, in the same way applies the preexistent logic developed with french fries to this new product, represented in advertisements as being dipped in a sauce before being eaten. Using junk food during fellatio and cunnilingus seems motivated not by love between partners but a desire to do something novel. As one kid said, "I guess its just like kind of an adventurous thing. . . . It's something new to do." Partners in a love relationship would not engage in sexual practices for the sake of novelty, but only to affirm the deep bond they share. In this and other texts, it is also suggested that the partners desire immediate pleasure (fast food) over long-term commitment and thereby seek to satisfy physical desires only. Such characteristics make up what teenagers classify as kinky sex.

Bondage, like other kinky practices, adds a commodity to the two bodies participating in straight sex and, in addition, emphasizes novelty over love. It differs from other kinky practices because it involves asymmetrical rather than reciprocal exchange between partners.

But these stories can also be read for the other element that emerges. At least until Debbie and Jack broke up, their kinky practices were framed within an explicit love story. Informants go so far as to interweave elements of the Romeo and Juliet story into that of Debbie and Jack, perhaps to ease their discomfort that two people who love each other would do such things. Like Romeo and Juliet, Debbie and Jack go to great lengths to see each other even when forbidden to do so. Both sets of parents forbid their association, though not because of family differences.

Thus, whether letting one's boyfriend dip french fries into one's vagina is a "kinky" and unredeemed search for physical pleasure or whether it is a form of romantic rebellion against accepted mores, it is not "normal." On this point the chorus of peers and parents agrees. And yet in the process of constructing kinky sex, normal sex and love are also constructed. Being able to differentiate natural or normal from unnatural and abnormal sexual practices provides kids with the analytical tools to make moral judgments on them, as Melissa's statement above indicates. Emphasizing novelty seems to deemphasize love while resting upon an understanding of what love entails.

Kinky sex differs from sexual practices fusing physical with emotional desires to affirm the bond of love between partners. The stress on asymmetry in the bondage story contrasts with mutuality in straight sexual intercourse. Most important, creating the category kinky sex by negating and transforming values that in other ways constitute straight sex enables kids to draw a line between kinds of sexual practices—at least with reference to what other kids do. The creation of difference between kinds of sexuality rhetorically enables kids to more clearly constitute the normatively desirable category. Constructing a category of practices that transgress the boundaries places limits on and elaborates values constituting the previously unbounded and ambiguously demarcated category of proper sexual practices.

And yet these stories defy the line they establish. Debbie embodies what most high-school girls want—good looks, a good figure, and social grace. However, her sexual practices do not match her social presentation of self. The discrepancy between Debbie's appearance and her practices is disconcerting; girls are led to wonder "about every other girl in school." While stories about Debbie seemingly provide a framework ordering teenager's sexual practices, the figure of Debbie herself contradicts this somewhat idealized framework. Girls also are troubled that these kinky practices at least initially occurred in a love relationship. If they happen in casual relations, they can be dismissed as expressive of a nonlove relationship. Their occurrence in a love relationship makes girls uncertain about who does what or ought to do what behind closed doors. They are unsure whether couples who love each other engage only in straight sexual practices.

These texts *seem* to articulate how to proceed and establish boundaries in sexual practices. However, they also suggest that this process and these boundaries are not at all straightforward. The line that is drawn between discordant features is tenuous. These contradictions indicate that girls use these texts to construct an alternative reading of their own sexual practices. That is, Debbie's defiance of preexistent representations of the female's place in sexual practices creates a space in which they can be differently interpreted. She gives new meaning to the values of equality and reciprocity and to psychological motivations representing love. Her practices suggest in part that girls, like boys, have physical desires motivating their engagement in intimate sexual contact. They want desires satisfied, and thus they seek equality and mutuality at the level of physical desires alone.

This new representation, however, remains partial; it occurs in a text of extraordinary sexual practices. It is presented as an anomaly that is difficult for girls to incorporate in their construction of their own sexual conduct. The discordant readings of Debbie's practices are set in a narrative structure emphasizing the traditional reading. The narrative structure places Debbie's practices in the foreground, thereby making it seem as though what happens is what she lets happen to her and thus providing the basis for morally evaluating only *her* actions. Consequently, ways her partner constructs this interactive social situation are not considered, nor are his actions morally evaluated. This socially constructed interactive situation is presented as if Debbie acts solipsistically. Her male partner is kept behind the scenes, while she occupies center stage. But it is not just the narrative structure of the kinky sex texts that resolves contradictions produced by components of Debbie's sexual practices. The story of Debbie's gang rape functions in part to more firmly assert traditional values about sexuality and thereby temporarily resolve these contradictions.

Stories of Rape

Debbie was raped on Saint Patrick's Day, the only schoolday when teenagers publicly and excessively engage in leisure pleasures usually performed privately and somewhat more moderately—pleasures only adults can appropriately engage in. They skip school, take the train to the nearby city where there is a parade, and publicly drink alcohol and smoke pot from the early morning onward, until extremely inebriated and high. They perhaps see some of the parade and they display their debauched selves in front of adults working in the city. Saint Patrick's Day is thus a day of ritual inversion.

This teenage manipulation of adult leisure pursuits on a holiday mirrors themes heralded in teenage "splatter films," suggesting that both sets of representations are constructed with values functioning for the same purposes. In splatter films, most commonly directed toward and seen by teenagers, "nice, middle-class kids [are] getting hacked and punctured . . . by darkness-dwelling crazies" (Herron 1984, 145) for violating traditional sexual taboos on holidays. As Herron observes, situating these morality stories in holidays "serves nicely to symbolize decadence. . . . tradition appropriates violence thematically, reading its presence . . . as visible evidence for the failure of liberation narratives, for the imperative need of managerial controls" (1984, 165). On these holidays male maniacs reaffirm traditional morality by acting violently toward females who transgress proper sexual boundaries and leaving alone females who do not do so. Females are bifurcated into good and bad—by actions they choose to engage in—while males' violent actions against them on a holiday reaffirm the traditional moral values that place females in these two categories. Good girls do not engage in wrongful sexual practices, and bad girls get what they deserve and presumably have been asking for by their conduct.

Some of these themes occur in the story of Debbie's rape. Like the "bad" teenage protagonists of splatter films, Debbie goes too far sexually. She too is violently attacked for sexual transgressions—by familiar white boys, not darkness-dwelling crazies, which perhaps reflects the less violent and final "real" rather than filmic solutions to teenage transgressions. Males representing traditional values literally impose themselves and their values on her during this holiday of indulgence. As Singer (chap. 5) and Myerhoff and Mongulla (chap. 6) suggest, holidays explicitly express a group's values. On Saint Patrick's Day, when one group's perspective is represented as common to all, a group of local boys impose their notions of right and wrong sexual practices on a girl known for having gone wrong sexually. Their actions enact and reaffirm traditional moral dicta about sexuality. Those who go beyond the bounds are brought back into the fold—violently, if need be.

Although the darkness-dwelling crazies of splatter films are not morally evaluated for appropriating violence in the service of traditional values, these local boys may be castigated for acting violently on Debbie, as indicated by the possibility that she might file a legal complaint against them. The ambiguity about whether Debbie did or did not bring charges suggests that these acts may be morally ambivalent, unlike those of splatter film maniacs.

This narrative is constructed like that of Debbie's kinky sexual practices. It focuses on and morally evaluates only Debbie's response. Thus the listener is made to look for motives not in the situation but in Debbie. Since no motives are explicitly presented and all listeners know Debbie's history of sexual looseness, it is this history that implicitly impels the narrative event. The structure of the text brings listeners to consider that these boys chose her as the object of their physical desires on a day when anything went because they knew she had a reputation for engaging in strange sexual practices. The narrative, like those of kinky sex, deemphasizes the role of the six boys. Their drunkenness on a holiday of indulgence seemingly absolves them of responsibility while allowing them to do what they want to do and what they think ought to be done to the girl with the singularly most tainted sexual reputation. Kids represent alcohol as a substance that frees people of inhibitions, enabling them to externally express their "true" internal feelings: "when you're drunk, it's what you feel inside. If you're raging up anger . . . when you get drunk, it comes out. . . . You can't lie when you're drunk. . . . I mean, you get somebody drunk, it's like putting them on a lie detector test, or giving them a truth serum." Thus, Debbie's rape poses these six boys as local heroes rightfully enacting internal moral convictions on the girl flouting proper sexual boundaries. As such, it fits with American legends about bad girls' sexual practices' leading to and actually providing the impetus for basically good males to act violently on them (Brunvand 1981).

This text also reproduces traditional assumptions about rape; for example, rape does not occur if a woman does not desire it, so if it does occur, the woman is "asking for it" (Brownmiller 1975). Males are absolved of guilt because this female, unlike others, provoked them. The end of the story, that Debbie has lustful desires, in part motivates the beginning frame of males raping Debbie. If Debbie did not have a renowned history of fulfilling kinky desires, she presumably would not have been their target. If she were not "asking for it" and "wanting it" all along, she could have stopped it or not enjoyed it.

More dramatically than texts on kinky sex, this text of gang rape delineates by negation kinds of sexuality and characteristics of girls engaging in them. "Good" girls do not engage in kinky sexual practices and thus are not targets for rape. If they were "asking for it" as "bad" girls do, boys would "give it to them" as they did to Debbie. This gang rape indicates that "good" girls do not have active sexual desires and only engage in straight sexual practices with their boyfriends. But gang rape is not kinky sex. And this difference is what makes their similar structures so telling. Kinky sex is represented in this textual discourse as volitional because it occurs between consenting partners. The term "gang rape," in contrast, indicates that more than one male forcibly has sexual intercourse with one female. Using this term in this text indicates that the situation represented is one of coercive asymmetrical relations between the genders.

However, in this gender-imbalanced situation, Debbie is shown responding to her male assailants as if she were in a love situation. Her response is made to redefine the situation as volitional, and thus the inappropriateness of her response is revealed. Such revelation further suggests that she responds inappropriately not just in this situation but perhaps in all sexual situations. More clearly than in texts of kinky sex, Debbie is constituted here as structuring the situation by responding only to internal lustful desires. By so constituting her, this text dramatically displays Debbie more generally as the person responsible for what happens in situations of sexual encounters.

However, components of this text also contradict this traditional reading. Debbie's possibly filing charges against her partners indicates she may not accept the traditional definition of females as bearing sole responsibility for actions in which they and males participate. However, the narrative presentation of her filing charges as a possibility rather than an actuality suggests that this alternative reading remains ambiguous. Another part of this alternative reading is suggested by Debbie's response to local moral arbiters' attacks on her. Her virulent assertion of willful lustiness that sets her even further apart from other females may represent female refusal to comply with the moral dictates that males establish. As the Knack say, "Good girls don't, but I do."

Thus far this analysis has been concerned with moments in girls' construction of the sexual domain when they place kinds of girls and sexualities in neat categories and seemingly resolve the ambiguities and dissonances they create when first introduced. These texts follow the "culturally dictated chain of reasoning" that Vance articulates, through which "women become the moral custodians of male behavior, which they are perceived as instigating and eliciting. Women inherit a substantial task: the management of their own sexual desire and its public expression. Self-control and watchfulness become major and necessary female virtues" (1984, 4).

The tragedy of the texts above is that in them girls represent themselves as moral custodians of male behavior. No matter what role males play in the events told about—and that role cannot be ascertained from data analyzed here—this analysis indicates that females construct their sexual practices in terms that put the onus of responsibility and definition on them. They construct sexual practices in the terms of a limited discourse that makes it difficult—though not impossible, as alternative readings of Debbie's practices suggest—for them to question or go beyond these limits.

However, these texts were produced in a certain temporal order, which provides further clues about their significance. The first and most pervasive text produced was that of the french fries. It was the only one that circulated alone during the entire period of my fieldwork. This text presented Debbie as letting her partner in a love relationship do what he wanted to her. It was followed by the text on gang rape, which also circulated widely. In the latter text Debbie let her partners in an explicitly coercive nonlove relationship do what they wanted to her. She is presented as responding as she had in the initial text—only later to reconstruct the situation by filing charges against her partners. The final set of texts produced were variants on the initial kinky practices. However, in addition to articulating what she lets her partner do to her, these texts also relate what she does to him. Moreover, some of these kinky practices now occur in nonlove relationships.

An implicit logic motivates the order in which these texts were produced. The first text is the most ambiguous. It suggests that Debbie engages in kinky sexual practices as part of a love relationship and thus that she and her boyfriend Jack defy traditional boundaries of sexual practices expressing love. Thus it provides a new definition of loving sexual relations: they can include kinky sex. At the same time, it questions the true "lovingness" of the relationship. The second text is also ambiguous, but it places kinky sex outside love. This text generates two contradictory representations; a girl can engage in sexual intercourse for physical pleasure without having an emotional bond with her partner(s), and a girl who previously engaged in kinky sexual practices is represented as a sexual monster voraciously seeking to satisfy physical appetites even in a situation clearly demarcated as asymmetrical and coercive. Unlike the first text, which resolves the relation between kinky sex and loving sexual intercourse by combining them, this text polarizes these aspects of sexual practices. Whether Debbie's practices are interpreted as "slutty" or those of a girl seeking to fulfill physical desires only, they are outside love. This second text suggests that there are two kinds of sexual relationships: physical and love-based. It thereby moves toward reestablishing the line drawn between kinky and loving sexual practices by the first text. The third set of texts further elaborates the implications in the second text. It more clearly draws the line between kinky and loving sexual practices by representing Debbie in various kinky practices transgressing the boundaries of a love relationship. Here she plays active rather than just passive roles (ice cubes during fellatio) as well as more explicitly passive roles (bondage). She also engages in such practices in nonlove relationships. This set of texts repositions the line between kinky and nonkinky sexual practices back where it had been originally. While these texts and the second suggest that females as well as males can have physical desires apart from emotional ones, they simultaneously indicate that the expression of such desires is not part of a love relationship.

The temporal order of these texts suggests later texts re-create the line between kinky and loving sexual practices that was disrupted in the first text. However, the reconstructed line introduces further problems. By suggesting that females as well as males can have physical relationships without an emotional bond, it makes it difficult to bifurcate females into two moral categories. Since drawing the line between proper and improper sex concomitantly separates good girls from bad girls, erasing moral judgments of females calls into question the segmentation of sexuality on which it is based. This continual production of contradictions suggests the girls have not resolved how to proceed and where to draw the line in their representations of proper and improper sexual practices of others. If they represent themselves as uncertain about this, is it not likely that they are also uncertain about drawing such a line in their own sexual practices?

By analyzing infrequently told private texts of their own sexual practices produced by girls who do not consider themselves sluts, we can depict their positioning of such practices. The following texts that Melissa generates provide the basis for an analysis of how such girls construct their own sexual practices and enables a broader articulation of the ways girls represent the sexual domain.

Melissa's Dilemmas

"Melissa" is a short, thin, pretty high-school junior. She and her girl friends are among the most popular girls. They date more frequently than other girls, and the boys they date are the most popular. Melissa articulated two positions on her own sexuality in many of our conversations. The following analysis examines two texts she produced in one conversation. Each exemplifies one position. The first text articulates how love, as a value, functions in discourse. It poses equality and reciprocity leading to the formation of a group—of two—that is then affirmed unproblematically in and through intercourse.

This representation is unproblematic. It is produced at a time when

Melissa speaks of relationships *apart from* her experience. The more problematic second text indicates that the values constituting the process of love cannot adequately account for her experiences. Although the narrative structure of this text explicitly represents sexual intercourse as expressing physical and emotional bonds and is thus still framed by "love," components suggest that these bonds are divided by gender. It alludes to gender-differentiated motives, inequality, and lack of mutuality. Because this text represents the sexual encounter only with cultural operators that constitute the discourse of romantic love, other cultural operators cannot be clearly delineated.

In the first text Melissa articulates the position I heard from many girls in the high school, that heterosexual relationships potentially embody romantic love: "When you're in love and you know that you love him, then you want to spend all your time with him . . . and you get along great. There's a lot of communication and love. . . . I kind of look at it [sexual intercourse] as if, I mean, you know, if you love the guy and then you know it could be something beautiful." Melissa represents partners in heterosexual relationships as aiming to acquire the state of mind idiomatically expressed as "being in love." Partners in love share similar psychological motives; they "get along great" and have "a lot of communication." Their mutuality and equality are expressed through sexual intercourse. Sexual intercourse between partners sharing similar psychological motives in a reciprocal relationship can be "beautiful"—that is, a sublime and harmonious experience. It can be so beautiful because they *know* they are in love. They both have assessed how they feel about each other and their relationship. The physical union reserved for such relationships tangibly expresses and affirms the state of being in love. However, partners do not logically realize they have achieved this state. Melissa and others demarcate the movement to the state of being in love as "falling in love." Falling in love is a vertiginous, undefinable process bringing one to view oneself relationally. Kids liken it to "magic" and "chemistry," which connect entities previously separated and are known primarily by effects rather than causes.

This text represents sexual intercourse as a physical act expressing a prior emotional bond between partners. Partners who have fallen in love—that is, experienced the irrational process leading them to the state of being in love—enact and affirm their relationship of mutual exchange as equal, like-minded persons in and through sexual intercourse. In this text, unlike the cautionary tales above, components do not contradict their encompassing narrative structure. Clear-cut and explicit boundaries between sexual practices are represented as easily transformable when the relationship between partners changes. Because gender is never explicitly considered, different positions each gender may occupy in the text are not represented. Because relations between partners are presumed equal, mutual, and motivated by shared psychological dispositions, ways in which these relationships are unequal and nonreciprocal and reflect partners' different internal motives cannot be articulated.

This text complements the narrative structure of cautionary tales in at least two ways. While cautionary tales explicitly present clear-cut examples of wrong sex—and, by negation, right sex—this text represents how right sex ought to happen and what its components are. In addition, this text and cautionary tales both represent experience at some distance from the speaker. Cautionary tales speak about "the other kind" of girl. This text speaks of practices of "this kind" of girl *apart from* any specific situation.

However, significant differences separate cautionary tales and this text. The former, speaking to sexual practices concerning which the line between proper and improper is drawn, reveal ambiguities beneath the surface of kinds of sexuality. This text, in contrast, speaking to proper sexual practices only, is one-dimensional. Here girls are presented as having no problem knowing what to do when and with whom, and moral judgments of actors are not made.

In the second text, Melissa constructs her sexual experiences using the discourse of love at a time when love is not present and when this discourse seems quite misleading. There is no way that she can present her experience as idyllically affirming a communicating partnership, as the values operating in the first text suggest. Rather, the encounter is depicted as a power struggle between herself and the boy:

J. C.: What does a guy do that makes you feel that he really, that he wants sex more than you want sex?

Melissa: *He keeps trying, you know, he keeps on asking you.*

J. C.: Well, what about you saying no. You, like, moving a hand away or something.

Melissa: *But it's like [lowered voice] "What's wrong: . . . What's wrong with you?" [regular voice tone] "Nothing's wrong with me, I just, I just don't want to." [lowered voice] "Ah, gee." [regular voice tone] And then you feel like you've ruined his night, you know? . . . As if it was like, all planned.*

J. C.: Yeah. But what about him ruining your night? Uh, is that less important—at that time?

Melissa: *At that time, at that time, yeah. I think I feel as if I've ruined*

his night more than he's ruined mine. . . . . *And then I get home and I turn it and I'm like, "I'm not the wrong one, he is," you know?*
J. C.: *You said that if you say no you're going to ruin his night and if you say yes, you're going to ruin your night, not that he's going to ruin your night.*
Melissa: *Right.*
J. C.: *In other words, you're putting all the burden on yourself.*
Melissa: *Yeah.*
J. C.: *So, do you feel that the situation, either way you lose?*
Melissa: *Well, I think that I can control the situation all by myself.*
J. C.: *How?*
Melissa: *I can say yes or no. I can regret it or I can enjoy it. I, um, I don't have to satisfy anybody out there, you know, I really don't.*

Melissa does not speak of sexuality and love fused but speaks only of sexuality. She represents her partner's and her own physical and emotional desires as differentiated by gender. The boy wants to have sexual intercourse and she does not. Unlike his articulated desire for a physical relationship, Melissa is mute about her desire for an emotional relationship underlying such a physical relationship. She responds to her partner's request to satisfy his desires by saying no and uncomfortably states that she does not want to. Despite the separation of sex from love and the gender-based division of desires, Melissa represents this situation with a narrative structure where partners have a relationship in which each can ask for what he or she wants. She constructs her partner as desiring a physical relationship with her and herself as being able to do what she wants in response; she can "say yes or no."

However, components of this situation suggest that these values function differently than Melissa indicates. Melissa's statement reveals that her partner's desires for a sexually intimate relationship with her are those that are negotiated. Yet his desires only provide background for textual action centering on her response to his articulated desires. Centering on *her* response prevents her from seeing how it is structured by *his* request to satisfy his desires.

By so ignoring the determining framework, Melissa cannot articulate why she wants to say no to his request. She positions the boy as assuming something is wrong with her for not wanting to engage in sexual intercourse. Despite her protestations that "nothing's wrong with me," she accepts a discussion of the possibility and deals with it as if the matter at hand were an emotional one. She does not know why she wants to give this answer; she can only state she does not "want to." This brings her back to the discourse of romantic love; she cannot have sex without love. Her inability to articulate the asymmetries in the situation is made into an affirmation of her independent agency as an individual who "doesn't have to satisfy anybody, you know."

The discourse of romantic love hides other values in process. It masks the "double standard" that morally evaluates only a girl's sexual practices. Melissa applies to her discourse about her sexual practices the same logic she applies to her representation of practices of sexually loose girls like Debbie. As her earlier statement about a cutoff point indicates, she assumes girls' practices are morally evaluated based on where they draw this line. She fears saying yes too soon will position her on the side of the line where Debbie is. Girls having sexual intercourse *when they know* they are in love are represented as good, while those doing so without such knowledge are sluts. However, this discourse provides no clues about *how* to draw this line or what to do if one is uncertain whether one is in love.

Although knowledge of one's own and one's partner's internal motivations is necessary, Melissa's text implicitly illuminates how difficult it is to acquire this knowledge. She can assess her own internal motivations to decide if she loves her partner, but she cannot easily ascertain if he loves her. He does not have to articulate how he feels about her emotionally when he proposes sexual intercourse. On the other hand, her response to him in this situation rests on *her* assessment of her feelings about him and his about her. She will have intercourse only if she knows they love each other. Thus she represents this situation and its outcome as resting on her assessment of his unarticulated emotional desires and her articulation of her emotional desires. Given that he does not explicitly aid her in this assessment, she has difficulty deciding what to do.

Melissa positions the boy as setting the terms of the struggle. Despite this positioning, she does not consider herself powerless. She focuses on her decision to respond to this situation. She claims she "can control the situation" alone because she can "say yes or no." Her perception is accurate but limited. Given that the boy structures the situation to which she responds, this yea or nay capacity is a power; what happens next between them depends on her answer. However, by the time she reaches the point of making a decision she has already been vanquished. By focusing on her decision-making process, she is fighting on his turf and is unable to challenge his structuring of the situation.

Besides the issue of relative power that the discourse of love masks without erasing, there is also the issue of a gender-based division of desires. In Melissa's discourse, the boy desires physical intimacy but may or may not want emotional intimacy, while she desires emotional intimacy but may or may not want physical closeness. She attributes physical desire to her partner and emotional desire to herself and considers the site of negotiation between them as her turf. The emotional relationship she desires is unmentioned but presumed. To get the emotional closeness she wants she must provide him with physical closeness. To get what he wants, he only does what he wants. Only his desire for a physical relationship is articulated in this situation. That he might have emotional needs is not even implicit. Their relationship to date has been negotiated by her regulating satisfaction of his physical desires, which rests on her assessment of their emotional commitment to each other. Since she decides each step of their progressive physical involvement based on her assessment of their emotional involvement, it is up to her to determine his emotional involvement. She has few means of doing so because he does not have to articulate his emotional desires.

Even when Melissa leaves this situation, she cannot easily develop an alternative perspective to that constructed with the determining discourse of romantic love. She does redefine the situation somewhat when she leaves it, as shown by her remark that she wonders if she "is not the wrong one, he is." Nevertheless, she has few discursive tools for exploring this possible interpretation beyond solitary ruminations. As I discovered during fieldwork, Melissa and other girls have few if any social spaces in which they can discuss nagging doubts they may experience during and afterward. Neither can they talk about the power issues or about the possibility that they too might have physical desires. Girls repeatedly told me I was the only person they could talk with about sexual experiences and experimentation. They represented their parents as disapproving of such experimentation and their peers as considering them sluts for even thinking about it.

But Melissa is not just mute about her own sexual desires. When she does engage in intercourse she does not find it pleasurable. She and the several other nonvirgins I spoke with about their sexual practices regretted having "lost" their virginity—that is, having given something away without receiving something in return—as the idiomatic expression suggests. They also found sex boring and blamed themselves for its being so. When I asked Melissa if her boredom was anyone's fault, she said, "I think I should try to get involved in it more than I am." Because she has no discursive means of articulating sexual desire, she cannot comfortably place herself in a situation where she is supposed to express such desire. Thus her statement is in part correct; her muteness makes it difficult for her to get involved in a practice constructed as resting on both partners' enacting and expressing of sexual desires.

Love: The Encompassing Value

This analysis of two texts that Melissa produced indicates both are constituted with the discourse of romantic love. Ironically, the first text, produced apart from lived experiences, provides values in process that she uses in her representation of her practices in the second text. The first text assumes that partners' equality and reciprocity are affirmed and expressed in sexual intercourse signifying love. Values are connected harmoniously to affirm the formation of a group of two where before there had been separate persons. Nothing in the text negates the discourse of romantic love because it is articulated apart from lived experience. Consequently, Melissa assumes it naturally functions unproblematically to represent equal and mutual relations between partners with similar psychological dispositions.

Melissa uses the same value to construct the lived experience of her second text. The results are less than satisfying. The narrative structure of the first text assumes both partners have similar desires and responses. The narrative structure of the second text, in contrast, indicates ways their desires and responses differ. It distinguishes between one partner's desires— the male's—and one partner's responses—the female's. Thus Melissa represents her sexual practices with a gender-differentiated narrative structure that is nonreciprocal and unequal and that assumes she and her partner have different motivations. But the unproblematic discourse of love haunts her as a spectre of how things ought to be and would be if she could figure out what she was doing wrong. Representing sexual conduct with values functioning apart from practice prevents her from developing the multivalent textures of textual meaning functioning in her practices.

This analysis of publicly told and retold stories of Debbie's sexual practices and privately confided stories of Melissa's suggests that American middle-class teenage girls use the discourse of romantic love to represent all sexual practices. In Dumont's terms, love is the encompassing value (1980b [1966]). However, the discourse serves different purposes in different settings. Texts of Debbie's sexual practices represented with this discourse permit a line to be drawn between kinky and loving sexual practices. Elaborating what constitutes kinkiness—that is, transgressions of loving sexual practices—also clarifies romantic love. Texts of Debbie's kinky sexual practices emphasize novelty over love, asymmetry over reciprocity, and inequality over equality and add commodities to embodied loving relations—and they thereby implicitly rest on an understanding of the discourse of romantic love.

Nevertheless, texts about Debbie obfuscate as well as affirm the significance of romantic love. She is represented as having desires for novel forms of physical intimacy in a seemingly traditional loving relationship, enjoying a physically intimate relationship divorced from emotional intimacy, and insisting such enjoyment is legitimate. These representations suggest that girls are unclear about where to draw the line between proper and improper sexual practices and seek to express physical desires with and apart from emotional desires, as they represent their male partners as doing. Such representations serve to provide space where traditional boundaries of sexual practices can be contradicted and transformed. This ongoing transformation as evidenced in representations of Debbie seems to be part of a broader process of transformation in teenage girls' representation of their practices. This transformation is succinctly captured in the line of the Knack's song "Good Girls Don't," "Good girls don't, but I do." The double standard remains; girls want to be labeled morally good rather than bad, but as the "but" in the line indicates, even "good" girls may engage in "bad" practices. The effect of doing so calls into question the line being drawn between good and bad and suggests it be renegotiated.

Ironically, while the discourse of romantic love provides means by which girls can represent sexual practices of "the other" that permit boundaries of proper conduct to be renegotiated, it limits their construction of their own practices. It does so because these practices by definition remain within boundaries of what is proper. In addition, properness first is constructed apart from practices in abstract statements such as that made by Melissa. By presuming a line already has been drawn between kinky and loving sex, girls have few means of knowing how to draw such a line in their own sexual encounters. Because they posit equality, mutuality, and shared psychological dispositions, girls cannot clearly articulate and therefore cannot transform inequality, nonreciprocity, and different psychological motivations or desires separating their own and their partners' positions. Thus girls represent their sexual practices with a discourse that cannot account for all that falls between the extremes of kinky sex and an abstract depiction of romantic love. They have few means of articulating their own experience.

When you see me in the street
You always act surprised
You say "How are you? Good luck!"
But you don't mean it.
Bob Dylan,
"Positively Fourth Street"

I see friends
Shaking hands
Saying "How do you do?"
What they are saying is
"I love you."
"Oh, What a Wonderful
World"

10   "Drop in Anytime": Community and Authenticity in American Everyday Life

Hervé Varenne

Community as Symbol, Community as Problem

My first major work on American culture (Varenne 1977) dealt with three main themes: individualism, community, and love. These words were borrowed from the vocabulary I had encountered during my fieldwork and captured some of the exotic qualities I had experienced in my encounter with small-town life. Yet while I knew that these were powerful symbols for my informants, they remained somewhat empty. I could describe the properties of each and analyze the impact of their use on everyday experience. I knew it was very difficult for people to formulate the role of their friends and family played in their lives if the stage was set for "individualism" (as when they were asked about their life histories). I knew they had trouble expressing disagreement when the stage was set for displays of "community" (as in meetings of friends, church services, or the public meetings of government boards). However, I was not attuned to the anxiety that went with the performance of the symbols. I was not ready to confront the kind of questions the participants asked about the reality of their individualism, the cohesion of their communities, or the sincerity of their loves.

At the same time, I began to read Dewey, Royce, Riesman, and Slater. I listened in some wonder to the utopian enthusiasm of the sixties with its straining for both absolute individual liberty and perfect community. My interest in "love" had much to do with the prevalence of the word in the popular art of the era. What I did not understand was that by adopting the vocabulary that was so generally used I was being caught within the limits of the tradition. An analysis I had generated from the point of view of an altogether naive "outsider" was being used for "insider" conversations. I was asked to answer questions like, "Are Americans real individualists?" "Aren't they mostly conformists?" "What do you mean, 'love'?" To such questions, I had a stock theoretical answer. I outlined this answer in chapter 1. There I tried to clarify the grounds that prevent me from answering these questions in the terms they suggest. If individualism is a context for life in the United States, if it is a way of talking about experience that makes sense in conversation, then it is not a psychological property, and I cannot tell whether any American is, in a substantive sense, a real, rugged individualist. Neither can I say anyone is not.

This theoretical answer, however, begs the question that my experience suggested. I may try not to answer a question that is put to me, but *I cannot prevent people from asking it.* To the extent that they have asked the question, my response, including my refusal to answer, is framed by it. I cannot escape America as long as I interact within the United States. This creates a modicum of difficulty for me that, I propose, is a general condition of all life in society. There is evidence all around us, as well as in our own lives, that recent outsiders are not the only ones whose personal experience is best understood in terms of their struggles to express themselves. Although much recent anthropology has focused on what happens when interlocutors can be assumed not to "share" the "same" culture (Gumperz 1982), there is a need to investigate what might happen when this cannot be assumed. This should throw more light on the concept of culture as a social process of co-optation when an utterance is used by someone other than the original speaker, in a different setting, at a different time, and for a different effect.

The first step in such an endeavor is to accept that questions the most "encultured" participants (whatever this might mean) ask themselves about the reality of their individualism or their love are questions that reflect anxiety about the relation between their experience and the language at their disposal to express it. When Jefferson worried about the exact phrasing of the Declaration of Independence, when Dewey questioned the conditions that would make a democracy possible, they cannot be seen simply as "doing their culture." At the core of this essay is an analysis of a moment in American everyday life where uncertainty and anxiety surface. Questions are asked that go beyond rhetoric even as they are phrased rhetorically. We will see a college student struggle with the failure of a friend of a friend to extend an invitation at a moment when such an invitation might be expected. We will see him confront the possibility that he himself might be seen as responsible for the failure. As he thought about the moment, he ended up asking certain questions of the type: Was I friendly enough? Was my interlocutor hospitable?

I will not answer these questions. My informant could not, and there are no grounds for me to decide for him. What is interesting is that he should have to face such questions, use a traditional methodology to try to answer them, and still be left with a puzzle. What is interesting is the suggestion of an awareness that these were not "his" questions, at least not at the early stages of the original event. He describes a developing consciousness that something had already happened to him that he now had to deal with. His concerns, whatever they were at the time, had been co-opted. The interactional process that produced this situation is the central focus of this chapter: How did friendliness or hospitality come to be at issue, given that it seems neither speaker wanted to bring up such matters?

The case study focuses the general statement I want to make, which, in deed, constitutes the contribution this volume intends to make to the field of American studies. American culture is continually practiced in daily life. It is not to be found solely in the statements of certain cultural specialists or during special ritual moments. Above all, American culture is a social, institutional event. It is to be found *in* interaction because it arose *through* interaction. Advertisers and moviemakers, planners of ethnic parades, college and high-school students, all are involved in America and in symbolizing it in their most concrete practices because they are jointly caught in a historical situation. What is clear also is that the situation within which all these people interact is much broader than their face-to-face interaction, or even the history of this interaction. Concrete difficulties that two people may have with each other are never purely private affairs. They always echo, and are echoes of, other difficulties that have been at the center of the culture's concerns for a very long time. A person's visiting the town where his interlocutor lives can easily raise questions of hospitality.

("Will she invite me?" "Should I invite him?") Questions of hospitality can raise questions about authenticity. ("Did she mean the invitation?") Questions about the authenticity of hospitality are fully coherent with the kind of philosophical questions about the reality of communities that have been the staple of American intellectual debates, particularly in social theory.

I begin with a brief review of the history of the use of the word "community" in these debates. This leads to an outline of the operations we must perform to recapture a form of innocent wonder when encountering the word. The body of the essay starts with the problems that surround the concept of "meaning" (as in "Do you mean it when you say you love me?") as it can be identified by analyzing the verses from the songs I have used as epigraphs. The next section consists of the analysis of two texts produced by an informant, which allows us to glimpse what can happen while relaxing with friends. This is followed by some suggestion about correspondences between the co-optation of experience that occurred at that moment and what seems to happen repeatedly in American sociological discourse.

Community and the Social Sciences

Historically, the power of the American conversation about community moved the social sciences into new areas of investigation. I understand the pragmatic movement, of which John Dewey was the most articulate spokesman in the early years of the twentieth century, to be a renewal of the traditional American understanding of human life as people joining together to create societies according to principles they jointly produce. If human beings could best be understood in this way, rather than simply in terms of inner drives of whatever sort, then it made sense to argue that, to learn about them, one should look at them in what came to be known as their "naturalistic" environment—that is, in the midst of their communities.

This line of argument moved sociologists into the neighborhoods of Chicago. It sent anthropologists to Mexican villages. It vivified the field by opening vistas on areas of human life that had remained obscure. It challenged earlier understandings of the ways people live their everyday lives. It produced lively debates that ended in an impasse, as well they should. Within a few years of the various general statements summarizing the what, how, and wherefore of the community study as method (Arensberg and Kimball 1965; Redfield 1960 [1955]), Maurice Stein proclaimed the "eclipse" of community in America (1964 [1960]), that is, the impossibility of observing "community" in the sense the discipline started with. No-where in the world could it be shown that people lived in well-bounded, self-determined, consensual communities. It had to be said that all villages and neighborhoods were part of various kinds of "mass societies" that constrained local initiatives and allowed social functioning without con-sensus. Thus the conversation Dewey and G. H. Mead had started reached a stage that radically challenged their premises. Local units, it came to be said, are best understood in terms of the struggles that splinter them and of the differences that can be observed within them; they cannot be seen in terms of the "common-alities" that pragmatist premises made one expect should be typical of commun-ities. Clifford Geertz's aphorism said it all: "Anthropologists don't study villages . . . ; they study *in* villages." And, he explains, "You can study different things in different places, and some things . . . you can best study in confined localities. But that doesn't make the place what it is you are studying" (1973b, 22). What Geertz says of villages is true not only of "communities" but also of any interactional set-ting we can imagine. However spontaneous a social moment may seem to be, we must understand it as part of something larger to which it is a re-sponse.

Geertz's statement could stand as the epitaph of the community study—that is, of the study of "a" community. However one might want to approach community, whether as a "whole," an "ecological system," a "social structure," a "typical biography," a "kind of person," an "outlook on life," a "history," a "community within communities," a "combina-tion of opposites" (Redfield 1960 [1956], v), one has to face the fact that in anthropology the community has almost universally ceased to be an object *of* study. For a few who are interested in American culture, it has instead become a subject *for* study.

The first step in this endeavor is to recapture a sense of surprise and puz-zlement when encountering the word, its synonyms and antonyms, the euphemisms that can be used to modulate its implications, and so forth. It is for this task that the sensibility of a foreigner who is still new to the coun-try is most useful. When I first arrived in the United States, one of the many things that did surprise me was the use of the word "community" in con-texts where I was sure it was never used in France. The University of Chica-go, I was told, was a community. Hyde Park–Kenwood (the university neighborhood) was another such community. And not surprisingly, given that I entered the country in the late sixties, I was also told that the universi-ty "did not care for the community" and that "it should listen to the com-munity." Moving from Chicago to New York, and from the late sixties to the late seventies, I encountered the word in many other settings. Rambunctious black adolescents in the corridors of the university were proof that it was "open to the community." The program that teaches English to recent immigrants to the United States is called the "Community English Program." The department where I teach is called Family and Community Education. Since the Community English Program and my department are housed on the same floor, we have had to tell many puzzled Colombians, Haitians, and Koreans that we know nothing about the English program. It seems at least to suggest that these people had learned the rhetorical implications of the word. "Community education" is a different field from "higher education," and there is a rule of thumb that says, "If you are looking for a nonacademic program in a large university look under 'Community.'"

I have lost my initial surprise. I have learned the power of a reference to community. I can see through someone's use of "community" to refer to his environment. I have learned how to defend myself against a claim of community. I suspect this gives me the same kind of competence with the symbol as people who have lived longer in the United States. I know about true and false communities. I know how to pretend to demonstrate that I am part of a community. I believe I know how to convince people I am not pretending. I hope I can tell when my claim is legitimate.

I have also tried to keep in a corner of my memory the awareness that the French word communauté cannot be used in most of the contexts where "community" is appropriate in America. George Herbert Mead (1967 [1934]) cannot write about social organization without using "community" as a synonym for it. The word communauté seems never to come from Marcel Mauss's pen (1950). The Sorbonne is never a communauté. A local hospital is always l'hôpital de la ville; it is never l'hôpital communautaire. One cannot translate into French the phrase "community college" without destroying the system of connotations that make such a place at the same time not quite a real college and a proof of the open nature of American democracy.

This is but another instance of the necessity of the general communications rules stating that, in all natural languages, (1) an apparently similar object, the "referent" of a word, concept, or symbol, say a hospital, can be in one language, for example, French, qualified as the hospital de la ville while it is qualified in another language, for example, American, as the hospital "of the community," and (2) the same symbol, in our case "community," can be used to qualify many different kinds of referents (localities, groups, types of persons, feelings). This confirms the usefulness of the methodological rule affirming that we cannot understand the power of a symbol by looking at the external, objective referents it can be used to qualify. We cannot substitute an object for the symbol, even if we present the object as nothing more than a token of a type. The symbol of community can be understood only in terms of its use—that is, in terms of the contexts in which an observer encounters it.

The Problem of "Meaning it"

The statements above are general analytic principles that frame the following analysis of a central corollary to "community," the symbol of "meaning." While the word "community" is used to refer to a social group, it is in fact appropriate only when used for a *special* kind of group, a group that is more than a simple aggregate of strangers. Groups of strangers "become" communities as they achieve a certain "sense" of themselves. This sense is a psychological state that must be "shared" by the members of the potential community. This sense can be made manifest in various ways. Most important, it is possible and appropriate to question these external signs for their "meaning"—that is, for the extent to which the signs actually refer to the internal state they are supposed to signal. It is agreed that people may lie, that their attachment to the community may be superficial, inauthentic, or opportunistic. The corpus I will be using consists of several examples of conversations about the authenticity of an expression of community:

a. a few verses from two songs (see epigraph);
b. the transcription of a few seconds of taped conversation between two persons during their first meeting (text 1);
c. a statement written by one of the participants in this conversation as an exercise for one of my classes (text 2);
d. the transcription of the interview about b and c that I conducted with this person on a subsequent occasion.

The problem of "meaning" is most clearly outlined in Bob Dylan's song, "You say 'How are you? Good luck!' But you don't *mean* it." My immediate goal is to demonstrate how these words belong to the set that also includes "community." I will first show how the words "meaning" and "love" are related in the two songs I am using.

The songs, obviously, are just that—songs. They belong to an artistic genre. They are not equivalent to actual conversations. Both, however, *represent* conversations:

When you see me in the street, you always act surprised. You say:

"How are you? Good luck!"

I see friends shaking hands, saying "How do you do?"
In both cases the rhetorical shape is that of a description of an event. In one case the speaker is constructed as a participant, in the other as an observer. This is almost ethnographic in quality, except perhaps for the comments "you always act surprised" and the word "friends."

The songwriters, however, do not stop with a description of a conversation. They add:

But you don't mean it.

What they are saying is "I love you."
These statements are not presented as an observation of the same sort as the description of the encounter. This is an account of something that was *not* said by the protagonists. It is, however, something that *can* be said— but not anywhere. Given our own generalized cultural knowledge, we might say that, in a face-to-face casual meeting in the street, there is a rule against making statements like *"How are you? I don't mean it!"[1] And one cannot quite say "I love you" when the occasion calls for "How do you do?"

Yet a blanket statement of such a rule would be an overgeneralization. I am sure most Americans could think of situations when these could be said appropriately or actually were said with more or less serious consequences. Certainly, the unsayable can be said in a song. We will soon look at another such setting. What is certain, however, is that the statements about "meaning" and "love" are not quite equivalent to statements about "seeing." "Meaning" and "love" come *after* "seeing." They are marked as commentary. They are a restatement that balances the descriptive saying. The sequence has the following general shape:

One says   . . .   what [I say] one is "really" saying
[statement]   . . .   [commentary]

A dichotomy is thereby created between two aspects of the speaker(s): what is *outwardly* observable and what is also *inwardly* happening. The gap between the two is both accounted for and constructed by the symbol of "meaning." We would not need such a symbol were there no gap between what we can observe and what we know could be observed but is not available to our observation. The gap would have a different shape if the symbol had different properties.

One of the things we can "mean" when saying "How do you do?" is "I love you." Other things can also happen. In particular, we can *not* mean "it." What is this "it"? In Dylan's song, the "it" in "but you don't mean *it*" refers grammatically to the phrases "How are you? Good luck!" But these phrases are emptied of their semantic content by the commentary. The speaker does not doubt that a question about his state of being has been asked. He doubts the presence of the intention that should underlie the question. The "it" is the implied intention, not the greeting itself. On strictly structural grounds, it could be argued that this "it" is "love," if we take literally the other song about the real meaning of a handshake. Such an analysis might make us lose sight of the fact that it may be important that, in settings where "meaning it" is questioned, the "it" is precisely *not* specified. Strictly speaking, that is, purely in terms of the text under consideration, the possibility of "not meaning" implies the presence of an "it" (an object?) that is the referent to the greeting. This "it" is neither specified nor described within the greeting itself. This "unmentionable" "it," however, is rather well specified grammatically. A "meaning" has a *personal* subject and a direct personal object: a *person* means "it," which suggests that "it" points to a psychological state. "Meaning" concerns social interaction— and so does "love." This is enough to suggest that the structural analysis would not be stretched.

In fact, a general knowledge of American culture allows us to mention that there are settings within which the "it" that one means can be mentioned. There are conversations during which "it" can become the topic as one discusses "what did you mean?" (which implies an agreement about the possibility of "meaning" but no agreement about what was meant) or "do you mean what you said?" (which implies agreement on both counts but a doubt about the validity—or authenticity—of the claim). The case study I now turn to includes a text from such a setting when authenticity is appropriately discussed.

Dilemmas of Hospitality

There is a bit of wisdom that people "who know America" like to give European newcomers to the United States. It runs something like this: "People here will tell you after meeting you for the first time, 'Drop in [at our home] anytime!' But don't believe them! [They don't mean it]." I myself was told this a few times. Some Americans I have talked to about it have recognized it. I have also been the recipient of the ambiguous invitation. Through naïveté, ignorance, or self-serving callousness, I have "dropped in" on people whom I wanted to meet for ethnographic reasons, on the strength of their outward invitations—even when I had doubts about the sincerity of the invitation. In such situations, doors were never closed in my face. It is as if those who had given such invitations (even supposing they did not "mean" them) were trapped by them. They could not deny having given them. Some of my informants have in fact been outraged at the idea that people might systematically doubt their sincerity. As they tell it, when they say, "Drop in anytime!" they mean it. If they did not mean it, they would not say it.

We have here a new version of the sequence represented in the songs. There is a statement that is part of an interaction ("Drop in anytime!") and then a warning to consider "meaning." I would also like to bring in the issues of evaluation and rhetorical power that are closely tied to the issue of "meaning." They are of a different order, since the first is directly available to the informants in the settings when meaning can be specifically addressed, where as the second is not usually quite so available. For any one who knows Bob Dylan's "Positively Fourth Street," I will not have to belabor the point that not to mean a greeting is highly improper: the song is a powerful critique of normal American everyday life. Similarly, the bit of wisdom I quoted is generally framed as a criticism of America. The informants who were outraged certainly took it as such. It is altogether insulting to accuse someone of not meaning an expression of hospitality. The reaction of "Springdale" to Vidich and Bensman's book exposing the insincerity of parts of the people's lives is another well-documented case of the dangers inherent in telling Americans that they are not friendly (1968 [1958]; see particularly chap. 14).

Let us now look at an instance of what can happen when hospitality becomes an issue. The brief moment I use here was tape-recorded by one of the participants, "Ted," a student in one of my classes. His girl friend, a friend of hers ("Sally"), Sally's husband, and their eighteen-month-old child were together on an after-lunch outing to a park in Manhattan. Sally and her husband, who lived in San Francisco, had come to New York to visit relatives and had had lunch at Ted's. After lunch they all decided to go to the park. As Ted described it later, "We had what I'd call a standard sort of passing-the-time-talking conversation. Not terribly intimate, not terribly casual either." Ted remembers that the conversation regularly lapsed. Each time Sally introduced new topics to fill the blanks, always about her child. After twenty minutes in the park, Sally asked Ted about a nephew of his whom he had visited in Texas. This led Ted to remark that he had made the visit while on a trip to San Francisco. The brief exchange of interest to us followed:

TEXT 1

Ted: **Then**, *I went to San Francisco.*
Sally: *Oooohh*
Ted: *That was my first time.*
Sally: *So,* **we** *were ¡there!*
  Near there
  Anyway
Ted: *Yeah*
  Near there
  I was there [laughter] for a conference.
Sally: *Well*
  Next time you go there
  We'll
  Now you **know** *us*
  [nervous (?) laughter]
Ted: *Yeah*
  I don't think
Sally: *Mmm*
Ted: *I don't have any plans to go there again.*
Sally: *Oh, it was that bad?*
Ted: *No, it was very nice*
Sally: *Mmmm*
Ted: *But I just don't have any plans*

The conversation then moved on to other things.

The corpus includes two other sets of texts. Ted had taped the conversation as part of an exercise that included transcribing a recording and writing "expansions/interactions" in the style of Labov and Fanshel (1977). Typical of what he wrote is the following passage where he expands on the utterance from text 1, "So *we* were ¡there!":

TEXT 2

TEXT	CUE
Sally: So, **we** were ¡there!	*Contrastive emphasis on "we";* *laughter in voice on "there."*

EXPANSION

You were in California at the same time we [my husband, son, and I] were. But I'm not sure how much further I want to talk about this, since it might carry a question of hospitality. You know that we live there.

INTERACTION

1. We're not too keen on house guests, and we don't know you very well or the extent of your friendship with our close friend [your girl friend], so I don't want to invite you directly just now until we know each other better.

OR

2. and your girl friend had told us that you might telephone us when you were there. But you didn't. In fact, you didn't even mention it. Perhaps you didn't (or still don't) want to bother with us? So we won't make a commitment to you either.

Those who know Labov and Fanshel's work will recognize that Ted is rather far from producing what they expect an expansion or interaction to look like. Labov and Fanshel understand the task of the discourse analyst as making explicit (1) the information shared by the participants, but implicit in their actual speech (expansion), and (2) the actions actually being performed through the speech (interaction). What Ted did was to interpret all this as a call for writing a version of what he reported later as his internal speech during the conversation. The actual text presented here clearly *represents* this text in a quasi-literary fashion. It is interesting as a token of what an informant can produce.

What fascinates me in these two texts is the contrast between the apparent topics, between what is said and not said in both. While Ted presented these texts as a simultaneous whole ("what was said and what was meant"), it remains that these are *two* distinct texts that are linked together by a cultural act that affirms—against all rules of cohesion—their mutual coherence. Notice that in text 1 there are no specific utterances extending an invitation or rejecting it. On the basis of this text only, one would be hard pressed to make a case for its containing such an invitation and rejection. Strictly speaking, the utterances are generally declarative. They state facts:

I went to San Francisco.

We were ¡there!

I don't have any plans to go there again.

One might wonder about the contrastive stress on "we" or the laughter on "¡there!". But this would not lead us very far. There are a few obscure utterances:

Next time you go there, we'll . . . Now you know us [laughter].

I don't think . . .
Something, clearly, is not said here. But what?
I do not know whether any person confronted solely with the transcript,
even a well-enculturated American, could easily fill in the blanks left by
the protagonists and produce what Ted is certain were the messages:
   *Next time you go there we'll have to get together.

   *I don't think I would call you if I ever went back to San Francisco.
I believe I can assume, however, that once the unspoken has been made
explicit in this manner the new text frames the first as something that the
first text might plausibly have been about. I even suspect that, once the
expansion has been made, it becomes extremely difficult to argue for the
possible validity of another expansion, probably for the same reasons that
make it difficult to "see" alternative shapes in a gestalt experiment once
one has been found. The second text is fully coherent with the first. It is
something that can be produced by an informant, whatever may be our
opinion of Ted's grounds for producing it (e.g., we might say that his interpretation is "strained," that he is overblowing Sally's hesitation, that he
might be altogether "wrong" about what she meant). We may not be convinced that Ted was fully aware of all the possibilities that he later uncovered while working on the transcript. In fact, we should deliberately doubt
the accuracy of his recall. The only thing we know for sure is that both he
and Sally encountered some kind of difficulty subsequent to his mentioning that he had gone to San Francisco and her redundantly affirming that
she does live there.

Things appear clearer in Ted's expansion. This makes it even more imperative that we take a skeptical stance not simply about the relationship
between Ted's tale and the event, but also about our own relationship to
his tale. What are we doing to Ted and the tale when we accept, or reject,
it? Clearly, the expansion does not represent the "truth" of the event, even
for Ted. It might be said that it represents the truth it had for him in his memory. Such a statement, however, would also be distanced from the event
(the expansion) as something that we, as outsiders to the time and place of
Ted's writing of the expansion, are doing to his text. In all cases, the passage of time and the shift in setting are of the essence, with the effect that
uncertainty remains with us, albeit in different locations. A secondary text
may make explicit some matters that remained implicit in the original and
in so doing appear to clarify it. In the process, however, the secondary text
will necessarily rely on further premises that will remain implicit, thereby
compounding uncertainty.

That Ted wrote the expansion after the completion of the original sequence allowed him to read the first utterances of the transcript in terms of
later ones. He may thus see himself (or Sally) as already aware of the nature
of the difficulty at a moment in the interaction when we may doubt that,
historically, such a clear awareness was possible. Ted's interpretation
would appear much less convincing if something had interrupted them
right after Sally's "So we were there!" Given the new position of Sally's
utterance (from being an immediate response demanded by a previous
statement to being an introduction to a text that prefigures what follows),
Ted can now elaborate and affirm the relevance of matters that were not
(could not?) have been explicitly brought out at the time.

What Ted brings out are the matters of hospitality, friendship, and commitment. However, we cannot stop here, for these matters do not stand by
themselves as referential objects, the presentation of which closes the
analysis. Ted's text (text 2) should be set in its own context as an utterance
in the conversation he had with me as my student. One of the social goals
of the text was to convince me. To do this Ted assumes my understanding
of a set of conventions for establishing coherence in texts about invitations.
Thus he assumes that it makes sense to question whether an invitation is
seriously stated. He assumes the utility of a kind of ethnosemantic analysis
that could be shown to adopt the same epistemological premises as mainstream American structuralist semantics. He is sure he is entitled to be unsure whether it was. (He had little choice in this matter, since I insisted that
students be unsure!) He is rather certain that what was meant, eventually,
turned out negative (that the invitation was not made and that it was refused). But he is not certain of the exact statement of this meaning. Not
surprisingly, he would rather blame Sally for starting the sequence improp-
erly. We can assume Sally would not agree about his characterization of
her internal speech (and this would probably make her doubt the accuracy
of his rendering of his own speech).

In other words, the expansion process displaces the apparent location
of interactional uncertainty without clearing it. Whether Ted and Sally
"meant" what they did to each other is an area of absolute uncertainty for
the participants. This uncertainty would remain even if we conducted the
kind of detailed discourse analysis associated with Labov and Fanshel, at
the end of which it is claimed that "what really happened" in a conversation can be specified. In fact, the more people we bring to bear on the conversation, the less sure we could be. Indeed, it may be that the "reality" of
the conversation was only available to the participants in the original situa-

tion and that any attempt at specifying it destroys it. To bring in more participants (as Ted did by inviting me in as he offered me the transcript, and as I am doing when I invite my readers to respond to this essay) is only to increase uncertainty about the original event.

The original event, however, is not what concerns us. We are not concerned about Ted's "meaning" in the way the culture suggests to us it should be discovered. Rather, we are interested in the process that links utterances, and texts, as plausible responses to some earlier utterance or text. Our unit of study is the ensemble of the texts that were objectively created in response to Ted's original *"Then,* I went to San Francisco." I have focused on the link between text 1 and text 2, but the references I have just made to my own activity, and that of my readers, should make it clear that I do not consider this text (my essay), or the texts my readers may produce in response to it, as privileged in any way. What is important is that they should be produced and make sense in some social setting with some social effect.[2]

Similarly, we are not directly interested in the cultural competence that Ted, Sally, myself (?), and my readers (I hope), possess. Although I have presented Ted as competent, we might also focus on the incompetence he displayed when he failed to salvage the original situation. We are more interested in the fact that at the time he expanded the original text for me, and now, his contributions could be given enough sense to maintain the conversations. Whatever happened initially, whatever Ted's or Sally's intentions, they co-opted each other as I am now co-opting them and as my readers will co-opt these sentences. Uncertainty about what a person means, what some like to call a "failure to communicate," does not by itself prevent social life from proceeding. Social life seems to be responsible for it and, perhaps, to thrive on it.

We are back to society and to a cultural system ("America") for dealing with certainty and uncertainty. In this system, "topic" is certain in that it can easily be specified. The necessity of a search for meaning also is certain. The nature of the meaning itself is not at all uncertain: it will be about a questionable psychological property of the subject ("I am not sure," "I want," "We're not keen," "we don't know," "you didn't want to bother," "commitment"). It is the specification of the meaning that is made uncertain, thereby transforming a social event into a psychological one. The logic of this progression is not the only one possible, but in the United States it is very difficult to escape it. The statement of the logic of this progression (my "analysis") is itself bound by the conversation I have with an intellectual tradition that gives me words to use and will soon restate my own texts.

From Greetings and Invitations
to Hospitality, Friendship, and Community

A partial goal of the preceding analysis was to present another performance of the pattern we began identifying through our look at the two songs. I have wanted to make the case that the apparently philosophical issues raised by the songs are in fact simplified versions of common anxieties. The songs, or philosophical treatises about similar issues,[3] have the advantage, from an author's point of view, that they can be edited and that the audience is not continually providing a response that reframes his statement. In crafted statements, we can construct a response and not have this construction immediately challenged. In conversation the situation is more difficult. The audience can escape the control of the speaker. No speaker, however competent, can prevent a hearer from transforming an "innocent" hesitation in making an invitation into a refusal to make the invitation. At this point the original speaker must defend himself for something he may not in fact have originally intended. He cannot deny that he could, *possibly*, have intended the slight.

What can be said of the offering of hospitality can also be said of the authenticity of a community. To be convinced of this on formal grounds, notice that all the issues raised by Ted and Sally are triggered by the fact that:

1. a group of persons,
2. finding themselves in the same locality,
3. must do something together
4. while displaying a state of mind that is relevant to their congregation.

Issues of community are triggered by the same factors. Look at Dewey's statement about the foundation of a truly human society: "Persons do not become a society by living in physical proximity. . . . Individuals do not even compose a social group because they all work for a common end. . . . If, however, they were all cognizant of the common end and all interested in it so that they regulated their specific activity in view of it, then they would form a community" (Dewey 1966 [1916], 4–5). "Community" is relevant to persons who live together, who act together, and above all, who develop a shared state of mind. These assumptions have been at the heart of the sociology of community ever since.

In my earlier work (Varenne 1977, 157), I quoted a few lines from the paragraph that precedes the one I just quoted. Dewey said for me, "Men live in a community in virtue of the things which they have in common" (1966 [1916], 4). He said of the social process in abstraction what I wanted to say about the concrete premises of the American cultural construction of the social process. At the time, I mainly wanted to suggest the existence of a formal isomorphism between several types of texts (those produced by friends partying together, churchgoers worshiping together, and politicians legislating together). As I mentioned at the beginning of this chapter, I would now like to go further. The formal isomorphism between the structure of Ted's text and the structure of Dewey's does not simply reveal the operation of a single concept, notion, symbol, theme, category, or what have you. These words can be useful in labeling what we are talking about in texts such as this one—that is, in intellectual conversations. Both Ted and Dewey are involved with "community"—and so am I. Such words as symbol or theme can also distort our understanding of the scenes and texts where "community" is performed if they lead us to write as if those who are involved are simply "performing."

John Dewey, Ted, and Sally are not performing a drama for the edification or entertainment of an audience. They are not "actors" in a play that is proceeding according to traditional conventions. They are participants in a historical moment whose future is completely cloudy. For participants, the problem lies with establishing coherence between what has just been said to them, what they may want to accomplish, the symbolic tools at their disposal, and the utterance they are about to produce. Participants in an American context thus must worry that, while "thoughtlessly" talking about a trip across the United States, they will suddenly find themselves embroiled in a dispute about the authenticity of the community that someone might hold them accountable for being. What we mean by "full enculturation" or "competence" in this respect refers to the fact that most people in the United States probably do not worry about being "caught in community." Most informants, like Ted, accept the right of the audience to hold them accountable for being community-minded. Their concern is transferred to the matter of the authenticity of the community claimed, so that they will ask, Is this group a community? Can the signs the participants performed be trusted? These are questions that can be asked in everyday life, as the songs we looked at—or Ted's case—reveal. They are also concerns for sociologists, as Dewey shows.

In some cases, of course, the sociologist, like anybody else, may assume that, simply by virtue of living together, some group had to have been transformed into a community. This is not surprising, since the concern for community is both a model "of" and a model "for" behavior. Retrospectively, it is a framework for interpretation, as it was for Ted. Prospectively, it is the model for future dramatic performances—as it was for Los Angeles Jews when they planned their parade (Myerhoff and Mongulla, chap. 6) or for college students when they were threatened with accusations of racism (Moffatt, chap. 8). In all such cases, however, such a distance remains between the actual event and the abstract yardstick as to leave the participants in doubt. They must doubt that they have achieved community, if only because someone will always doubt their sincerity. Think, for example, about the controversies that surround the construction of the Moonies and other sects as proper communities. Think about the difficulties the Los Angeles Jews had in affirming themselves as such.

In any case, it should be clear that in America a concern for community is a concern one may legitimately have about some social grouping *whether or not the people involved are interested in being seen as "a community."* In fact, this concern is best understood as being generated by forces that are not, strictly speaking, psychological events. Community will concern you when you are in the United States, whether it has been internalized as a "belief," a "value," a part of an "ethos," a "character structure," an "ideology," or even a "culture." People are caught within the symbolism of community. Whether they believe in it or not, whether they value community or not, is another matter altogether. Indeed, "community," in its full complexity, cannot be fully "valued" as good things are valued. Like those Indian goddesses whose most fearsome aspects are but another side of their most beneficial aspects, community is as much a danger to American life as it is the foundation upon which relations are built. Community is as much a weapon in social struggles as a way to resolve such struggles. As such, it is a particularly effective tool for power in the United States that impinges even on those who "do not understand" the implications of the symbol, including those who may have internalized, for whatever reason, a "culture" other than the dominant one.

Community and American Culture

I opened the chapter with some reflections on the evolution of my own experience of what makes America American. From the position of an outsider enjoying the patterned exoticism of a foreign drama, I have moved to the position of an insider who has found himself, time and again, caught within the drama, manipulated and manipulating in terms that, I could see afterward, transformed my intense effort to deal with an immediate ambiguous experience into a fully appropriate American performance. I could look around me—at home, with my neighbors, colleagues, and students—and see others caught as I was. How often did I tease people by telling them "How American you have just been!" only to be answered more or less angrily, "It's fine for you to say, but it's irrelevant to the problem at hand." Some have even told me that friendship could be at stake if I persisted. Indeed, this essay is difficult to present to an audience that includes friends whose hospitality I have enjoyed.

Such experiences have led me to look for an alternative way of stating the American character of America. In the first chapter, I detailed a way of doing this that frees people who live in the United States and perform America symbolically from being treated as "oversocialized" robots. One can have lived for a long time in the United States, one can have performed America from one's infancy, and still doubt the ultimate efficacy of the interpretational structures that are one's sole resources. There is something optimistic in Dewey's general statement that men must have aims, beliefs, aspirations, knowledge in common in order to form a community or society (my paraphrase; 1966 [1916], 4). There is also something that could lead to pessimism if we expect, or assume, that consensus will necessarily develop when people live together. Ultimately, I would find it chilling to have to say that consensus is the condition of social life.

In fact, even here American culture offers an interpretative frame. After all, it is well known that the converse of the concern with consensus is the concern with the oppressiveness of a successful consensus. How is consensus to be differentiated from conformity? Shouldn't we be at work creating social forms that preserve the possibility of following different drummers? What about "freedom," a cultural symbol that is another attempt to deal with cultural arbitrariness, symbolic domination, external constraints, and uncertainty? From the point of view of freedom, lack of consensus is not something to fear. It is something to hope for.

Let us then hope for freedom, for the preservation of a cacophony of voices, including the voice that, somewhere inside us, tells us that all is not quite as we tell it. Let us incorporate within our theories of culture the fact of freedom—that is, uncertainty. As Sartre once told a journalist at the end of his life:

> The idea which I have never ceased developing is that, finally, everyone is always responsible for what has been made of him—even if he cannot do more than assume this responsibility. I believe that a man can always make something out of what has been made of him. This is

the definition I would today give of freedom: the little movement which makes out of a totally conditioned social being a person who does not give back the totality of what he has received from his conditioning. This is what makes a poet out of Genet, even though he had been rigorously conditioned to be a thief.

A degree of alienation from one's culture, a deep exposure to other world views and even a temporary period of living "as others" may indeed be necessary for heightening one's perception about the culture and society one is born into. For this very reason, anthropologists may be eminently qualified for the study not so much of other societies but of their own.

Sudhir Kakar 1982, 9

Epilogue: On the Anthropology of America

John L. Caughey

This volume is more than a collection of essays demonstrating the considerable interest symbolic anthropology holds for the study of our own culture. The book also challenges us with an important question: What should an anthropology of America consist of? Generally, of course, it has been assumed that anthropologists are especially qualified to study someone else, usually the people of traditional, small-scale, nonwestern communities. As Hervé Varenne observes, the whole discipline has been shaped by ethnographic study of "the other." And yet we can argue, as does Sudhir Kakar, that the experience elsewhere gives anthropologists a special opportunity to contribute something important to the study of their own society—in our case that of the United States. But just how is it that anthropologists are qualified, and just how should they proceed? There are many complex issues here—they have come up in the past and they will probably be raised again in the future.[1] But given the amount of anthropological work being done in the United States—and the relative lack of reflection on it—these questions merit more discussion now. Varenne has made a significant contribution by identifying many of the issues involved in bringing anthropology back home. In framing the essays of this volume as he does, he also offers them as examples of how American anthropologists can proceed in studying their own culture. In this chapter, I would like to follow up on some of the issues raised by Varenne, add some reflections of my own, and consider how these essays stand up as models for the anthropological study of American culture.

My own perspective on the anthropology of America has been influenced by both my research and my teaching. Trained in anthropology at the University of Pennsylvania, I have had two major field experiences with "the other." In 1968 I did eleven months of research on one of the Trukese islands of Micronesia (Caughey 1977, 1980). In 1977 I did six months of fieldwork with a band of Sufi fakirs in the Margalla hills of northern Pakistan. However, since 1970 I have spent most of my academic career in American Studies departments—at the University of Pennsylvania's Department of American Civilization, at the University of Islamabad's Institute of United States Studies, and at the University of Maryland's Department of American Studies. Here I have been working with colleagues and students from other disciplines who have kindly but firmly invited me to show just how anthropology is helpful in the study of American culture and how its methods and theories might be integrated with their own work in social history, the sociology of literature, popular culture studies, and so forth. During this time I have also carried out several field projects in the United States. The first two were in somewhat "exotic" settings, an Old Order Mennonite community in Lancaster County, Pennsylvania, and the locked psychiatric ward of a public hospital in Philadelphia. Most recently and most extensively, I did a field project on the consciousness and fantasy life of middle-class informants in my own social circles, mainly students, colleagues, and staff at two universities in the eastern United States (Caughey 1984). Each field excursion, but especially the fantasy project, has also confronted me with the special characteristics, problems, and possibilities of doing anthropology at home in America.

Anthropology: Away and at Home

To make a special issue out of the anthropological study of our own society is to suggest that such research is significantly different from traditional research elsewhere. Sometimes this point is denied; more often it is simply ignored. By their lack of attention to this issue some writers imply that research in the United States is a direct extension of our fieldwork with "the other"—and requires no special reflection. I disagree—the situational contrasts at home involve some fairly complex methodological and epistemological consequences. No one wants to paralyze anthropological research in the United States with excessive methodological introspection. But if we fail to take account of the special characteristics of research at home we hamper our ability to take advantage of the special opportunities available.

For my purposes, anthropological research can be understood as a special set of "social relations." First, the ethnographer assumes the role of participant observer and interviewer in relation to a set of others who more or less cooperate in the role of informants and subjects. Next, the ethnographer assumes the role of analyst in relation to a body of data, usually his or her records of local social behavior. Finally, the ethnographer takes the role of author and constructs a written communication, an ethnographic statement, aimed at a set of others who are to assume the role of audience / reader.

In the traditional situation, the ethnographer goes to an exotic nonwestern community and assumes the role of participant observer vis-à-vis strangers. As Varenne notes, the ethnographer usually has no previous experience with the situation studied, must struggle for minimal competency in the language, stays only a year or two, and never attains full membership and adult status in the community. The anthropologist's advantage is in his distance from the system, his comparative perspective, and his analytic methods. Usually the ethnographer relies heavily on key informants who are relatively aware of their own culture and who can directly inform or teach him about aspects of it. The anthropologist also seeks to use his data and outsider perspective to go beyond what people can tell him in order to uncover hidden tacit aspects of the culture. As for data, typically the ethnographer is restricted to the analysis of observational and interview records that he or she generates. Finally, the anthropologist constructs an ethnographic statement aimed not at the informants but at an audience of anthropological colleagues who share many understandings with the ethnographer but have little firsthand knowledge of the community described. Typically, the communication is intended to be descriptively informative in terms of anthropological assumptions about relevant ethnographic information and to contribute to current anthropological "conversations" within the particular theoretical camp with which the ethnographer happens to be affiliated.

When American anthropologists enact the role of ethnographer at home in the United States, the social situation of their research changes. It seems least different when anthropologists succumb to what Varenne calls "the temptation of the exotic," that is, when they turn to the study of American "fringe" groups that are "clearly differentiated from the mainstream." Just what mainstream American culture consists of is a complex problem that I will return to later. For the moment I will simply follow Varenne and note that anthropologists at home rarely study ordinary middle-class groups, situations, and roles. Rather, they study tramps, drug addicts, schizophrenics, Old Order Mennonites, reservation Indians, street-corner men, distinctive ethnic groups, or whatever—that is, people of groups and roles that "appear to intellectual middle-class eyes almost as exotic as the people anthropologists normally study" (Varenne, chap. 2). This kind of American research seems to parallel classic nonwestern fieldwork: the subjects' lives and understandings seem drastically different from the ethnographer's, the anthropologist reports to anthropological colleagues who have little or no contact with the group studied, and so on. In fact, such research is already different from traditional anthropology because even fringe, deviant, and countercultural groups usually have many important connections to the dominant mainstream culture.

As Spradley observes, the study of nonwestern cultures provides an "unparalleled opportunity for cultural discovery" precisely because "both the ethnographer and the informants are naive about the other's culture" (1979, 20). Because of their multiple links to the dominant sociocultural system, American fringe groups are usually far from naive about mainstream American culture. Spradley (1970) showed various aspects of this in his classic study of Skid Row tramps. Although tramps have a distinctive way of life on the fringe of American society, they are linked to the mainstream through activities such as panhandling and seasonal jobs and especially through their frequent experiences with dominant cultural institutions such as jails, courts, rehabilitation centers, and missions that seek to control them. Tramps do operate with distinctive cultural knowledge, including exotic systems of categories for aspects of their environment ("jungle," "flop," "bucket," etc.) as well as values contrary to those of the mainstream, such as rejection of occupational achievement. However, they also have extensive understanding of mainstream culture. Even their deviant values have a structural connection of opposition to the dominant culture; they are partially trying to reject something they know. Through their "translation competence" they can switch linguistic and conceptual codes and speak and act in standard mainstream ways with middle-class persons. Where it is strategically useful they can also play along with mainstream values, as by offering contrition for their drinking or expressing intentions of getting a job. At another level, they genuinely share many basic assumptions and orientations with the mainstream and hence with a middle-class American ethnographer. Few if any tramps were born to their current way of life. Most of them have "dropped out" of lower-middle-class life only as adults.

Something similar is true of the Old Order Mennonites. Despite their desire to lead a "separate life," they are intricately linked to the dominant culture through their farming practices, which involve numerous economic transactions with outsiders, and through their use of dominant culture institutions such as stores, hospitals, and public transportation. Also, like the tramps, some of their seemingly distinctive practices represent oppositional reactions to mainstream culture patterns. Not only are the Old Order Mennonites currently subject to mainstream influences, they have been so subject for more than two hundred years. Their focal religious traditions are also directly rooted in the European Protestant version of the Judeo-Christian tradition — the same tradition that underlies many aspects of the mainstream culture they seem to oppose. Even the psychotics of the psychiatric ward I studied are really very American. Their delusionary and hallucinatory systems are laced with American concepts, values, and orientations, including Judeo-Christian religious elements, standard materialism and success fantasies, and scientifically oriented delusions. Locked up for occasional acts of conspicuous deviance, they yet pass much of their day interacting in standard American ways with other patients and staff, and they spend large amounts of time absorbing mainstream information and images in front of the dayroom television.

Anthropological research with fringe American groups is different from the classic nonwestern situation because the members of such groups are neither isolated from nor naive about the mainstream culture with which the American ethnographer is likely to be affiliated.[2] Among other important consequences, this may lead the ethnographer to miss or to ignore cultural understandings that he or she shares with the fringe group as well as the audience of professional colleagues — understandings he would be much more likely to uncover if they were different from his own. As this process is repeated, each ethnographer focusing on what is distinctive about the group studied while overlooking similarities, it may well contribute to an exaggerated picture of the pluralistic nature of American society.

Varenne views the anthropological study of American exotic groups with ambivalence. He concedes that such work has value similar to the ethnography of nonwestern cultures: it adds another case to the ethnographic record, it may shed light on social and cultural processes, and so forth. Also, since these groups exist within the borders of our own nation, an understanding of their lifeways may have beneficial "applied" or "political" consequences. Spradley's study of Skid Row tramps led to legal reforms that helped alleviate some of the negative ways tramps were treated by institutions of the dominant culture.[3] But Varenne argues that the study of American exotic groups is not sufficient for a truly valuable anthropology of America. He insists that American anthropologists should also do the kind of study they have usually avoided—that is, they should bring anthropology all the way back home and take on the American mainstream: the suburbs, the middle class, the dominant "national culture" institutions.

In Search of the Mainstream

The anthropological neglect of the mainstream stems in part from an orientation to the study of exotic cultures. It may also connect to anthropologists' identity dynamics. As Gulick observes, "I think that middle-class American culture is probably the last culture in the world that most American anthropologists would be willing to study objectively by participant observation. This is because most of them are emotional refugees from this very culture" (1973, 1012). There is probably something to such explanations. But to characterize anthropologists as refugees from the mainstream is probably an exaggeration. As Varenne suggests, "We [anthropologists and other such intellectuals who like to place themselves at the margin] are not at the fringe, we are the center" (p. 37). I would guess that the truth lies somewhere in between. Most anthropologists function reasonably successfully within middle-class institutions—whether engaged in academic or practicing anthropology. But this does not mean that their attitudes and life-styles are not systematically different from those of many other middle-class professionals.

In a way this is part of the problem we are considering. It is a legitimate question about American culture to ask the extent to which some degree of alienation plus cross-cultural experience affects the way a particular class of professionals—anthropologists—play their various professional and domestic roles. But while Gulick, Varenne, and I know something about this issue from our participation in anthropology, none of us is offering anything we would accept as serious anthropological research evidence on this issue. We are simply offering impressionistic speculations. If we want to understand these and other issues, we are going to have to do some serious anthropological research on our own culture—which is just what Varenne is calling on us to do.

Why should American anthropologists engage in more extensive research on the American mainstream? First, we can never fully understand the fringe groups of America without a better understanding of the dominant culture to which they are linked and from which they receive so many important influences. Second, the American mainstream not only is one legitimate subject within the array of possible United States cases—a description of which ought to be added to the ethnographic record—it is a particularly important case. It is a massive, complex system that, as Varenne notes, is a dominant power not only on the national level but also internationally. To provide a full contribution to the scholarly interpretation of contemporary society, anthropologists need to take on the mainstream as well as the exotic.

Another, more controversial reason for studying the mainstream is that it seems to many of us to be a seriously flawed system. In studying elsewhere, our obligation or even right to criticize is at least debatable. But when we see our own culture as flawed it is "our problem" in a variety of compelling ways. First, to the extent that we personally experience our own culture as "spurious," it seems important not to turn away but to make it an object of critical inquiry. I use "critical" here not in the negative but in the literary sense of the term. If our own culture is a "text," then we should seek to understand its structure in order to identify its strengths—with an eye toward consolidating them—and to identify its flaws with an eye toward alleviating them. This principle applies to our personal understanding of how culture shapes our own thoughts, emotions, and behavior and to our understanding of how culture impinges on the lives of those we personally care about. It also applies to the understanding of cultural problems on the national and international levels. This kind of problem-centered anthropology is what Messerschmidt calls the "anthropology of issues" (1981, 5). He sees it as both a characteristic and a desirable trend in modern anthropological studies of America.

It might be objected that this rationale for studying the mainstream is itself an expression of the mainstream's deeply rooted and naively idealistic moral orientation as specifically shaped by recent experiences in the 1960s and 1970s. Probably so; but as a rationale for ignoring the mainstream, this interpretation not only would have to show the cultural origin of this impulse, it would have to show that it is futile, delusionary, or scientifically inappropriate. And that too would call for more careful research on our own culture. So it seems to me that any ambivalence or alienation we feel toward the mainstream should be reconceptualized as a reason for studying it, not ignoring it. Certainly many of our fellow scholars of America are not dissuaded by alienation. In fact, as Kakar (1982, 9) suggests, a degree of alienation may be beneficial—it can help us to maintain the "distance" that is often important in the study of one's own culture.

For the anthropology of the mainstream, an important but still unresolved and controversial issue is just what kind of entity the mainstream is as a cultural system. Even if we might agree on the identification of many American groups as "fringe"—that is, not mainstream—we are likely to find it much more difficult to agree on just what mainstream culture is, or even whether it exists at all (cf. Agar 1980, 42). Past debates have too often involved simplistic arguments about sharing versus diversity: Does America possess a single unitary culture, or is it a pluralistic, multicultural society? As the Americanist Murray Murphey has observed, this issue needs to be resolved through careful cultural research, both historical and contemporary, not ideological polemics (1979, 2).

Certainly those who approach culture as a system of knowledge have demonstrated that at a certain level of analysis there is considerable cognitive diversity within the American mainstream. To pass acceptably as a member of most standard mainstream occupational roles such as lawyer, psychiatrist, Mercedes Benz car salesman, or anthropology professor requires mastery of a distinctive body of official and unofficial operating knowledge that is widely shared within a particular role but largely unknown outside it. Similar variation is associated with religious organizations, voluntary associations, age and sex roles, and ethnic groupings. It is in this vein that Wallace suggests that cognitive nonsharing is not only a characteristic but a "functional prerequisite" of complex cultural systems (1970, 34).

At the same time there is also strong evidence for a good deal of similarity in cultural knowledge across the various sectors of the American mainstream. This includes various assumptions, rules, information, beliefs, and values. For example, there is widespread emphasis on complex conceptions of the desirable, such as occupational achievement, romantic love, and materialism, the conceptual organization of which is quite characteristically American. In my own work on imaginary dimensions of mainstream experience, I collected fantasy material from more than five hundred Americans with a good deal of diversity in ethnic affiliation, occupation, age, sex, region, religion, and the like. Along with some significant variation, I found striking similarities in fantasy life cutting across the various sectors of the mainstream. Many of these similarities were directly linked to widespread cultural values and themes mentioned above (Caughey 1984, 163–85). Like other kinds of cultural sharing, this similarity can be traced to various social forces that counter the centrifugal, pluralistic tendencies in American society: the national standardized educational, legal, political, and ritual systems and, in this case particularly, the standardized mass communications system. Many fantasy scenarios are lifted from television and movie productions, and the fantasy self often meets or even is transmuted into favorite media figures.

Varenne too argues for the presence of a distinctive American culture that is geographically widespread and historically deep. Building his definition of the mainstream around the idea of institutional constraints that make a difference in everyday social interaction, he suggests that themes like individualism and friendliness are important aspects of the structure. He shows, for example, that friendliness is a significant issue in American social interactions even when it might appear to be absent. Varenne does not paint a simplistic portrait of American uniformity. He fully recognizes that regional, class, ethnic, family, and individual variations exist. He argues, however, that many apparent differences should be conceptualized as variations of the dominant structural pattern. This approach represents an advance over what has been implied in some previous pronouncements about the presence of a single, unitary American culture. To an interesting extent it also converges with some of the more complex models of cultural structure advanced by cognitive theorists such as Goodenough (1981). Although we urgently need ethnographic work directly addressed to issues of mainstream cultural structure, it seems evident that in complex ways similarity, variation, and diversity will all prove valid and important.

The Mainstream Research Situation

With such a general notion of the mainstream in mind, we can see how research at home differs from research in traditional nonwestern settings. There are significant differences in our relations to our informants, to our data, and to our audience.[4] Let us assume, for example, that a middle-class American anthropologist is doing a comparative study of middle-class anthropologists and Social Security bureaucrats in Washington, D.C. He wants to determine if differences in their work roles are linked to differences in their social life outside work. Many aspects of the work of bureaucrats, with their extensive knowledge of Social Security policies, regulations, and procedures, will be unknown to him. In this respect—because of mainstream cultural variation—his research will parallel research with exotic American subcultures. In many other ways, however, the bureaucrats will be much closer to him. There may be significant variation, but he is likely to share with them many past experiences with similar kinds of families, schools, and colleges. They will share current kinds of friendship, marital, and economic relationships as middle-class professionals living in the suburbs of the same city. Here—and even more with the anthropologists—the ethnographer will "know" much of the culture he studies, in the sense that he is already fluent in many of the pertinent cultural domains. But as with language, to know a culture in the sense of being fluent in it is not the same as knowing its underlying structure. Like natives elsewhere, natives at home—and we among them—may not recognize the existence of linguistic and cultural structures that govern their lives. They may even deny that such structures exist. Significant aspects of our own culture are hidden from our awareness. They may be hidden because, like linguistic structuring, they are tacit or unconscious. They may be unknown because they are so familiar that we cannot "see" them. Or they may be obscured by our own biases, assumptions, myths, emotional involvements, and delusionary "folk beliefs." This is a major characteristic and a major problem of mainstream research at home.

On the other hand, cultures are such complex systems that our native fluency in the system we are studying is a tremendous advantage. In studying exotic cultures, we rarely obtain anything like full adult competency in the system. At home in the mainstream we have full adult status and a lifetime of cultural experience in the society we are studying. This gives us a wealth of knowledge we could obtain only by decades of involvement in a foreign culture. Also, much of this knowledge is more or less "explicit"— it involves aspects of culture that we can readily grasp analytically (Spradley and McCurdy 1975, 31–32). And even in relation to hidden aspects of the culture our fluency gives us many potential clues and leads—a significant advance over the ignorance that obscures our understanding of a foreign system. A useful aspect of this situation is that at home in the mainstream I not only can operate in the role of ethnographer, I can also act as my own informant. Through memory and introspection I have the opportunity to make my experience of America part of my data.

Our relationship with other informants is also different. It is true that people at home may sometimes not tell us certain things—perhaps because they think we should already know them, perhaps because they think we may draw unflattering conclusions an outsider might not. Our fluency in rules of interaction may prevent us from making those useful blunders that elsewhere are so revealing of unspoken constraints and rules. But there are many advantages at home as well. Being fluent in the language and rules of communication often makes it easier to build rapport. Knowing subtle cues, we can sense when we are treading on sensitive ground and take advantage of familiar strategies for alleviating anxiety or mistrust. In short, we can play our social relationships more smoothly.

At home, our relationship with our data is also different. When dealing with conventional observational notes or interview transcripts, we may fail to see patterns in the data because we are too familiar with the material to discover them or because we mistakenly believe that we already know its significance. On the other hand, we are less likely to make gross misinterpretations that are probably all too characteristic of work on exotic data, especially when interpretations are not checked by a fluent native. For example, I suspect that an outsider would have a very difficult time sorting out the complex attitudes toward kinky sex and romantic love that Joyce Canaan nicely handles (chap. 9). Our situation is also different in that we have access to—in fact, are likely to be flooded by—data that are traditionally not available in nonwestern research. For example, in studying Social Security bureaucrats one will encounter a mass of written material: huge telephone-book-sized tomes on esoteric aspects of bureaucratic procedures as well as in-house magazines and newsletters, business letters, official records and forms, and personal written material such as letters, diaries, fictional writing, and the like, not to mention various supplementary media material including the informants' favorite television programs, movies, novels, newspapers, and comic strips. A still further fund of data includes the massive historical record—archival materials as well as official and analytic historical treatments. This wealth of material obviously constitutes an advantage, if it can be integrated successfully with traditional ethnographic data. Carol Greenhouse's study (chap. 7) provides a fine example of how a rich source of historical data can be handled ethnographically.

Finally, as Varenne observes, the situation at home is different because the professional colleagues who constitute the audience are also natives of the culture anthropologists are writing about. This changes the level of communication used in the relationship. Consider the following ethnographic statement: "They bring their self-propelled metal vehicles, or 'cars,' to a halt when a boxlike device called a 'traffic light' displays the color red." Such a statement parallels information often provided about exotic cultures, and it would be very "informative" to an outsider, say a New Guinea highlander, interested in American culture. But to an American audience such statements will be utterly trivial. When talking to the native audience one cannot ignore the obvious, but one must develop a level of analysis that is informative. This is an advantage in that it encourages us to move into deeper aspects of cultural structuring. The audience's familiarity with the material discussed also provides a welcome check on the accuracy of information and interpretation. The natives can and will talk back from an experienced perspective: "I know that's not right because when I . . ." or the "Yes!" shock of recognition when a problematic aspect of the familiar is suddenly illuminated. Yet it is also evident that, as with any other native audience, their agreeing or disagreeing does not always prove an interpretation is correct or mistaken. The natives' folk beliefs, biases, and ethnocentrism, may render it difficult for them to recognize or accept interpretations that run counter to their deeply ingrained images of themselves and their culture. But a successful ethnographer should be able to point out such cultural barriers in presenting material that contradicts them. As in all those areas that make the study of the mainstream distinctive, we need to explore carefully the special factors involved and then adapt our research methods to take advantage of the opportunities and avoid the dangers.

In thinking about the anthropology of America, Varenne suggests that anthropology "must remain true to itself" in order to "contribute a kind of knowledge different from that offered by the disciplines traditionally focused on modern society" (pp. 40–41). One might question this. Why must anthropology remain distinctive? Isn't this an example of our own dubious concern with archaic "disciplinary" boundaries? It may well be that anthropologists working at home will sometimes produce work that is closely similar to that of other "Americanists." If such work is good, what is wrong with it? On the other hand, it does seem well worth drawing on what we do best, on what is distinctively strong in our own disciplinary traditions. As elsewhere, anthropologists should be creative in dealing with the situations they encounter. At home this often will mean adapting traditional methods to the special situations of mainstream research. It is in this sense that I fully agree with Varenne that we need to "reconstruct" anthropological research at home. This means thinking carefully about the anthropology of the mainstream as an ethnographic, comparative, and theoretical enterprise.

Ethnographic Approaches

Much of what is strong in anthropology is clearly based on methods for carrying out in-depth participant observation studies with manageable sets of human beings who represent a distinctive social sector or scene. It will usually be important to keep this ethnographic orientation at home. Several fine essays in this volume are ethnographic in a nearly traditional sense of the term. Moffat's study of college dormitory racism (chap. 8) and Myerhoff and Mongulla's work on an urban pilgrimage (chap. 6) have taken anthropology to nontraditional research settings, but they have carefully applied intensive ethnographic methods. Both studies depend in part on mainstream variation. They involve work with mainstream situations that are significantly different from those in which the researchers currently live. This allows them to set up relationships with their informants that in part approximate the traditional ethnographic model. At the same time, they are working with widespread mainstream themes, and I think their success also stems in part from their sensitive analytic orientation to cultural themes with which they are personally familiar. Thus they can play their familiarity against a variant form of the same theme in a different social context. But it is their solid ethnographic evidence from specific social scenes that confirms and makes convincing their insights and interpretations of mainstream issues. Many strong anthropological contributions to the study of America are likely to follow this pattern.

This does not mean we should not expand our conception of "ethnography" to take advantage of special opportunities at home. An important example would be studies of American mass communication such as Beeman's analysis of television advertising (chap. 3) and Drummond's interpretation of popular films (chap. 4). Certainly the data offer interesting possibilities, being rich and abundant, public and accessible. Through the wonders of videotape it can be recorded and replayed again and again and thereby subjected to the most intensive, fine-grained analysis. Furthermore, such data parallel the expressive materials often given attention by symbolic anthropologists elsewhere. Beeman nicely reveals an important appeal of advertising. Like personal fantasy, it magically resolves cultural contradictions — here the cultural imperative to "be individualistic and unique" but also to "conform and fit in." Drummond illuminates an important mainstream fear, the pervasive and varied threat technology constantly presents. Bond's appeal, he suggests, stems in part from his mastery and destruction of technological material culture. Both studies show how media dreamtime worlds provide an illuminating point of access to tacit themes in the mainstream culture.

However, neither essay is ethnographic in the sense of participant observation research. Further work on these topics would have benefited from such research. Beeman takes good advantage of one additional source of data, advertising how-to-do-it manuals. But it would also be of great interest to have some data from a participant-observation study of one of the advertising agencies that produces this kind of television advertising. Certainly such a situation would be perfectly manageable in terms of ethnographic methods. It would almost certainly produce rich additional insights. It would also further distinguish this work from studies of mass communications by other scholars who produce interpretive media studies similar to Beeman's. We should also pay participant-observation attention to the consumers of mass communication. This may help confirm—or disconfirm—interpretations advanced and should also generate other insights. In Drummond's case, for example, it would be valuable to know if different sectors of the mainstream make different "use" of the same Bond materials. An important development in recent writing on mass communication is the call for observational and interview work on the consumption of mass media materials in natural social settings—as in observations of television use in the home (Meyer, Traudt, and Anderson 1980). This call is seen as "nontraditional" and innovative since it is a new departure for scholars who have either ignored audience research or pursued it through laboratory or survey research and who usually lack any background in ethnographic methods. Here, clearly, is an area where the application of anthropological ethnography could add something important to the general scholarly understanding of a complex dimension of mainstream American culture.

I think we should also expand the traditional notion of ethnography in such a way as to take full advantage of our personal experiences as natives of the mainstream. Drummond takes a step in this direction. His nice rendering of the opening of a Bond film draws on his personal appreciation of the scene. But explicitly, at least, he does not use his experience as a Bond "fan" much further. I suggest that in studying any aspect of the culture we are personally involved in we should make explicit, systematic, rigorous use of our experiences. In anthropology emphasis is often placed on grasping "the native's point of view" (Geertz 1976). This involves some degree of direct participatory involvement by the ethnographer, but it usually implies a good deal less than "complete participation." However, the most radical advocates of the "inside" approach argue that partial participation produces only partial understanding: that the ethnographer "must begin by becoming the phenomenon" he studies (Mehan and Wood 1975, 225). Thus the anthropologist David Hayano argues that to obtain an adequate understanding of the culture of professional poker players, he had to become a professional player himself (1982, 155). This may be a rather stringent and debatable injunction for studying many American roles, including those of drug addict, schizophrenic, or Mafia hit man. But whatever advantages complete participation involves—and who can deny that they are considerable?—these are already available to us when we study mainstream scenes or roles in which we are experienced natives. Here we already are the phenomena we study. What is needed is a means of systematically using reflexive, introspective observations and integrating them with other kinds of ethnographic data.

Within the culture of anthropology, introspection has often been considered taboo. Jacques Maquet expressed the conservative view when he asserted that "anthropological techniques exclude introspection" (1971, 2). This objection may stem in part from the traditional assumption that anthropology is the study of "other cultures" and hence that introspection by the researcher is irrelevant. The objection also arises from the traditional social science prejudice that introspection invariably produces false data. In fact it has become increasingly recognized in many fields that in certain circumstances introspection is a reliable method. Certainly this is true in ethnography. As Wallace has shown, introspection is and always has been central in standard anthropology (1972, 311). In the field, ethnographers routinely ask questions that require their informants to engage in reflective self-scrutiny on aspects of their own thinking and cultural experience. This may involve trying to articulate explicit aspects of culture, and it may involve trying to dredge up, from memory, appropriate texts that allow the informant and ethnographer working together to make explicit the tacit knowledge implicit in the text. Far from excluding introspection, many anthropological reports are based on it (Caughey 1982, 119). As Wallace goes on to suggest, introspection may also be used as a technique by which the researcher studies his own culture, using himself as the informant; "for the anthropologist to record by writing or dictating his own thoughts about his own culturally relevant behavior involves only a minor difference from standard procedure" (1972, 311). Wallace illustrates the approach by uncovering and analyzing complex data on the cognitive processes involved in a familiar mainstream role, commuting to work. Those of us who have experimented with the approach in other areas have also found that it can be highly productive. One can gain obser-

vational access here to culturally rich inside experiences, internal dialogues, daydreams, and emotional reactions that one can never get at so
directly with any other informant. Although it is difficult to be objective
about sensitive aspects of our personal experience, there are vast areas of
many cultural domains where this is not a problem. For example, we can
potentially make good use of our experience of occupational, marital,
friendship, and kinship roles. We can also monitor our own reactions to
symbolic productions. As Bennett Berger points out, this process parallels
a favorite analogy of symbolic anthropology, the literary critic and his text:
"In the nature of the case, critics are interpretive; but they are reflexive
when they use their own response to text or image as more data for analysis
of the experience of the art work; I was particularly moved (or not) by this
or that sequence . . . why was I moved? How was it done to me?" (1981,
238; cf. Myerhoff and Ruby 1982).

It may be objected, of course, that such self-ethnography or "auto-
ethnography" is problematic because it is confined to a sample of one, and
a possibly interested or biased researcher at that (Hayano 1979, 103). Here
the solution is simple enough. Just as we can stop during or after an event
and analyze our reactions to it, so we can ask any number of other informants to do the same. Such an approach allows for systematically check-
ing and comparing independent introspective reports about the same experience (Caughey 1982).

An important aspect of this introspective process—as in other ethnographic work at home—is the problem of finding significance in what is so
personally ordinary. As Aguilar observes, "the conduct of research at
home often inhibits the perception of structures and patterns of social and
cultural life. Paradoxically, too much is too familiar to be noticed or to
arouse the curiosity essential to research" (1981, 16). Thus all the advantages of fieldwork at home—linguistic fluency, rapport, reflexive opportunities—may be negated by our failure to "see" the patterns we are en-
trapped in. This problem is often mentioned, but it needs to be explored
and analyzed further. Certainly one aspect of the methodology needed to
find significance in the ordinary involves systematically bringing to bear, at
home, another aspect of traditional anthropology—its cross-cultural,
comparative dimension.

Comparative Perspectives

One of the traditional rationales for doing ethnography elsewhere, in an
exotic setting, is the idea that as a stranger one can see another culture bet-

ter. Such heightened perception depends on comparison. It is enculturation in American society that provides the contrastive frame that highlights
distinctive features of the exotic system.

This aspect of comparison is important to Michael Agar's recent her-
meneutic examination of the ethnographic process. Emphasizing that
ethnography typically involves a special social encounter between an
ethnographer operating with one cultural tradition and a set of informants
operating with an alien tradition, Agar stresses the importance of "breakdowns." These are situations in which the ethnographer runs into something, say an instance of customary behavior, that does not seem to "make
sense," that surprises him, that violates his expectations (1982, 783). Agar
considers such moments a crucial point of entry into an alien system. In
fact, this notion of breakdowns can be expanded to include anything that
catches our attention about the alien system, including anything that
evokes positive or negative emotional reactions. Any such instance can
provide a means of discovering distinctive features of the alien culture.
Turning this around, we can see that one of the problems of the anthropology of the mainstream—especially in studying familiar scenes, roles, and
institutions—is that such situations are minimally productive of "breakdowns."

But this is true only if we do not go away, to do ethnography of the
other, before studying the American mainstream. With cross-cultural experience behind us, we are in a much better position to see patterns in our
own culture. Drawing on a paper by M. N. Srinivas, Victor Turner provides a nice account of this process. Our "first birth," he says, is our natal
origin in our own culture. Our "second birth" is our move from the familiar to do fieldwork "in a far place." "The third birth occurs when we have
become comfortable within the other culture—and found the clue to
grasping many like it—and turn our gaze again toward our native land.
We find that the familiar has become exoticised; we see it with new eyes.
The commonplace has become the marvelous. What we took for granted
now has power to stir our scientific imaginations. Few anthropologists
have gone the full distance. Most of us feel that our professional duty is
done when we have 'processed' our fieldwork in other cultures in book or
article form. Yet our discipline's long-term program has always included
the movement of return, the purified look at ourselves. 'Thrice Born' anthropologists are perhaps in the best position to become the 'reflexivity' of
a culture" (1978, xiii–xiv).

If we think of the anthropological journey this way, it will encourage us
to take fuller advantage of the possibilities. As breakdowns occur during

fieldwork elsewhere, we can try to treat them not only as clues to features of the other system, but also as clues to our own culture. What surprises us, interests us, or repels us is partly a product of our culture—the conditioning of emotional structures, modes of thought, and assumptions that leads us to perceive an alternative mode of behavior as alien. I remember many such experiences in my own fieldwork with the other, as when negative emotions welled up while I watched a group of young men torturing a white bird they had captured. Reflecting on the experience later, I found in myself an extensive set of orientations toward "pets" and other animals, ranging from the "Bambi complex" of middle-class childhood through experiences of hunting. I had acquired these orientations through my American enculturation, but I had not previously begun to grasp their complex cultural structuring. In such ways anthropologists might make interesting use of self-ethnography in the field, not only in monitoring our own perceptions and emotions, but also in attending to daydreams, anticipations, internal dialogues, and fantasies during fieldwork (Caughey 1982, 136). In anthropology we already have an emerging tradition of reflexivity during fieldwork, but this is usually advocated as a means of providing the reader with information on our field procedures, including the roles we played with informants. I am suggesting that we could also use self-ethnography to gain a better understanding of our culture by observing what happens when our version of American consciousness is subjected to a rather drastic experiment—year-long immersion in an alien cultural world. Just as we might treat any immigrant's reactions, fantasies, and breakdowns in a new social world as clues to his or her culture of origin, so too we can analyze our own reactions as clues to patterns in American culture. On returning home we might also seek to take more systematic advantage of the third stage, including the period of reverse culture shock, when formerly mundane aspects of American life stand out starkly as strange. To the extent that we have partially grasped another point of view, we should also sometimes be able to consciously assume it at home, as a deliberate research strategy, as a way of better seeing the American culture in and around us.

The anthropology of America would also be strengthened by more emphasis on traditional kinds of cross-cultural comparison. Most anthropologists would surely agree that an understanding of any topic of American life—whether legal procedures, kinky sex, reactions to popular culture, or greeting behavior—can be significantly enhanced by consideration of contrasting expressions of similar kinds of behavior in other cultures. Such contrasts are invaluable in exploring patterns at home. But in anthropological publications on United States culture, such comparison is offered much less often than one might expect. As a case in point, none of the essays in this volume is explicitly comparative. Of course, one cannot do everything in a single essay, but the pattern strikes me as unfortunate. Certainly any of the topics covered here could have been profitably placed in cross-cultural comparison with available evidence from other societies.

Why then, like many other anthropologists at home, did the authors not use comparative materials in these essays? In part this may be due to stylistic conventions. Just as we think, but rarely write, "In contrast to Americans who do *x*, tribe A does *y*," so in work at home we think but less often write, "in contrast to tribe A who does *y*, we Americans do *x*." Perhaps there is a feeling that the audience will already know how the American material stands out against the cross-cultural evidence. In fact, I think we should use comparative materials even more extensively when we are writing about our own society. This is because such material is so significant in revealing the cultural dimensions of the familiar, not only for the American researcher, but also for the American reader. And this is especially true in our writing on American culture, where our audience should be wider than fellow anthropologists. We cannot assume that other scholars, let alone the general public, will know how this or that topic varies in nonwestern cultures. By using comparison more, we can add something important and distinctive to general scholarly conversations about the nature of contemporary American culture.

Theoretical Orientations

Anthropology can be partially distinguished from other disciplines not only by its comparative, ethnographic traditions, but also by its culture theory. The various schools that have developed—symbolic, cognitive, adaptionist, and so on—as well as certain topics of theoretical focus—kinship terminology, social organization, religion, and others—have all been greatly influenced by traditional anthropological research with small-scale nonwestern communities. Because of this, a few writers have argued that anthropological theory is "inadequate" to handle contemporary American culture (Cohen 1977, 389). Whereas certain topics of traditional preoccupation, such as lineage theory, may be of little relevance, most anthropological theory, in social organization, economics, religion, and the like, has a much more universal orientation than such criticism implies; it is hardly restricted in its relevance to tribal or peasant communities. In fact, it can be more persuasively argued that our work elsewhere is what makes anthropological theory particularly valuable in understanding American culture. Unlike work in many other fields, our conceptualizations are not "single case" theories; they are based on something more extensive than information about Western society. On the other hand, as with our ethnographic methods, some adaptation of anthropological theory is necessary as we attempt to deal more extensively with social processes and situations at home.

One distinctive feature of anthropological theorizing at home—considerably different from our traditional situation—is that we are working on a society that has generated its own elaborate and incredibly extensive ethnosystem of scholarship aimed at self-understanding. Most of whatever we may choose to study already has a large body of literature, some done by other anthropologists. Singer's review of Warner's "Yankee City" materials (chap. 5) shows the good use that can be made of reexamining earlier anthropological studies. But most of the work on America has been done by scholars in other disciplines. As Varenne suggests, working at home we need to develop a more productive relationship to past and ongoing scholarship in other fields.[5] Instead of conversing only with fellow anthropologists, we need to both listen and speak to the current interdisciplinary conversation about the nature of American culture. On the one hand, there is what Varenne refers to as the "danger of parochialism." When Drummond seeks to "propose that the unserious fare of our popular movies has serious implications for the study of American culture" (p. 68). he is saying something new to some anthropologists. But he is also proposing something that has long been accepted, researched, and theorized about by scholars in other fields. At home, we need to orient our theories more toward what has been done in these fields, and in "popular culture studies," as in many other areas, this is extensive indeed.[6]

But as Varenne indicates, there is also the danger of overacceptance of the scholarship that does exist. Scholarship in America is a product of American culture, and it is sometimes adversely affected by an absence of cross-cultural awareness and by the presence of dubious, culturally constituted assumptions, biases, values, and political orientations. In this sense American scholarship becomes part of our data on American culture. One of our roles at home, as Varenne suggests, is to examine and question "the terms" with which the scholarly conversation at home is conducted (cf. Geertz 1984). Often this involves the use of what Anthony F. C. Wallace has called the anthropological "veto," the bringing to bear of cross-cultural evidence that exposes the false or limited nature of Western assumptions about human nature and social processes (1968, 42). Sometimes this may consist of presenting a single detailed case, as Margaret Mead (1928) sought to do with her work on Samoan adolescence. Sometimes it may involve analyzing materials from a variety of societies in order to test the conventional Western wisdom. For example, Peggy Sanday used a standard cross-cultural sample of 156 societies to demonstrate the false nature of scholarly assertions that rape is "inherent" in the societal relations between men and women. She not only found that many societies in the sample are "rape-free," but was also able to uncover social and cultural dimensions that correlate with rape-prone societies (1981, 25).

But it is all too easy for anthropologists to fall into their own trap here. Despite our work with other cultures, our own discipline has no fully privileged position. The anthropological concepts and theories we think with are closely linked to Western traditions. As Aguilar (1981, 26) notes, studies of other cultures by American anthropologists can tell us a good deal about American culture. The very categories by which we order cross-cultural materials—concepts like "religion," "rape," and "family"—are often partial projections of Western emic concepts rather than fully useful etic concepts. And as Varenne has argued, certain trends in American anthropological theorizing, such as our emphasis on the diversity within cultural systems, may stem from the influence on us of basic American values such as individualism (1984). An important aspect of bringing anthropology back home will be to bring it all the way back home. We need to consider anthropology as part of the general problem of how knowledge of our own social forms develops in relation to beliefs about real or imagined neighboring societies. In Hallowell's phrasing, we need to consider anthropology itself "as an anthropological problem" (1965). This will involve using cultural perspectives and ethnographic methods to study the history, current organization, and theories of the discipline as a subsystem of contemporary American scholarly culture. Here again we can obtain help from comparative perspectives, as by considering the work of other scholars on the emergence of other disciplines and on the development of Western social science generally. We can also get alternative perspectives from the work of nonwestern anthropologists and social scientists who have offered challenging critiques of many aspects of Western social science. And once again we can also make good use of our familiarity with traditional nonwestern thought worlds as a way of highlighting and questioning our assumptions about the proper mode of inquiry into the nature of human life. For example, the extensive body of knowledge in "Eastern philosophy" provides a rich source of parallels and contrasts.[7]

The issues involved in reconstructing an anthropology of America have far-reaching implications. Thinking about them offers us an exciting opportunity to look freshly at our own lives, our own society, and our own discipline. These issues challenge us to adapt traditional methods and to introduce new ones as we seek to advance our understanding of the culture we live in. Certainly the essays here demonstrate that an anthropology of the mainstream can contribute significantly to our understanding of American culture. As a native reader, I found that each essay offered something of that special sense of enhanced cultural awareness that good work at home provides—the recognition that, yes, this is an aspect of my life. Such illumination helps to confirm the value of this kind of anthropology. Given the extent to which our lives at home seem clouded by cultural complexities, confusions, contradictions, and poorly understood processes and forces, there is a clear need for further work of this kind.

Notes

Chapter 1. Creating America

1. I am drawing inspiration here from developments in ethnomethodology (particularly Garfinkel 1967). Elsewhere (Varenne 1983, chap. 12), I have explained at greater length the yield for cultural anthropology of ethnomethodological considerations about the relation of language to implicit knowledge. In essence I suspect it will prove helpful to look for cultural patterns in the way people "expand" symbolically on silence or on highly elliptical messages and in the order they give to what they mention (what comes first, what comes second, what is never mentioned unless there is much time or much prodding by an "outsider").

2. As Arensberg (1976, n.p.) puts it: "for cultural anthropology, three or more persons must be considered: the transmitter, the learner, and the sanctioner of cumulative tradition." I am grateful to Ray McDermott for suggesting to me that a fourth "person" should be included, what I call the "interpreter," that is, the institutions that frame the consequences in the appropriate rhetoric, thereby justifying the action of the sanctioner (my "enforcer"). For an application of this analysis, see chapter 10, note 1.

3. The Apache case is also interesting in that it shows how "different" cultures can make sense of each other. The Apaches can make something of American friendliness; that is, it is recognizable as a pattern that has power over them. It is also possible that we are being misled into thinking the joke I used is somehow "typical" of Apaches' ideas about friendliness. Basso may have included it, wittingly or not, because he knew it would be rhetorically effective with his (American) audience.

4. I mention the notion of "consequences," which I borrow from certain ethnomethodological writings, here in place of a statement about a "norm," what people "should do" under penalty of punishment. Such statements are often taken to mean that people will not do what they should and that their not doing it is evidence that they "reject" the norm or that they do not quite "belong" to the cultural group for which the norm is operative. I want to emphasize that no pattern is absolutely deterministic and that failure to perform the expected, whatever the reason,

can be handled in terms of the norm: it can have consequences in terms of the norm. This is an expansion of Bourdieu's (1977) analysis of honor in Kabylia. Not doing what one is supposed to do is not evidence that the norm is irrelevant to the group *unless it is demonstrated that the absence is not at issue.*

5. The argument I am making for the existence of a dominant culture in the United States is not simply a variation on Margaret Mead's old argument that, as Schneider puts it, "the middle class set the standard, stated the aspired goals, formulated the values which permeated every other strata of American society" (1980 [1968], 121). The middle class is interesting because within it American institutional constraints are least resisted, are least visible to the participants. Middle-class people are "dominant" because their refusal to revolt prevents the other classes and ethnic groups from succeeding in their attempts at revolt.

6. As against the various cognitivist understandings of culture, I do not think that culture has directly to do with "competence." Although the emphasis on competence makes common sense, our problem concerns above all *joint* (social) *performance.* The mystery resides in the fact that, when human beings come in contact, even when they know nothing about each other, they immediately begin to hold each other accountable for maintaining the interaction. In the process they organize this interaction, and it becomes possible to describe the institutionalized pattern analytically. This does not mean, however, that each protagonist will gloss this interaction in the same manner. The work of Gumperz and his students has shown that this is rarely the case. In this sense the "knowledge" each protagonist has of the other's "meanings" can be wrong without making it impossible for communication to proceed. What I mean by "culture" is the possibility of communication and its patterning and then institutionalization. I would define culture as "a historically constituted pattern of joint performance" (i.e., a *langue*—a social, not psychological, fact).

7. The normal anthropological mode, when writing about worldviews, particularly those more closely related to our own, has been critical. Our culture prevents us from seeing the other. It fosters ethnocentrism. This is true. It is also true that the converse of cultural blindness into certain areas of the human experience is a keener insight into other areas, a richer development of certain possibilities. America, like other cultures, is rich in particular human wisdoms.

8. In a recent article I explored at length the consequences of the search for the constitutive elements of the individual personality (Varenne 1984). My position is a much more radical rejection of what Shweder, in his introduction to the most recent summary of developments in cultural (symbolic) anthropology, calls the "five rules of thumb" or "heuristics" of the psychological sciences (Shweder and LeVine 1984, 3). The most basic of these heuristics is the third one: "What's real is inside the skin; the individual person is the sole unit of analysis." We all agree that this cannot be the case. We part ways in defining the central anthropological task. Shweder says that the volume "present[s] a . . . discussion of theories of culture, especially as those theories relate to current research issues *in the development of mind, self and emotion*" (my emphasis; Shweder and LeVine 1984, 1). Inescapably, in Western ideology, a concern with concepts like mind, self, and emotion is a concern with phenomena happening under the skins of individuals. A social or

interactional theory of the development of these leaves us with a (possibly "social") psychology, not with a sociology or an anthropology.

9. This phrasing implies, of course, that I see the census as one of the major institutions that appropriately represent America to itself. To do this effectively, it must present itself as a neutral mirror of social "realities." We do not have to accept this presentation of self!

10. It may, however, be politically necessary to "demonstrate" solidarity with "other" ethnic groups. The Los Angeles Jews, for example, decided to distribute green ribbons to signify their concern for the mass murder of black children in Atlanta. This demonstration of solidarity would not have been needed had the parade not been "Jewish."

11. This analysis is still preliminary and should be expanded. The domain of relevance of the issue of "competence" is probably broader than I suggest here. It seems clear, however, that "competence" is not universally relevant to all areas of family life (or school life, for that matter).

12. Interestingly, the "special" character of this response disappears as soon as the family becomes part of the "public" record through ethnographic analysis. At this point the family becomes the source for a new "next" behavior that is now controlled by the setting of the presentation on the family (e.g., the scholarly paper, the college classroom, the professional meeting). It is now easy for the uniqueness of the family to evaporate as it becomes a recognizable token of some well-known type.

Chapter 2. Doing the Anthropology of America

1. For an excellent recent review of this work see Spindler and Spindler 1983.

2. The reflective pieces by Wise (1979, 1983) are a good starting point for an exploration of American Studies and its evolution.

3. Clearly, the point here is not to adopt the Panglossian attitude that all is well in this best of all American worlds. Rather, it is to reach for a higher form of critical consciousness that becomes aware of the cultural grounds of our normal critical activities.

Chapter 3. Freedom to Choose

I wish to thank Elizabeth Bakewell, Roy D'Andrade, T. A. Durham, Michael Moffatt, Milton Singer, Hervé Varenne, and two anonymous readers from the University of Nebraska Press for discussion and comments that greatly improved this essay. I of course am responsible for any deficiencies that remain.

1. Schudson's insightful study of advertising (1984) maintains that advertising does little to increase sales. Rather, it reinforces existing patterns of economic consumption. Schudson does agree that advertising can adversely affect sales, especially when the product being advertised is poor.

2. Note Raymond Williams on the history of advertising: "The real business of the historian of advertising is more difficult: to trace the development from processes of specific attention and information to an institutionalized system of commercial information and persuasion" (1981, 170).

3. In preparing this study, the following professional advertising materials were consulted (these of course represent only a fraction of those available, but I attempted to cover roughly a fifty-year span to emphasize long-term cultural and historical trends): Advertising Age 1976; Baker 1961; Bauer and Greyser 1968; Benn 1978; Betancourt 1982; Brozen 1974; Buxton 1972; Caples 1957; Cowling et al. 1975; Lucas and Britt 1950; Malickson and Nason 1982; Martineau 1957; Paganetti and Seklemian 1982; Roman and Maas 1976; Sandage 1961; Starch 1923; Ulanoff 1979; Watkins 1959 [1949]. In addition, several studies of advertising by social scientists were also consulted, including: Geis 1982; Goffman 1979; McLuhan 1951; Packard 1981; Rothenberg 1962; Schudson 1984; Seabrook 1981; Williams 1981; Williamson 1978.

4. Schudson points out that demographic data are "the most consistently employed kind of data in advertising work" (1984, 64).

5. Schudson presents a diametrically opposed view. He writes: "the most evidently successful advertising is still advertising that abandons all efforts at psychological manipulation and just tells people that the product offered is on sale or has a low price" (1984, 64). Schudson's view is highly persuasive but at odds with those of most commentators on advertising. This diversity of opinion shows more than anything the uncertainty of observers inside and outside the industry about the utility and basic dynamics of advertising.

6. Note that the tendency of Americans to operate at a high level of generality was noted by Tocqueville: "The Americans use general ideas much more than the English and have a greater relish for them" (1969 [1848], 438).

7. Here Schudson is in some agreement with other commentators, though he still maintains that advertising is not very effective in making consumers do what they would not otherwise do anyway. He writes, "there is every intention of portraying social ideals, representing as normative those relatively rare moments of specialness, bliss or dreamlike satisfaction" (1984, 220).

8. One should remember that Tocqueville was not as favorably disposed to democracy as a social institution. He wrote: "Thus, not only does democracy make men forget their ancestors, but also clouds their view of their descendants and isolates them from their contemporaries. Each man is forever thrown back on himself alone, and there is danger that he may be shut up in the solitude of his own heart" (1969 [1848], 508).

9. Except in high fashion, where it creates antipathy, since it interferes with the rules for demonstrating individuality.

10. They can also be the most damaging influences on sales if the judgments are negative. Cases of this are numerous. Rumors that McDonald's added worms to its hamburger adversely affected sales in the Southeast. General Foods' "Pop Rocks" candy was rumored to cause cancer, and the manufacturer had to take out full-page ads in newspapers to combat the rumors (Schudson 1984, 94). Schudson claims that personal influence and word-of-mouth recommendations are far more important in affecting sales than mass-media advertising (1984, 95).

11. This is one of the oldest dicta in advertising, of course. It is summed up in the immortal phrase: "Sell the sizzle, not the steak."

12. Again, in keeping with his overall theme in analyzing the effects of advertising, Schudson maintains that such equations draw on established beliefs. Advertis-

ing merely invokes what consumers already believe. In particular, he analyzes the rise in women's cigarette consumption in the twentieth century, pointing out that this trend has strong social/cultural origins and is not really attributable to increased advertising (1984, chap. 6). Schudson's position is of course not inconsistent with the main point of this essay: that advertising messages in the United States draw heavily on themes that are already fixed beliefs in American culture.

13. Although Schudson believes advertisements that simply provide news of low prices or information about product attributes are more effective in influencing consumer choice than advertisements that sell images or rely on psychology, he also notes that price is itself a subjective variable in selling goods. Sometimes a higher price actually increases sales by enhancing the image of the product. The opposite is also true: "many marketers are reluctant to actively promote their products on the basis of price, with coupons or discounts or deals. They fear that such promotion, emphasizing low price, is ultimately destructive to the image and reputation of their product" (Schudson 1984, 114).

Chapter 4. The Story of Bond

1. Even in 1971 an interpretation of the Bond phenomenon as a British affair was inadequate, as Mordecai Richler's harsh criticism of Fleming illustrates (1971, 341–55). Richler thought Fleming a pretentious hack and his books execrable and attributed their popularity to their soothing effect on the ravaged self-esteem of the English. "James Bond is a meaningless fantasy cutout unless he is tacked to the canvas of diminishing England. . . . Little England's increasingly humiliating status has spawned a blinkered romanticism on the Left and on the Right. On the Left, it has given us CND (the touching assumption that it matters morally to the world whether or not England gives up the Bomb unilaterally) and anti-Americanism. On the Right, there is the decidedly more expensive fantasy that this offshore island can still confront the world as Great Britain. If the brutal facts, the familiar facts, are that England has been unable to adjust to its shriveled island status, largely because of antiquated industry, economic mismanagement, a fusty civil service, and reactionary trade unions, then the comforting right-wing pot-dream is that virtuous Albion is beset by disruptive Communists within and foreign devils and conspirators without. Largely, this is what James Bond is about" (1971, 350–51). It is difficult to see how Richler could have arrived at such a parochial interpretation of a craze then sweeping North America. Even in 1968, when his article originally appeared in *Commentary,* the Fleming novels and several movies had reached an immense audience across the Atlantic from "Little England." Did Richler really suppose that the seventeen-year-olds thronging movie houses in Omaha and Seattle (and even his native Montreal) had come to watch Sean Connery do battle with Rosa Klebb and Doctor No in order to revive their faith in a diminished England? The idea seems as improbable as Fleming's characters. Richler's distaste for Fleming and Bond are characteristic of the first-rate writer's feelings toward the second-rate. And his denunciations may carry some weight as political commentary as well as literary criticism. "It is possible to explain the initial success of the Bond novels in that if they came at a time when vicious anti-Semitism and neo-Fascist xenophobia were no longer acceptable in England, then a real need as well as a large audience

for such reading matter still existed. It was Fleming's most brilliant stroke to present himself not as an old-fashioned, frothing wog-hater, but as an ostensibly civilized voice who offered sanitized racialism instead. The Bond novels not only satisfy Little Englanders who believe they have been undone by dastardly foreign plotters, but pander to their continuing notion of self-importance" (Richler 1971, 354). As cultural analysis, however, this political diatribe does not begin to explain Bond's appeal to audiences—including the very "wogs" Fleming's "sanitized racialism" supposedly deprecated—removed in time and space from the concerns of postwar England. Unless one is content to explain away cultural productions with vague references to neofascist leanings and anticommunist bias, the task remains for cultural analysis to specify the particular appeal of the specific content of a movie, television show, sport, or style. Upon undertaking that task, one is immediately struck by the disdain Bond shows his superiors and their stuffy, bureaucratic rules; he seems far more interested in cars and women than in furthering a political doctrine of any sort. How Richler could have watched a Bond movie—if he ever went to one—with its endless chases, seductions, and flippant one-liners and come away with a gloomy vision of political intrigue and anti-Semitism testifies to the need for an anthropological effort where a literary attempt has fallen short. Whatever his political and historical antecedents, Bond is first and last a mythical hero in a saga that is continually rewritten to address the contemporary world.

2. For a discussion of the Dreamtime or Dreaming in its aboriginal context, see Stanner (1965). A translation of *alchuringa*, the concept embraces both a belief in a world dawn or genesis, when totemic ancestors were engaged in legendary deeds and the animal and human worlds were one, and a sense that those events are still going on, that genesis is not a once upon a time affair but, as Stanner phrases it, an everywhen. Although this concept has long been held up as a piece of anthropological exotica—a relic of extinct primitive culture—I find it particularly apt in discussing the mythology of twentieth-century America. The view of myth elaborated in the following pages consequently shuns the common interpretation of myth as the garbage can of history—quaint tales from the dead past—and espouses an interpretation of myth as a continuous rethinking of the fundamentals of culture. In this modern Dreamtime, our movie theaters are strikingly like Australian sacred caves, where initiates would sit entranced by the sounds and fleeting shadows of the totemic shades.

Chapter 5. The Melting Pot

1. Warner's definition of "ritual" makes all rituals symbolic: "The term 'ritual' means that the members of the association express in overt symbolic acts the meanings which socially evaluated objects have for them and that, at the same time, they also state in symbols what their relations are with such objects" (1953, 197). This usage and his distinction between "sacred ritual" and "secular ritual" derives from Radcliffe-Brown and Durkheim. The phrase "total social fact" derives from Durkheim and Mauss. For recent discussions see Lévi-Strauss 1976, 6 and Clifford 1983, 128–31.

2. The Western Electric study is described in Mayo 1933; Roethlisberger and Dixon 1939; and Homans 1950.

3. Warner sometimes refers to the "old Americans" as an "aristocracy" (Warner 1953, 55–56, 232), more usually as a "birth elite," the "old-family class," or "a superior lineage" (Warner 1963, 17). He also quotes Biggy Muldoon's reference to it as "the codfish aristocracy," a designation more congruent with Marquand's observation that there were only two families with authentic coats of arms (Marquand 1960, 265).

Warner's general terms "status hierarchy" or "class and caste hierarchy" are his usual polar opposites to "democracy" and "equality" but do not specify the specific racial, ethnic, and cultural hierarchy involved. For a rare expression of his personal attitude see Warner 1953, 105.

4. This social mobility theory of the melting pot makes use of the ecological conception of ethnic neighborhoods and successions initiated by the Chicago sociologists Robert Park and Ernest Burgess. See the reference in Warner and Srole 1945, 33n.

5. Specific textbooks are not cited, but Ernest Hooton, Harvard physical anthropologist and author of a textbook widely used in the 1930s, is acknowledged for advice on statistical analysis. Because Warner's rank hierarchy of "subordination" and "time-table for assimilation" use the racial classifications of the 1930s and distinguish invidiously between the "old" immigration from northwestern Europe and the "new" immigration from southeastern Europe, Africa, and the Orient, it seems likely that the Dillingham Commission reports of 1907–10 and the Laughlin report of 1922–23, which were the basis for legislative quotas in 1921 and 1924, were direct or indirect sources. Oscar Handlin, a foremost historian of immigration, has written of these reports that "by giving governmental and scientific validation to existing prejudices against the new immigrants, they helped to justify the discrimination against them in the laws of 1921 and 1924" (Handlin 1957, 109). Handlin also pointed out that this tightly intermeshed body of ideas, practices, and movements was shortly to vanish. "Somewhere in the mid-1930s there was a turn. Americans ceased to believe in race, the hate movements began to disintegrate, and discrimination increasingly took on the aspect of an anachronistic survival from the past rather than a pattern valid for the future" (Handlin 1957, 141).

The Yankee City fieldwork was conducted from 1930 to 1935, so the "timetable for assimilation" codified a "hierarchy of subordination" that was, in Handlin's view, destined to become an anachronistic survival by the 1950s.

Chapter 6. The Los Angeles Jews' "Walk for Solidarity"

The data for this chapter were compiled by Stephen Mongulla, who attended meetings of the Solidarity Walk Steering Committee from February through May 1981. On the day of the event, Barbara Myerhoff and students of Rita Lowenthal took part in participant observation. We wish to address special thanks to Alicia Gonzalez for bringing to our attention the material on the folklore of movement being done at the University of Texas—Austin and to Rita Lowenthal of Hebrew Union College, whose students assisted by interviewing various participants in the march. Thanks also are due to Marc Feldman of the United Jewish Federation Council of Los Angeles.

[Editor's note: This chapter is based on a draft written by Barbara Myerhoff for presentation to the American Anthropological Association meetings in December 1981. Tragically, illness struck her before she could revise it herself, and she asked me to do so for her. Death overtook her before she could read the essay as it now stands. I can only hope that I have not betrayed the confidence with which she honored me. It was a privilege to work with her material. All of us in anthropology and American studies profoundly miss her continued contribution.]

1. [Editor's note: Myerhoff and Mongulla's argument at this point should recall Dolgin's analysis of the Jewish Defense League (1977) as it attempted to establish its political presence by using the means inaugurated by the Black Power movement of the sixties, which itself based its action on a manipulation of the mass media's own structure, thereby either subverting the dominant cultural forms or falling prey to them.]

Chapter 7. History, Faith, and Avoidance

1. "Individualism" became a new word in English when Henry Reeve translated Tocqueville's *Democracy in America* in 1835. See Phillips Bradley's note to the 1945 edition (1: vi).

Anthropologists conventionally attribute this new usage for Tylor in 1871 or 1865 (for example, see Bohannan 1964, vii–ix). Williams, however, points to its development and application in the late eighteenth and early nineteenth centuries, as social commentators sought to distinguish the mental and moral life of humankind from the literal and figurative machinery of the new industrial age (Williams 1958, 16–18).

3. My fieldwork in "Hopewell," Georgia, took place from September 1973 through summer 1975 and in fall 1980. The first visit was funded by a training grant from the National Institute of Mental Health to Harvard University's Department of Anthropology. The second visit was funded by a faculty grant for research in the humanities from the College of Arts and Sciences, Cornell University.

4. All scriptural references are to *Good News for Modern Man,* a modern English edition of the New Testament preferred by most people I knew.

5. All references, unless otherwise noted, are to the White River Baptist Association *Minutes,* 1825–1911. Citations are to year and either page number or item number, depending on the density of references in any particular year.

6. Soon after the controversy over the abuses of the allegedly tyrannical majority in the minutes, the association began to record its votes—but only when they were unanimous.

7. Perin is referring to suburbanites in this sentence and contrasting them to city-dwellers.

Chapter 8. The Discourse of the Dorm

I thank Yanet Baldares and Susan Gal for help with many of the ideas presented here, developed in general discussions over the past several years; and I am grateful to Karen Predow, Randy Smith, and Sarane Boocock for useful discussions of the initial data. Specific thanks are due to Linda Nelson and Mwalimu Shujaa for a recent critical reading of an earlier draft of this essay and for making clearer to me the historical, political, and black perspectives on this material. At a cultural level, this essay attempts to draw on two rather different current approaches to the analysis of American culture: a cognitive approach that emphasizes modeling, precise replicability, and folk-conceptual "objects," which I draw most directly from the work of Naomi Quinn (as well as from Roy D'Andrade and others); and a structural, interactional, pragmatic approach best summed up in Hervé Varenne's recent work. I see the anthropology of American culture as making its valuable and distinctive contribution by rooting itself in the intense interactive small-group level that has traditionally been its chosen object, or in other sorts of close-grained empirical testing of what people "mean" (e.g., in well-designed interviewing contexts) rather than in free-floating interpretive work on American cultural materials. Financially, this research was done on a shoestring. My thanks to the Rutgers University Research Council for a small grant in 1978–79 and to the Rutgers housing office for a subsidized room/bed rental in 1984. Thanks finally to Dean Howard Crosby and his staff in 1978–79 and to Dean Stayton Wood and his staff in 1984.

1. "Erehwon" is a pseudonym—"nowhere" spelled backward. I am conducting similar research in 1984–85, though I am not residing on an interracial floor this time.

2. The whole floor—The Robeson section and the opposite section—had about sixty residents, almost equally divided by race and by sex. Twenty-two were first-year students, the focus of my research; sophomores, juniors, and seniors made up the remaining residents, in declining proportions. The residents, like the rest of the student body, were working-class to middle-class in family status and very local in their orientations; all but two of the first-year students were born in New Jersey, as were many of their parents, 22% of whom had finished college. The black students' class origins were skewed downward compared with the whites'; they were more often from urban than from suburban hometowns, and their parents had often been born in the South.

I am a WASP, and I went to a small private college. I was thirty-four when I first conducted this research. Apparently looking young for my age, I was often taken for a student in the college. Though known in the dorm to be a "professor" in the school, I was a teacher to only two students on the floor. I had a room with two student roommates on the white side and generally saw and heard things most spontaneously from the white point of view.

3. Thus, though floor membership was often not a matter of choice, especially for white residents, the structure of the floor emphasized its community status and hence its "friendliness." And out of this universe of friendly persons, the individual exercised "choice" in the selection of personal "friends." A personally chosen inner world was thus possible within a less chosen outer world. Otherwise stated: the floor was set up so people knew each other personally. People who know each other personally "ought" to act "friendly" toward one another. And from this group of "friendly people," one chooses one's "friends."

4. American folk metaphors suggest that friendship is an infinitely variable more than/less than phenomenon, for friendship "grows" and "dies" or "dissipates." On the other hand, no student informant had trouble giving a discrete answer to the question, "How many *real* friends, *close* friends, do you have?" After a short rev-

erie, most respondents gave a single number, averaging six or seven for white respondents.

5. The students' ability to ignore the history of race is consistent with their ahistoricity in other contexts, with the pervasive lack of historical reference in the general discourse of the dorm as I heard it. It is also consistent with more general history-denying tendencies in American culture. See, for instance, Carol Greenhouse's article (chap. 7) or Barbara Myerhoff's splendid description of the inability of an Americanized psychologist to comprehend or even listen to "history" in dealing with a schism within a group of elderly Eastern European-born Jews in Los Angeles (Myerhoff 1978, 153–95).

6. Quotations that are taken verbatim off a tape are italicized. Other quotations are from my field notes—my best memory of verbatim remarks, generally recorded within an hour or two of hearing them.

7. For the sake of clarity, the term "culture" in quotation marks ("culture") will refer to the students' concept of the term.

8. To be precise culturally, the white residents never spontaneously compared their theory (given in one context) that residents of different sides were from different cultures with their theory (given in other contexts) that sections ought to be friendly and that friendliness was an unproblematic "natural" relationship. They never considered the possibility that one factor generating felt unfriendliness between the sections might have been interethnic miscommunication of friendship cues between blacks and whites. In 1984 I asked a few students about this apparent contradiction. On a monoracial floor, I asked the suppositional question, "Imagine someone from a different culture lived on this floor and acted "friendly" in a different way than Americans do. Would he or she get along?" The male student answered that since this suppositional outsider was in "our" country, he or she would have to learn American patterns of friendliness first. (But then I said, "Does that mean that if you went to India you'd be willing to demonstrate friendship with other males by holding their hands in public? That's how they show friendship there." And he replied, "Oh, no, I'd never do that!") On the Robeson floor, I asked a black resident the same question, but he declined to agree that blacks and whites were really different in any "cultural" way. If they were, he continued, he could not see how that would affect potential friendliness between them. This particular informant had made a close white friend on the other side the year before.

9. The two exceptions were two hardworking junior-class males relatively uninvolved in floor social life, who knew they would get a conveniently central room if they asked to be on the floor—since it was requested by so few white students.

10. My thanks to Roy D'Andrade for making this simple but important point in a comment on this essay at the meetings of the American Anthropological Association in November 1983.

Chapter 9. Why a "Slut" Is a "Slut"

I would like to thank David Schneider for his encouragement and assistance in helping me initially present data on this rather delicate topic. Of course, without *American Kinship* this analysis would have been impossible. Katherine Bowie helped clarify the first draft. Comments by Bruce Kapferer and John MacAloon on the first draft presented at the 1983 American Ethnological Society meetings were insightful. I would also like to thank Jean and John Comaroff for enabling me to present this first draft to their class on ideology in winter 1983 at the University of Chicago and for their feedback as well as that of their students. Judith Farquhuar's perceptive reading added much to this final version. Finally, Hervé Varenne's close reading of the first draft and his incisive and encouraging comments on the second helped me take this essay as far as I could.

1. Both of these terms are those my informants use to refer to themselves. They call themselves teenagers when talking about themselves formally and kids when doing so informally. I will follow their usage in this chapter.

2. I have begun such examinations of both genders' practices (1984). This examination suggests that girls' and boys' representations of their bodies and sexuality are hierarchically interrelated, with those of boys encompassing those of girls.

3. Sheepshead is a pseudonym for the community where research was conducted. I have also used pseudonyms for the two girls discussed below, Debbie and Melissa.

4. These and the preceding figures cover the 1980—81 school year during which I conducted most of my fieldwork. They are derived from the following sources: Bureau of Government Research 1980, State Municipal Data Book 1981, and the unpublished work of Dorothy Unrath. I have omitted state and local names to keep the community's identity confidential. It should also be noted, for comparative purposes, that Sheepshead is a few miles from the high schools studied by Varenne (1983) and Goldman (1982) and that the communities share very similar characteristics.

5. The otherness central to my position as anthropologist gave these girls one place where they could explore—and then rather timidly on their part and mine for most of my fieldwork—a very problematic area of their lives.

6. My informants use the terms slut and whore interchangeably. Since in teenage slang virtually all terms for categories of persons refer only to teenagers and primarily to those teenagers in one's school (Canaan 1983), slut and whore refer to high-school girls whose sexual behavior departs too far from what is considered the norm.

Chapter 10. "Drop in Anytime"

1. An asterisk before a quoted sentence indicates that the sentence is not one I have ever heard or read. It is not part of the data base. It is, however, useful to highlight properties of sentences that are part of the data.

2. The analysis of the anthropologist's unit of study I outlined in chapter 1 (p. 19) could be illustrated here by mentioning that what happened between Ted and Sally that afternoon in the park also involved any person who would interpret for them— or force them to interpret in particular ways—what happened ("the interpreter"). Finally, it involved any person who might reward or punish them for what they were interpreted as having (not) done ("the enforcer"). I seem to have been cast as the enforcer, for we can imagine that Ted did not want to appear unfriendly in what he wrote for me. There is no direct "interpreter" in the situation as I know it. We are safe in suspecting that Ted did not invent his interpretation and that it was suggested

to him as appropriate by all the people who had told him about the world since he was born and by the reactions of the enforcer, imagined (when Ted was writing) and actual (in the subsequent interview).

3. Although songs and philosophical treatises belong to different genres from improvised conversation, they can be seen as variations on the expression of the same theme. Any cultural theme can be expressed in any number of forms, from the most "reduced" (as in proverbs or songs) to the most "expanded" (as in philosophical or psychological writing)—to use a vocabulary suggested by Hill and Varenne (1981). In the process of reduction or expansion much changes, both in the statement itself and in the organization of the relationship between speaker and audience. The coherence system that allows the statements to make traditional sense may remain constant, as is the case in our examples.

Epilogue: On the Anthropology of America

1. For earlier discussions of the anthropology of America, see Lantis 1955; Gillen 1967; Jorgensen and Truzzi 1974; Messerschmidt 1981; and Spindler and Spindler 1983.

2. An American anthropologist at home may not come from a mainstream, middle-class background, but the undergraduate and graduate training he or she undergoes is likely to provide a definite mainstream influence (Aguilar 1981, 24).

3. For a discussion of some of the political effects of Spradley's (1970) study, see Spradley and McCurdy 1975, 638–40.

4. For discussions of the problems and possibilities of "studying up," see Ablon 1977 and Emerson 1981, 371.

5. Anthropologists working on American society may find it useful to connect with the American Studies movement. Begun in the 1930s as a literary and historical enterprise, the field now takes an interdisciplinary approach to American culture past and present. Its combination of humanistic and social science orientations will seem congenial to many anthropologists. The American Studies Association, based at the University of Pennsylvania, holds a biennial convention and publishes the major journal in the field, *American Quarterly*. The current editors are sympathetic to strong anthropological contributions. Another, somewhat looser branch of the movement involves the American Culture Association and Popular Culture Association based at Bowling Green University. They hold a joint annual convention and publish a number of journals including the *Journal of American Culture* and the *Journal of Popular Culture*. For an overview of the American studies movement, see Wise 1979.

6. For a review of the general literature on popular culture studies, see Mintz 1983.

7. For provocative discussions of parallels and contrasts between American culture and Eastern philosophy, see Ornstein 1972; Capra 1983; and O'Flaherty 1984.

References

Aaker, David. 1982. The social and economic effects of advertising. In *Consumerism: Search for the consumer interest,* ed. D. Aaker and G. Day, 190–209. New York: Free Press.

Ablon, Joan. 1977. Field methods in working with middle class Americans. *Human Organization* 36:69–72.

Advertising Age. 1976. *How it was in advertising: 1776–1976.* Chicago: Crain Books.

Agar, Michael. 1980. *The professional stranger.* New York: Academic Press.

———. 1982. Toward an ethnographic language. *American Anthropologist* 84: 779–95.

Aguilar, John. 1981. Insider research: An ethnography of a debate. In *Anthropologists at home in North America,* ed. Donald A. Messerschmidt, 15–26. New York: Cambridge University Press.

Arens, William. 1976. Professional football: An American symbol and ritual. In *The American dimension,* ed. S. Montague and W. Arens, 3–14. Port Washington, N.Y.: Alfred.

Arensberg, Conrad. 1976. Generalizing anthropology: The recovery of holism. Columbia University.

Arensberg, Conrad, and Solon Kimball. 1965. *Culture and community.* New York: Harcourt, Brace and World.

Baker, Stephen. 1961. *Visual persuasion: The effects of pictures on the subconscious.* New York: McGraw-Hill.

Bakhtin, Mikhail. 1968 [1936]. *Rabelais and his world.* Trans. H. Iswolsky. Cambridge: MIT Press.

———. 1981. *The dialogic imagination..* Trans. C. Emerson and M. Holquist. Austin: University of Texas Press.

Basso, Keith. 1979. *Portraits of "The whiteman": Linguistic play and cultural symbols among the western Apache.* New York: Cambridge University Press.

Bateson, Gregory. 1958 [1936]. *Naven.* Stanford: Stanford University Press.

————. 1972. *Steps to an ecology of the mind.* New York: Ballantine Books.

Bateson, M. C., J. B. M. Kassajian, H. Safavi, and M. Soraya. 1977. Safa-yi batin: A study of the interrelations of a set of Iranian ideal character types. In *Psychological dimensions of Near Eastern studies,* ed. L. Brown and N. Itzkowitz, 257–74. Princeton, N. J.: Darwin Press.

Baudrillard, Jean. 1984. Oublier Foucault. In *Theoretical strategies,* ed. P. Botsman, 188–214. Sydney: Local consumption Publications.

Bauer, Raymond, and Stephen Greyser. 1968. *Advertising in America: The consumer view.* Cambridge: Division of Research, Graduate School of Business Administration, Harvard University.

Beeman, William. 1971. *Interaction semantics: Preliminaries to an observational study of meaning.* M.A. thesis, Department of Anthropology, University of Chicago.

————. 1976. Status, style and strategy in Iranian interaction. *Anthropological Linguistics* 18:305–22.

————. 1977. The hows and whys of Persian style: A pragmatic approach. In *Studies in language variation,* ed. R. Fasold and R. Shuy, 269–82. Washington, D.C.: Georgetown University Press.

————. 1982. *Culture, performance and communication in Iran.* Tokyo: Institute for the Study of Languages and Cultures of Asia and Africa.

————. 1986. *Iranian interaction styles.* Bloomington: Indiana University Press.

Bellah, Robert, et al. 1985. *Habits of the heart: Individualism and commitment in American life.* Berkeley: University of California Press.

Bellah, Robert. 1970. *Beyond belief: Essays on religion in a post-traditional world.* New York: Harper and Row.

————. 1975. *The broken covenant: American civil religion in time of trial.* New York: Seabury Press.

Benn, Alec. 1978. *Twenty-seven most common mistakes in advertising.* New York: American Management Associations.

Berger, Bennett. 1981. *The survival of a counterculture.* Berkeley: University of California Press.

Berman, Ronald. 1981. *Advertising and social change.* London: Sage.

Betancourt, Hal. 1982. *The advertising answerbook: A guide for business and professional people.* Englewood Cliffs, N. J.: Prentice-Hall.

Boas, Franz. 1940. *Race, language and culture.* New York: Free Press.

Bohannan, Paul. 1964. Editor's introduction. In E. B. Tylor, *Researches in the early history of mankind and the development of civilization,* ed. and abridged by Paul Bohannan, vii–xvii. Chicago: University of Chicago Press.

Boon, James. 1982. *Other tribes, other scribes: Symbolic anthropology in the comparative study of cultures, histories, religions, and texts.* New York: Cambridge University Press.

Bourdieu, Pierre. 1977. *Outline of a theory of practice.* Trans. R. Nice. New York: Cambridge University Press.

Bourdieu, Pierre, and Jean-Claude Passeron. 1977 [1970]. *Reproduction: In education, society and culture.* Trans. R. Nice. Beverly Hills, Calif.: Sage.

Bowles, Samuel, and Herbert Gintis. 1976. *Schooling in capitalist America.* New York: Basic Books.

Brownmiller, Susan. 1975. *Against our will: Men, women and rape.* New York: Bantam Books.

Brozen, Yale. 1974. *Advertising and society.* New York: New York University Press.

Brunvand, Jan. 1981. *The vanishing hitchiker: American urban legends and their meanings.* New York: W. W. Norton.

Burdus, J. Ann. 1981. Communication or persuasion. *European Research* 9:103–8.

Burnett, Leo. 1961. *Communications of an advertising man.* Chicago: Leo Burnett.

Buxton, Edward. 1972. *Promise them anything.* New York: Stein and Day.

Canaan, Joyce. 1983. Learning to lust: How American suburban middle class teenage girls constitute sexual desires. Paper presented at the 1983 American Anthropological Association meetings.

———. 1984. Building muscles and getting curves: Gender differences in representations of the body and sexuality among American teenagers. Paper presented at the 1984 American Anthropological Association meetings.

Caples, John. 1957. *Making ads pay.* New York: Dover.

Capra, Fritjof. 1983. *The Tao of physics.* Boulder: Shambhala.

Caughey, John. 1977. *Fáánakkar: cultural values in a Micronesian society.* Philadelphia: University of Pennsylvania Publications in Anthropology, no. 2.

———. 1980. Personal identity and social organization. *Ethos* 8:173–203.

———. 1982. Ethnography, introspection, and reflexive culture studies. In *Prospects: The annual of American cultural studies,* ed. J. Salzman, 115–39. New York: Burt Franklin.

———. 1984. *Imaginary social worlds: A cultural approach.* Lincoln: University of Nebraska Press.

Clifford, James. 1983. Power and dialogue in ethnography: Marcel Griaule's initiation. In *Observers observed: Essays on ethnographic fieldwork,* ed. G. Stocking, 121–56. Madison: University of Wisconsin Press.

Cohen, Yehudi. 1977. The anthropological enterprise. *American Anthropologist* 79:388–96.

Coulson, Margaret. 1980. The struggle for femininity. In *Homosexuality: Power and politics,* ed. Gay Left Collective, 21–37. New York: Schocken Books.

Coward, Rosalind, and John Ellis. 1977. *Language and materialism: Developments in semiology and the theory of the subject.* Boston: Routledge and Kegan Paul.

Cowling, Keith, J. Cable, M. Kelly, and T. McGuinness. 1975. *Advertising and economic behavior.* London: Macmillan.

Csikszentmihalyi, Mihaly, and Eugene Rochberg-Halton. 1981. *The meaning of things: Domestic symbols and the self.* New York: Cambridge University Press.

Davis, A., and B. and M. R. Gardner. 1941. *Deep South: A social anthropological study of caste and class.* Chicago: University of Chicago Press.

Dewey, John. 1930. *Human nature and conduct: An introduction to social psychology.* New York: Modern Library.

———. 1966 [1916]. *Democracy and education.* New York: Free Press.

Dolgin, Janet. 1977. *Jewish identity and J.D.L.* Princeton: Princeton University Press.

Drake, St. Clair, and H. R. Cayton. 1945. *Black metropolis.* New York: Harcourt, Brace.

Drummond, Lee. 1977a. On being Carib. In *Carib-speaking Indians: Cultural continuities and change,* ed. E. Basso, 76–88. Tucson: University of Arizona Press.

———. 1977b. Structure and process in the interpretation of South American myth: The Arawak dog-spirit people. *American Anthropologist* 79:842–68.

———. 1978. Transatlantic nanny: Notes on a comparative semiotics of the family in English-speaking societies. *American Ethnologist* 5:30–43.

———. 1980. The cultural continuum: A theory of intersystems. *Man* 15:352–74.

DuBois, Ellen, and Linda Gordon. 1984. Seeking ecstasy in the battlefield: Danger and pleasure in nineteenth century feminist thought. In *Pleasure and danger: Exploring female sexuality,* ed. C. Vance, 31–49. Boston: Routledge and Kegan Paul.

Dumont, Louis. 1980a [1961]. Caste, racism and stratificaton. In *Homo hierarchicus,* trans. M. Sainsbury, rev. ed., 239–58. Chicago: University of Chicago Press.

———. 1980b [1966]. *Homo hierarchicus.* Trans. M. Sainsbury. Rev. ed. Chicago: University of Chicago Press.

Durkheim, Emile. 1947 [1912]. *The elementary forms of the religious life.* Trans. J. Swain. New York: Free Press.

Eco, Umberto. 1979. *The role of the reader: Explorations in the semiotics of texts.* Bloomington: Indiana University Press.

Emerson, Robert. 1981. Observational fieldwork. *Annual Review of Sociology* 7:351–78.

Ewen, Stuart. 1976. *Captains of consciousness: Advertising and the social roots of the consumer culture.* New York: McGraw-Hill.

Feinberg, Richard. 1979. Schneider's symbolic culture theory: An appraisal. *Current Anthropology* 20:541–60.

Fields, George. 1983. The Japanese communication base: The art of saying it without words. *Japan Marketing/Advertising* 23:67–76.

Foucault, Michel. 1978. *The history of sexuality,* vol. 1. Trans. R. Hurley. New York: Pantheon Books.

Frake, Charles. 1980. *Language and cultural description.* Essays selected and introduced by A. S. Dil. Stanford: Stanford University Press.

Freilich, Morris, ed. 1970. *Marginal natives: Anthropologists at work.* New York: Harper and Row.

Friedrich, Paul. 1979. *Language, context and imagination.* Stanford: Stanford University Press.

Galanter, Marc. 1983. Reading the landscape of disputes: What we know and don't know (and think we know) about allegedly contentious and litigious society. *UCLA Law Review* 31:4–71.

Garfinkel, Harold. 1967. *Studies in ethnomethodology.* Englewood Cliffs, N. J.: Prentice-Hall.

Geertz, Clifford. 1973a [1971]. Deep play: Notes on the Balinese cockfight. In *The interpretation of cultures,* 412–53. New York: Basic Books.

———. 1973b. *The interpretation of cultures.* New York: Basic Books.

———. 1976. "From the native's point of view": On the nature of anthropological understanding. In *Meaning in anthropology,* ed. K. Basso and H. Selby, 221–37. Albuquerque: University of New Mexico Press.

———. 1984. Anti anti-relativism. *American Anthropologist* 86:263–78.

Geis, Michael. 1982. *The language of television advertising.* New York: Academic Press.

Gillen, John. 1967. More complex cultures for anthropologists. *American Anthropologist* 69:301–5.

Glazer, Nathan, and Daniel Moynihan. 1963. *Beyond the melting pot: The Negroes, Puerto Ricans, Jews, Italians, and Irish of New York City.* Cambridge: MIT Press.

Goffman, Erving. 1971. *Relations in public.* New York: Harper and Row.

———. 1979. *Gender advertisements.* New York: Harper Colophon.

Goldenweiser, A. 1910. Totemism, an analytic study. *Journal of American Folklore* 23:1–115. Ed. V. F. Calverton.

Goldman, Shelley. 1982. *Sorting out sorting.* Ph.D. diss., Teachers College, Columbia University.

Goodenough, Ward. 1981. *Culture, language and society.* Menlo Park, Calif.: Benjamin/Cummings.

Gorer, Geoffrey. 1948. *The American people: A study in national character.* New York: W. W. Norton.

Greenhouse, Carol. 1979. Avoidance as a strategy for resolving conflict in Zinacantan. In *Patterns of conflict management,* ed. K. -F. Koch, 105–23. Milan: Dott A. Guiffre Editore; Alphen den Rijn: Sijthoff and Noordhoff.

———. 1982. Nature is to culture as praying is to suing: Implications of legal pluralism. *Journal of Legal Pluralism* 20: 17–35.

Gulick, John. 1973. Urban anthropology. In *Handbook of social and cultural anthropology,* ed. J. Honigmann, 979–1029. Chicago: Rand McNally.

Gumperz, John. 1982. *Discourse strategies.* New York: Cambridge University Press.

Hallowell, A. I. 1965. The history of anthropology as an anthropological problem. *Journal of the History of the Behavioral Sciences* 1:24–38.

Handlin, Oscar. 1957. *Race and nationality in American life.* Garden City, N.Y.: Doubleday.

Hayano, David. 1979. Auto-ethnography: Paradigms, problems and prospects. *Human Organization* 38:99–104.

———. 1982. *Poker faces.* Berkeley: University of California Press.

Heath, Stephen. 1984. *The sexual fix.* New York: Schocken Books.

Herron, Jerry. 1984. On feeling blue: Sex, Reaganomics, violence and taboo. In *Forbidden fruits: Taboos and tabooism in culture,* ed. R. Browne, 145–76. Bowling Green, Ohio: Bowling Green State University Popular Press.

Hicks, George. 1976. *Appalachian valley.* New York: Holt, Rinehart and Winston.

Higham, John. 1974. Hanging together: Divergent unities in American history. *Journal of American History* 61:5–28.

Hill, Clifford, and Hervé Varenne. 1981. Family, language and education: The sociolinguistic model of restricted and elaborated codes. *Social Science Information* 20:187–228.

Homans, George. 1950. *The human group.* New York: Harcourt, Brace.

Hsu, Francis. 1972. American core values and national character. In *Psychological anthropology*, ed. Francis Hsu, 241–62. Cambridge: Cambridge University Press.

Hymes, Dell. 1974. *Foundations in sociolinguistics*. Philadelphia: University of Pennsylvania Press.

Jacobs, P. H. 1968. *Front and center: The legend of Bossy Gillis*. Newburyport, Mass.: Newburyport Press.

Jakobson, Roman. 1960. Concluding statement: Linguistics and poetics. In *Style in language*, ed. T. Sebeok, 350–77. New York: Wiley.

Jorgensen, Joseph, and Marcello Truzzi, eds. 1974. *Anthropology and American life*. Englewood Cliffs, N. J.: Prentice-Hall.

Kael, Pauline. 1968. *Kiss kiss bang bang*. New York: Atlantic Monthly Press.

Kakar, Sudhir. 1982. *Shamans, mystics and doctors: A psychological inquiry into India and its healing practices*. New York: Knopf.

Katz, Michael. 1971. *Class, bureaucracy and schools: The illusion of educational change in America*. Cambridge: Harvard University Press.

Keely, Ann. 1982. Research identifies eight underlying rules of consumer choice. *Marketing News* 16:10.

Kidder, Tracy. 1981. *The soul of a new machine*. New York: Atlantic Monthly Press.

Konig, David. 1979. *Law and society in puritan Massachusetts, Essex County, 1629–1692*. Chapel Hill: University of North Carolina Press.

Labov, William. 1972. *Sociolinguistic patterns*. Philadelphia: University of Pennsylvania Press.

Labov, William, and David Fanshel. 1977. *Therapeutic discourse: Psychotherapy as conversation*. New York: Academic Press.

Lakoff, George, and Mark Johnson. 1980. *Metaphors we live by*. Chicago: University of Chicago Press.

Langer, Susanne. 1951. *Philosophy in a new key*. New York: New American Library.

Lantis, Margaret, ed. 1955. The U.S.A. as anthropologists see it. *American Anthropologist* 57:1113–1295.

Lasch, Christopher. 1977. *Haven in a heartless world: The family besieged*. New York: Basic Books.

Leach, Edmund. 1958. Concerning Trobriand clans and the kinship category *tabu*. In *The developmental cycle in domestic groups*, ed. Jack Goody, 120–45. New York: Cambridge University Press.

Leichter, Hope. 1978. Families and communities as educators: Some concepts of relationships. *Teachers College Record* 79:567–658.

Lévi-Strauss, Claude. 1963a [1958]. *Structural anthropology*. Vol. 1. Trans. C. Jacobson and B. Schoepf. New York: Basic Books.

———. 1963b [1962]. *Totemism*. Trans. R. Needham. Boston: Beacon Press.

———. 1966 [1962]. *The savage mind*. Chicago: University of Chicago Press.

———. 1976 [1958]. *Structural anthropology*. Vol. 2. Trans. M. Layton. New York: Basic Books.

Linton, Ralph. 1924. Totemism and the A.E.F. *American Anthropologist* 26:296–300.

Littleton, Scott. 1966. *The new comparative mythology: An Anthropological assessment of the theories of Georges Dumézil*. Berkeley: University of California Press.

Lockridge, Kenneth. 1970. *A New England town: The first hundred years*. New York: W. W. Norton.

Lubin, Aasta. 1984. The language of success: The successful career woman and mother in New York City. Ph.D. diss., Teachers College, Columbia University.

Lucas, Darell, and S. H. Britt. 1950. *Advertising psychology and research*. New York: McGraw-Hill.

Lukes, Stephen. 1973. *Individualism*. New York: Harper and Row.

Lynd, Robert, and Helen Lynd. 1937. *Middletown in transition: A study in cultural conflict*. New York: Harcourt, Brace and World.

———. 1956 [1929]. *Middletown: A study in modern American culture*. New York: Harcourt, Brace and World.

McDermott, John. 1976. *The culture of experience: Philosophical essays in the American grain*. New York: New York University Press.

———. 1983. America? The loneliness of the quest. *Teachers College Record* 85:275–90.

McDermott, R. P., and Kenneth Gospodinoff. 1979. Social context for ethnic borders and school failure. In *Nonverbal Behavior,* ed. A. Wolfgang, 175–95. New York: Academic Press.

McDermott, R. P., and Henry Tylbor. 1983. On the necessity of collusion in conversation. *Text* 3:277–97.

McLuhan, Herbert. 1951. *The mechanical bride: Folklore of industrial man*. New York: Vanguard.

McRobbie, Angela, and Jenny Garber. 1976. Girls and subcultures: An exploration. In *Resistance through rituals: Youth subcultures in post-war Britain,* ed. S. Hall and T. Jefferson, 209–22. New York: Holmes and Meier.

Malickson, David, and John Nason. 1982. *Advertising: How to write the kind that works*. Rev. ed. New York: Scribner's.

Malinowski, Bronislaw. 1946 [1923]. The problem of meaning in primitive languages. In *The meaning of meaning,* ed. C. Ogden and I. A. Richards, 296–336. New York: Harcourt, Brace.

Maquet, Jacques. 1971. *Introduction to aesthetic anthropology*. Reading, Mass.: Addison-Wesley.

Marcus, George. 1986. Some contemporary problems of ethnographic writing in the modern world system. In *The making of ethnographic texts,* ed. J. Clifford and G. Marcus. SAR Santa Fe Seminar Volume.

Marquand, J. P. 1951. *Point of no return*. New York: Grosset and Dunlap.

———. 1960. *Timothy Dexter revisited*. Boston: Little, Brown.

Martineau, Pierre. 1957. *Motivation in advertising*. New York: McGraw-Hill.

Marty, Martin. 1970. *Righteous empire: The Protestant experience in America*. New York: Dial Press.

Marx, Leo. 1964. *The machine in the garden: Technology and the pastoral ideal in America*. London: Oxford University Press.

Mauss, Marcel. 1950. *Sociologie et anthropologie*. Paris: Presses Universitaires de France.

Mayo, E. 1933. *The human problems of an industrial civilization.* New York: Macmillan.

Mead, George Herbert. 1967 [1934]. *Mind, self and society.* Chicago: University of Chicago Press.

Mead, Margaret. 1928. *Coming of age in Samoa.* New York: Morrow.

————. 1965 [1942]. *And keep your powder dry: An anthropologist looks at America.* New York: W. Morrow.

Mehan, Hugh, and Houston Wood. 1975. *The reality of ethnomethodology.* New York: Wiley.

Meillassoux, Claude. 1981. *Maidens, meal and money: Capitalism and the domestic community.* New York: Cambridge University Press.

Mercer, Colin. 1983. A poverty of desire: Pleasure and popular politics. In *Formations of pleasure,* ed. Editorial Collective, 84–100. Boston: Routledge and Kegan Paul.

Merleau-Ponty, Maurice. 1973 [1969]. *The prose of the world.* Trans. J. O'Neil. Evanston: Northwestern University Press.

Merry, Salley. 1979. Going to court: Strategies of dispute management in an American urban neighborhood. *Law and Society Review* 13:891–926.

Messerschmidt, Donald, ed. 1981. *Anthropologists at home in North America: Methods and issues in the study of one's own society.* New York: Cambridge University Press.

Meyer, Timothy, Paul Traudt, and James Anderson. 1980. Nontraditional mass communication research methods: An overview of observational case studies of media use in natural settings. *Communication Year* 4:261–75.

Miller, Perry. 1965. *The life of the mind in America.* New York: Harcourt, Brace and World.

Miner, Horace. 1975 [1956]. Body ritual among the Nacirema. In *The Nacirema: Readings on American culture,* ed. J. Spradley and M. Rynkiewich, 2–13. Boston: Little, Brown.

Mintz, Lawrence. 1983. Recent trends in the study of popular culture. In *Sources for American studies,* ed. J. Kellog and R. Walker, 489–507. Westport, Conn.: Greenwood Press.

Moffatt, Michael. 1979a. Harijan religion: Consensus at the bottom of caste. *American Ethnologist* 6:244–60.

————. 1979b. *An untouchable community in South India: Structure and consensus.* Princeton: Princeton University Press.

Montague, Susan, and Robert Morais. 1976. Football games and rock concerts: The ritual enactment. In *The American dimension,* ed. W. Arens and S. Montague, 33–52. Port Washington, N.Y.: Alfred.

Murphey, Murray. 1979. Comments on the session "Fieldwork in modern America: Anthropologists and Americanists meet." Paper presented at Seventh biennial convention of the American Studies Association, Minneapolis.

Murrin, John. 1972. Review essay. *History and Theory* 11:226–75.

Myerhoff, Barbara. 1974. *Peyote hunt: The sacred journey of the Huichol Indians.* Ithaca: Cornell University Press.

————. 1976. Return to Wirikuta: Ritual reversal and symbolic continuity among the Huichol Indians. In *The reversible world,* ed. B. Babcock. Ithaca: Cornell University Press.

———. 1977. "We don't wrap herring in a printed page": Fusions and continuity in secular ritual. In *Secular ritual,* ed. S. Moore and B. Myerhoff, 199–224. Amsterdam: Van Gorcum.

———. 1978. *Number our days.* New York: Simon and Schuster.

Myerhoff, Barbara, and Jay Ruby. 1982. Introduction. In *A crack in the mirror: Reflexive perspectives in anthropology,* ed. J. Ruby, 1–35. Philadelphia: University of Pennsylvania Press.

Myrdal, Gunnar. 1944. *An American dilemma: The Negro problem and modern democracy.* New York: Harper and Row.

Nakane, Chie. 1968. *Japanese society.* Chicago: University of Chicago Press.

Nichols, George. 1867. Wild Bill. *Harper's New Monthly Magazine* 34:273–85.

Novak, Michael. 1971. *The rise of the unmeltable ethnics: Politics and culture in the seventies.* New York: Macmillan.

O'Flaherty, Wendy. 1984. *Dreams, illusions, and other realities.* Chicago: University of Chicago Press.

Ornstein, Robert. 1972. *The psychology of consciousness.* New York: Penguin.

Packard, Vance. 1981. *The hidden persuaders.* Rev. ed. New York: Pocket Books.

Paganetti, Jo Ann, and M. Seklemian. 1982. *The best in retail ads: 401 newspaper ads and why they work.* New York: Retail Reporting Corporation.

Peirce, C. S. 1955 [1940]. *Philosophical writings of Peirce.* Ed. J. Buchler. New York: Dover Publications.

Perin, Constance. 1977. *Everything in its place.* Princeton: Princeton University Press.

Phillips, Ulrich. 1968 [1902]. *Georgia and states' rights.* Yellow Springs, Ohio: Antioch.

Piaget, Jean. 1968. *Le structuralisme.* Paris: Presses Universitaires de France.

Quinn, Naomi. n.d. Understanding the experience of marriage in our culture. Working paper, Duke University.

Radcliffe-Brown, A. R. 1948 [1922]. *The Andaman islanders.* Glencoe: Free Press.

———. 1965 [1940]. *Structure and function in primitive society.* New York: Free Press.

Rapson, R., ed. 1967. *Individualism and conformity in the American character.* Boston: Heath.

Ravitch, Diane. 1977. The revisionists revised: Studies in the historiography of American education. *Proceedings of the National Academy of Education* 4:1–84.

Redfield, Robert. 1960 [1955]. *The little community.* Chicago: University of Chicago Press.

Richler, Mordecai. 1971. James Bond unmasked. In *Mass culture revisited,* ed. B. Rosenberg and D. White, 341–55. New York: Van Nostrand Reinhold.

Ricoeur, Paul. 1976. *Interpretation theory: Discourse and the surplus of meaning.* Fort Worth: Texas Christian University Press.

Riesman, David. 1955. *Individualism reconsidered.* Glencoe, Ill.: Free Press.

Riesman, David, with N. Glazer and R. Denney. 1961 [1950]. *The lonely crowd:*

A study of the changing American character. New Haven: Yale University Press.

Roethlisberger, F. J., and W. J. Dickson. 1939. *Management and the worker.* Cambridge: Harvard University Press.

Roman, Kenneth, and Jane Maas. 1976. *How to advertise: A professional guide for the advertiser.* New York: St. Martin's Press.

Rothenberg, Jerome. 1962. Consumer's sovereignty revisited and the hospitality of freedom of choice. *American Economic Review* 52:269–83.

Rougemont, Denis de. 1956. *Love in the Western world.* Trans. M. Belgion. New York: Pantheon Books.

Rubin, Gayle. 1984. Thinking sex: Notes for a radical theory of the politics of sexuality. In *Pleasure and danger: Exploring female sexuality,* ed. C. Vance, 267–319. Boston: Routledge and Kegan Paul.

Ruskin, Francine, and Hervé Varenne. 1983. The production of ethnic discourse: American and Puerto Rican patterns. In *The sociogenesis of language and human conduct,* ed. B. Bain, 553–68. New York: Plenum.

Sandage, C. H., ed. 1961. *The promise of advertising.* Homewood, Ill.: Richard D. Irwin.

Sanday, Peggy. 1981. The socio-cultural context of rape: A cross-cultural study. *Journal of Social Issues* 37:5–27.

Schneider, David. 1969. Kinship, nationality and religion in American culture: Toward a definition of kinship. In *Forms of symbolic action,* ed. Victor Turner, 116–25. Proceedings of the Annual Meeting of the American Ethnological Society. Seattle: University of Washington Press.

———. 1970. American kin categories. In *Echanges et communications,* ed. J. Pouillon and P. Maranda, 370–81. Paris: Mouton.

———. 1980 [1968]. *American kinship: A cultural account.* Chicago: University of Chicago Press.

Schudson, Michael. 1984. *Advertising, the uneasy persuasion: Its dubious impact on American society.* New York: Basic Books.

Seabrook, Jeremy. 1981. The end of great expectations. In *The bedside Guardian.* Manchester: Manchester Guardian.

Shweder, Richard, and Robert LeVine, eds. 1984. *Culture theory: Essays on mind, self, and emotion.* New York: Cambridge University Press.

Singer, Milton. 1977. On the symbolic and historic structure of an American identity. *Ethos* 5:428–54.

———. 1978. For a semiotic anthropology. In *Sight, sound and sense,* ed. T. Sebeok, 202–31. Bloomington: Indiana University Press.

———. 1980 [1972]. *When a great tradition modernizes: An anthropological approach to Indian civilization.* Chicago: University of Chicago Press.

———. 1984. *Man's glassy essence: Explorations in semiotic anthropology.* Bloomington: Indiana University Press.

Slater, Philip. 1970. *The pursuit of loneliness: American culture at the breaking point.* Boston: Beacon Press.

Sollors, Werner. 1980. The rebirth of *all* Americans in the great American melting pot. *Prospects* 5:79–110.

Spindler, George. 1963 [1959]. The transmission of American culture. In *Educa-*

tion and culture, ed. George Spindler, 148–72. New York: Holt, Rinehart and Winston.

———. 1977. Change and continuity in American core cultural values: An anthropological perspective. In *We the people: American character and social change,* ed. G. De Renzo, 20–40. Westport, Conn.: Greenwood.

Spindler, George, and Louise Spindler. 1982. Roger Harker and Schoenhausen: From familiar to strange and back again. In doing the ethnography of schooling: Educational anthropology in action, ed. George Spindler. New York: Holt, Rinehart and Winston.

———. 1983. Anthropologists view American culture. In *Annual reviews in anthropology,* 12:49–78. Palo Alto, Calif.: Annual Reviews.

Spradley, James. 1970. *You owe yourself a drunk.* Boston: Little, Brown.

———. 1979. *The ethnographic interview.* New York: Holt, Rinehart and Winston.

Spradley, James, and D. McCurdy. 1975. *Anthropology: The cultural perspective.* New York: Wiley.

Stanner, William. 1965. The dreaming. In *Reader in comparative religion,* 2d ed., ed. W. Lessa and E. Vogt, 158–67. New York: Harper and Row.

Starch, Daniel. 1923. *Principles of advertising.* New York: McGraw-Hill.

Steele, Edward D. 1957. The rhetorical use of the "American value system" in the 1952 presidential campaign addresses. Ph.D. diss., Stanford University.

Stein, Maurice. 1964 [1960]. *The eclipse of community.* New York: Harper and Row.

Stocking, George. 1968. Franz Boas and the culture concept in historical perspective. In *Race, evolution and culture: Essays in the history of anthropology,* ed. George Stocking, 195–233. New York: Free Press.

Strout, Cushing. 1974. *The new heavens and new earth: Political religion in America.* New York: Harper and Row.

Thernstrom, Stephan. 1971 [1964]. *Poverty and progress.* New York: Atheneum.

Tocqueville, Alexis de. 1969 [1848]. *Democracy in America.* Trans. G. Lawrence. Garden City, N.Y.: Doubleday.

Turner, Kay. 1980. The Virgin of Sorrows procession: A Brooklyn inversion. In *Folklore papers of the University Folklore Association,* ed. K. Turner, no. 9: 1–26. Austin: Center for Intercultural Studies in Folklore and Ethnomusicology.

Turner, Victor. 1969. *The ritual process: Structure and anti-structure.* Chicago: Aldine.

———. 1978. Foreword. In *Number our days,* by Barbara Myerhoff. New York: Simon and Schuster.

———. 1979. *Process, performance and pilgrimage: A study in comparative symbology.* New Delhi: Concept.

Ulanoff, Stanley. 1979. *Advertising in America: An introduction of persuasive communication.* New York: Hastings House.

Vance, Carole. 1984. Pleasure and danger: Toward a politics of sexuality. In *Pleasure and danger: Exploring female sexuality,* ed. C. Vance, 1–27. Boston: Routledge and Kegan Paul.

Varenne, Hervé. 1977. *Americans together: Structured diversity in a midwestern town.* New York: Teachers College Press.

————. 1978. Is Dedham American? The diagnosis of things American. *Anthropological Quarterly* 51:231–45.

————. 1982. Jocks and freaks: The symbolic structure of the expression of social interaction among American senior high school students. In *Doing the ethnography of schooling*, ed. George Spindler, 210–35. New York: Holt, Rinehart and Winston.

————. 1983. *American school language: Culturally patterned conflicts in a suburban high school*. New York: Irvington.

————. 1984. Collective representation in American anthropological conversations about culture: Culture and the individual. *Current Anthropology* 25:281–300.

Varenne, Hervé, Vera Hamid-Buglione, R. P. McDermott, and Ann Morison. 1982. *"I teach him everything he learns in school": The acquisition of literacy for learning in working class families*. New York: Teachers College, Columbia University, Elbenwood Center for the Study of the Family as Educator.

Varenne, Hervé, and R. P. McDermott. 1986. Why Sheila can read: Structure and indeterminacy in the reproduction of familial literacy. In *The acquisition of literacy*, ed. P. Gilmore and B. Schieffelin. Norwood, N. J.: ABLEX.

Vidich, Arthur, and Joseph Bensman. 1968 [1958]. *Small town in mass society: Class, power and religion in a rural community*. 2d ed. Princeton: Princeton University Press.

Wallace, Anthony F. C. 1968. Anthropological contributions to the theory of personality. In *The study of personality*, ed. E. Norbeck, D. Price-Williams, and W. McCord, 41–53. New York: Holt, Rinehart and Winston.

————. 1970. *Culture and personality*. New York: Random House.

————. 1972. Driving to work. In *Culture and cognition*, ed. James Spradley, 310–26. San Francisco: Chandler.

Warner, W. Lloyd. 1937. *A black civilization: A social study of an Australian tribe*. New York: Harper and Row.

————. 1952. *Structure of American life*. Edinburgh: University of Edinburgh Press.

————. 1953. *American life: Dream and reality*. Chicago: University of Chicago Press.

————. 1959. *The living and the dead: A study of the symbolic life of Americans*. Yankee City Series 5. New Haven: Yale University Press.

————. 1963. *Yankee City*. Abridged ed. New Haven: Yale University Press.

Warner, W. Lloyd, et al. 1949. *Democracy in Jonesville*. New York: Harper and Row.

Warner, W. Lloyd, R. J. Havighurst, and M. B. Loeb. 1944. *Who shall be educated?* New York: Harper and Row.

Warner, W. Lloyd, and J. O. Low. 1947. *The social system of the modern factory*. Yankee City Series 4. New Haven: Yale University Press.

Warner, W. Lloyd, and Paul Lunt. 1941. *The social life of a modern community*. Yankee City Series 1. New Haven: Yale University Press.

Warner, W. Lloyd, M. Meeker, and K. Eells. 1949. *Social class in America: A manual of procedure for the measurement of social status*. Chicago: Science Research Associates.

Warner, W. Lloyd, and L. Srole. 1945. *The social system of American ethnic groups.* Yankee City Series 3. New Haven: Yale University Press.

Watkins, Julian. 1959 [1949]. *The one hundred greatest advertisements: Who wrote them and what they did.* New York: Dover.

Whalen, Bernie. 1983. Semiotics: An art or powerful marketing research tool? *Marketing News* 17 (10 section 1): 8–9.

Williams, Raymond. 1958. *Culture and society, 1780–1950.* New York: Pelican Books.

———. 1977. *Marxism and literature.* New York: Oxford University Press.

———. 1981. Advertising: The magic system. In *Problems in materialism and culture,* 170–95. New York: Schocken.

Williamson, Judith. 1978. *Decoding advertisements: Ideology and meaning in advertising.* London: Marion Boyars.

Wise, Gene. 1979. Some elementary axioms for an American culture studies. *Prospects* 4:517–47.

———. 1983. From "*American* studies" to "American *culture* studies": A dialogue across generations. *Prospects,* 8:1–10.

Z/G. 1980. *Special issue on sado-masochism 7.*

Zangwill, Israel. 1911. *The melting pot: Drama in four acts.* New York: Macmillan.

Zaretsky, Eli. 1976. *Capitalism, the family and personal life.* New York: Harper and Row.

Zuckerman, Michael. 1970. *Peaceable kingdoms: New England towns in the eighteenth century.* New York: Knopf.

Contributors

William Beeman is associate professor of anthropology at Brown University specializing in sociolinguistics and communication in culture. He is the author of *Culture, Performance and Communication in Iran* (1982), *Language, Power and Strategy in Iran* (1986), and numerous articles on culture and communication in the Middle East, Japan, India, and the United States. He is also associate editor of Pacific News Service, San Francisco, and contributing editor to *Performing Arts Journal*.

Joyce Canaan is a visiting fellow at the Centre for Contemporary Cultural Studies (University of Birmingham). She recently earned her Ph.D. in anthropology from the University of Chicago. Her research interests include gender and sexuality, youth, popular culture, social history of education, and methodology. She is coeditor of and contributor to the forthcoming book *The Politics of Research and Methodology* (Hutchinson University Library).

John Caughey is associate professor in the Department of American Studies at the University of Maryland. He has done fieldwork in Truk, Pakistan, and the United States. He is interested in the cultural dimensions of consciousness, social organization, and mental illness. His publications include *Fáánakkar: Cultural Values in a Micronesian Society* (1977), *Imaginary Social Worlds* (1984), and a variety of articles in journals such as *Ethos, Prospects,* and *American Quarterly.*

Lee Drummond is associate professor of anthropology at McGill University. He has worked extensively in Guyana and has published several papers on aspects of this work, focusing particularly on ethnicity, myth, and symbols. He is now working on a book on movies and myth.

Carol Greenhouse is associate professor of anthropology at Cornell University. Her research in "Hopewell" merges her interests in the anthropology of law and the anthropology of the United States. Recent publications include articles on cultural norms, mediation, and remedial choicemaking; a forthcoming book expands on the ethnographic and historical issues in her contribution to this volume.

Michael Moffatt is an associate professor of anthropology at Rutgers University. He is the author of *An Untouchable Community in South India* (1977) and *The Rutgers Picture Book* (1985) and the senior translator and editor of *A South Indian Subcaste* by Louis Dumont (1985). His interests include American and Indian culture, culture theory, ethnography, anthropology and history, and interdisciplinary education.

Steve Mongulla is a graduate student in anthropology at the University of Southern California.

Barbara Myerhoff was professor of anthropology at the University of Southern California. She died in January 1985. She published extensively on a range of matters: symbolic anthropology, myth and ritual, aging, ethnicity, Jewish anthropology, and women studies. Two of her major publications are *Peyote Hunt* (1975) and *Number Our Days* (1979). Since 1982 she had been studying the Jewish community in Fairfax, Los Angeles.

Milton Singer is professor emeritus in the Department of Anthropology and Paul Klapper Professor Emeritus of the Social Sciences at the University of Chicago. He has published extensively on culture theory, India, and more recently, on American culture. His most recent book is *Man's Glassy Essence: Explorations in Semiotic Anthropology* (1984), which brings together his continuing interest in philosophy, culture theory, and Peircean semiotics.

Hervé Varenne is professor of education at Teachers College, Columbia University. He is the author of *Americans Together* (1977), *American School Language* (1983), and articles on aspects of everyday American life. He has also worked on literacy in the United States. His current work focuses on the cultural structuring of natural conversations in family settings. Other interests are the writing of anthropology, culture theory, and new technologies for publishing ethnography (videodisc, CD-ROM, etc.).

Subject Index

Author Index